Crimson

KIRSTEN FARRIS

Crimson

Kirsten Farris
Crimson

All rights reserved.
Copyright © 2024 by Kirsten Farris

Published by Spines
ISBN: 979-8-89383-633-2

Dedicated to Evan and Luke Farris

Kirsten Farris

Kirsten Farris is a talented artist, a painter for almost 20 years and an author in the drama/thriller genre. She is a champion for women artists/authors. With a background in Interior Design and motherhood, she discovered a passion for painting. Now, she is ready to share her novel "Crimson" that she wrote on train rides to and from college in Manhattan.

Prologue

WOKEN from a deep sleep she was sure she heard something loud coming from outside. The incoming gusting wind was banging something on the rooftop of the house. Was that the sound she heard?

The window was slightly open, and papers flickered up and down on the desk as the wind pushed air into the room. The silvery blue drapes rippled as gusts of wind blew forward. The wind whistled and howled as it whipped through the space. She felt nervous, and she clenched her blanket. She lifted her head above the blanket and peered out to quickly scan the room. Her sister lay silently in her bed.

Her sister's breathing was steady, undisturbed by the chaotic symphony playing outside their window. But she couldn't shake the feeling of being watched, of unseen eyes peering through the darkness. Every gust of wind seemed to carry a message, a warning that she couldn't quite understand.

The creaking of the old house intensified as the eerie wind continued to batter the walls. Shadows danced across the room, flickering ominously in the dim light. It was as if the house itself was alive, whispering secrets that she could not decipher. A sense of unease crept over her as she strained to hear what she thought was a heated commotion.

As the shadows deepened and the wind grew more frenzied, she knew that sleep would elude her tonight. A loud crashing sound echoed up the stairs.

She sat straight up in her bed. Out the window, she could see the long gravel driveway beneath the house, which stretched across the field, giving way to blackness. The trees were swaying heavily in the wind, whistling and cracking. Gusts of wind twisted the long, overgrown grass back and forth, bending and swaying it, almost as if they were going to break free. A horse was whining in the distance. "Is it only the storm that's making those sounds?" she thought to herself. Tension filled the air, mingling with the fear that crept up her spine like icy fingers in the night, as she strained to hear any other mysterious sounds that may be lurking in the darkness.

Her breath seemed to fill the room, her chest rising and falling with each heartbeat. Her sister, frozen in place, didn't even flinch as more loud noises erupted from below. The distant yelling grew more urgent, more menacing, yet remained incomprehensible to her ears. Who could it be shouting like that? The forceful wind outside howled mercilessly, rattling the window panes with increasing intensity.

Then, in a sudden burst of light, the sky illuminated as if struck by lightning. *BANG!* She sat up on her knees, stretching her body to see. She looked out the window again. A blinding silver glow enveloped the scene. The trees were swaying back and forth. The room felt suddenly suffocating, the air heavy with an unspoken threat. She wondered where all the oxygen had gone.

Bang! A deafening boom followed, its reverberations rippling through the night with a savage intensity that made her heart skip a beat. She was now breathing hard. Still, no rain fell from the ominous black clouds that now loomed threateningly in the moonlit sky, their edges tinged with a ghostly iridescence.

It was as if the heavens themselves were bracing for something foreboding, something unknown but undeniably sinister. At that moment, a shiver ran down her spine as a sense of dread settled in, casting a long shadow over her already uneasy heart.

Large clouds had now enveloped the moon, and she could no longer see the outline of the driveway. She could hardly make out the contours of the flowered wallpaper. The wind was still pumping through the window. The drapes seemed ghostly, swaying back and forth. A bright light filled the room, and then darkness. Intense booming sounds engulfed the black sky. Her heart raced with a mixture of fear and curiosity as she struggled to piece together the strange occurrences happening around her.

Screaming. She heard screaming. What should she do? The front door slammed against its frame. Again, yelling. Noises were coming from the front porch — stomping noises and then the crackling of thunder. With a sense of urgency, she threw the covers off, her heart racing as she ran towards the window. Desperation gnawed at her, compelling her to witness the unfolding commotion outside. Why had the clouds gathered so quickly? She saw a figure standing outside. The figure was illuminated by dim moonlight. She gasped in terror as she realized the figure was staring directly at her. Goosebumps erupted on her skin as she instinctively dropped her head, her hands trembling with fear. Was the figure pointing at her?

She turned around and looked behind her. What she saw made her blood run cold. The red object hanging in the closet was a tattered dress stained with what looked like dried blood. She blinked and realized it was just clothes. What? Panic gripped her as she noticed that she was sweating with fear. Her mind raced as she struggled to comprehend the sinister feelings enveloping her.

With a sudden burst of courage, she turned back to the window, ready to confront the mysterious figure outside. But to her horror, the figure was now lying on the ground. What should I do?

Before she could make sense of it all, she found herself on the floor, her elbow throbbing in pain. Blood trickled down from a deep cut just behind her elbow. Her sister had pulled her down, her eyes filled with fear and uncertainty. The atmosphere was charged with suspense, leaving her bewildered and on edge, unsure of what would happen next.

"You might be seen. Don't look out the window,"

She whispered urgently to her sister, her voice speaking in a hushed tone.

She struggled to pull herself free from her sister's grasp.

Her sister was strong and determined, refusing to let her peek outside.

"Why won't you let me see?"

She questioned. Her curiosity mingling with trepidation.

Sounds from below were muffled, drowned out by the ominous drumming of the darkened sky.

"We should be careful. It's not safe,"

Her sister replied, her tone intense.

Then, in a moment of fleeting defiance, she managed to break free. As she did, a bolt of lightning tore through the darkness, illuminating the scene below for a brief instant.

As the woman lay on the muddy ground, limp, the woman's eyes closed, a figure emerged from the side of the house. A tall, menacing silhouette stood motionless, obscured by darkness and the pounding rain. The sound of heavy footsteps approached her, echoing ominously in the stormy night.

The suspense hung heavy in the air. She looked with a final glance mingling with the rain and thunder, as the figure vanished into thin air. All she could say for sure was that she knew deep down that the nightmare haunting them was far from over.

CHAPTER 1

Coming Home

"YOU SEEM UPSET."

"Yeah?" Her voice sounded unsettled.

"Tell me why you're feeling upset."

"I don't know why really." She shifted slightly.

"Try putting your finger on it."

"I don't know. I keep having more weird dreams."

"Ah."

"I keep having this really strange dream. I had it again last night," her body shivered as she thought about it.

"Unfortunately, I usually can't remember mine."

"Well, you will remember this dream."

"Tell me about it. Everything you can remember."

She paused for several seconds, trying to adjust to the light, while her eyes gazed around the dimly lit room. The room was filled with what seemed like grand furniture, nostalgia, and a

hint of mystery. She slowly walked through the shadows to a
desk that sat in the middle of the room. With a sense of
curiosity, she picked up a notebook from the desk and tried to
read the handwriting. Barely able to read the words, she placed
the notebook back onto the desk, she tried to jog her memory as
to why she was in this room, and why a rush of familiarity
washed over her? The details remained just out of reach.
The dim glow made it hard to see the room's surroundings. The
barely smoldering flames cast eerie shadows on the walls. She
turned to the fireplace, determined to reignite the logs.
Searching for a piece of paper to aid in lighting the fire, she
rummaged through a stack of old letters on a nearby shelf. With
a sense of excitement, she found a large, dusty envelope and tore
off pieces to use as kindling.
Returning to the fireplace, she carefully held the paper near the
simmering logs, watching as the paper and logs slowly reignited
into a bustling flame. A warm glow spread throughout the room
as the fire crackled to life, casting a comforting light around her.
The room seemed to come alive with the dancing flames,
illuminating the forgotten corners of the familiar yet eerie
space.
There, in the gleaming light, was an old cognac leather chair. It
looked comfortable. She felt tired, as if she had journeyed a long
distance to get here. As she settled back into the cozy armchair
by the fire, enveloped in its gentle warmth, she couldn't shake
the feeling that there was more to this room than meets the eye.
Allowed herself to sink deeper into the inviting surroundings,
eager to unravel the mysteries that lay hidden within its walls.
Sensing something familiar, she glanced around the room,
trying to make sense of the situation. Had she been there before?
She couldn't help but wonder if she was imagining things.
Wasn't there a wood door there before? Maybe it was just a trick
of the light, or perhaps she was more tired than she realized?
But no, the door was now gone. Her heart started to race as a
chill crept down her spine. She took a deep breath, trying to

calm herself. After all, there must be a logical explanation for this...

Then she realizes that every time she blinks, something else disappears. She tries not to blink, but she can't stop herself. It was like a twisted game of hide-and-seek where everything she looks at fades away, leaving her with a growing sense of unease. She needs to

find a way out of this before it's too late. Everything had now vanished except for the single light bulb hanging in the middle of the room. It cast long shadows on the bare walls, creating a surreal atmosphere. She takes a deep breath, trying to steady her nerves It's like something out of a horror movie.

This room did not resemble the one it was just a few moments ago. It stood barren now, except for a small wooden chair also in the middle of the room. She walks over and sits down, trying to gather her thoughts.

This chair was far less comfortable than the previous leather armchair. What is happening? How did I end up here? She tries to remember, but the memories are fuzzy, like a dream just out of reach.

Outside, she can hear muffled sounds, a stark contrast to the eerie quiet of this strange room. She wonders if anyone else is out there, if anyone even knows she's trapped in this doorless room. Her mind races with a million questions, but no answers seem to come.

She shifts in her seat, the wooden chair creaking beneath her. The light bulb above her swings gently, casting flickering shadows. It's mesmerizing in a way, the way the light plays against the darkness.

She closes her eyes, trying to block out the uncertainty that surrounds her.

She focuses on the soft hum of the light bulb, letting it lure her into a strange sense of calm. Maybe, just maybe, there is a way out of this?

Then the light goes out.

The woman leaned back in her chair. She looked puzzled.

"What do you think it means?"

"I don't know. You're the doctor."

The doctor smiled. She placed her hands on her lap on top of her notebook.

"Why do you think the dream bothers you so much?"

"I'm not sure. Maybe because I felt trapped, and I couldn't get out."

"Do you think you had another one of your panic attacks?"

"No."

"Are you still taking your medication?"

"Yes."

"Good. How have your headaches been lately?"

"Better."

"Dreams are your subconscious way of dealing with day-to-day stress. Is there something recently that has made you feel trapped?"

"Nothing I can think of."

"Okay. I'm sure this will work itself out. You're doing great. You should be proud of yourself."

The doctor wrote something down in her notebook. Then she looked at her watch.

"Time is up. See you next time."

* * *

THE WATER FELT smooth and cool against her body as she sliced through the pool with elegant strokes. Gliding effortlessly, she moved quickly through its mass. Her mind focused on the rhythm of her breathing and the sound of water splashing around her.

She had been swimming since the age of seven. She was like a fish in water. It was a great stress reliever for her, and she was good at it, which was a bonus. She had earned a partial scholarship, which made her parents proud. Her father practically drooled all over himself when she got the acceptance letter.

Her heart was pounding in her chest as she neared the end of her swim. She had been swimming for almost an hour, and she only had a few more laps to go. As she propelled herself forward, her thoughts drifted to her upcoming trip home.

The semester had been long and tough, and she dreaded the thought of having to make up incomplete classes over the summer. Her visit home wasn't going to be a long visit, but she was determined to make the best of it. She knew she would have to deal with her father, who always had a way of pushing her buttons. It was his way or the highway.

Charlie, her boyfriend, only added to an already difficult situation. A few days of seeing him were better than nothing, she thought to herself. She felt like she could never make everyone happy. It felt like nothing she did was ever good enough. She seemed to always make someone mad.

She wanted to be excited to go home, to see her family, especially Charlie. Maybe things would go better than she was anticipating.

Pushing those nagging thoughts aside, she focused on the sensation of flowing through the water. The coolness of her skin was a welcome distraction from her worries. As she reached the end of her final lap, a sense of understanding washed over her. She would have to deal with whatever came her way. She emerged from the pool, the water dripping from her body, a smile playing on her lips. She was going to make the best of it no matter what happened.

* * *

"You ready?" Sarah asked, glancing over at her best friend, Lou, who was busy packing her bags in the trunk of her car.

"I think so," Lou replied. "I can't believe I'm not coming back."

Sarah chuckled, shaking her head. "I wish I could say the same thing. But hey, I'll be out of here soon enough."

Lou nodded. "Nothing like another few months of not working a real job."

"Well, at least I'll finally get to be with Charlie for a few days," Sarah cheered out loud. The anticipation had been building up for months, and now the moment had finally come. After eight months of being apart, she was on her way to reunite with her boyfriend, Charlie.

As they neared the airport, Sarah couldn't contain her excitement. Lou glanced over at her with a knowing smile, understanding the mixed emotions that Sarah was feeling. With the windows partially down, the wind ruffled through their hair, carrying with it a sense of freedom and adventure.

The airport parking lot was bustling with activity as they found a space and unloaded Sarah's belongings.

"What am I going to do without you, Lou?

"You might fall apart," Lou joked, trying to lighten the mood.

Sarah smiled, a mix of nostalgia and excitement crossing her face.

"Oh, I'm sure you'll find a way to survive without me." Lou poked Sarah in the arm.

Hugging Lou tightly, Sarah expressed her gratitude for all the support and friendship she had received throughout the year.

"Call me."

"I will."

With a last hug, she grabbed her luggage and headed towards the entrance.

Inside the airport, the sound of chatter and footsteps echoed around her. Sarah's heart hastened with anticipation as she navigated her way through the terminal. Finally, she reached the arrival gate. As the passengers began to disembark the plane at the gate, Sarah scanned the crowd eagerly, waiting to reunite with her loved ones and get home already. She also wanted to take a long, much-needed nap. She hadn't gotten much sleep these past few months. She was surprised that she hadn't gotten sick. Usually, when she didn't get enough sleep, she would end up in bed for a week.

Time seemed to slow down as they boarded the plane. So many people. The plane was much too crowded for her liking. People bumped into each other at every turn. She had unfortunately gotten a middle seat. She hoped that the people sitting next to her would leave her alone.

The only thing holding her together was knowing that she was going to see Charlie. She imagined herself giving him a big hug and a sloppy wet kiss. The long distance had only made their relationship weaker, and now she was ready to try to embark on a new chapter together with only one more obstacle to get over. Charlie wasn't happy about her having to go back to summer school. Neither were her parents.

As the plane was ready to take off, the pilot announced there was a slight delay. Sarah could already feel her impatience growing. The delay was frustrating enough, but the stifling heat inside the aircraft made it nearly unbearable. The promised quick fix had somehow spiraled into a seemingly endless wait, and Sarah found herself stuck next to an elderly man who seemed intent on sharing stories from his past.

"Almost there," the captain's voice crackled over the intercom, but Sarah doubted the veracity of that statement. The old man next to her had already shared a handful of anecdotes, each one more random than the last.

"You look like my granddaughter," he said, his eyes twinkling with nostalgia. "I would guess you are almost the same age."

Sarah, exhausted from the day's events, forced a smile. "I'm about to turn 21," she replied, hoping to steer the conversation towards a rapid conclusion.

The man chuckled, his eyes taking on a faraway look. "Ah, the legal drinking age," he mused. "I remember those days..."

Sarah felt her eyelids grow heavier with each passing second. She tried to focus on the man's words, but all she could think about was finding a way to escape the conversation and slip into a much-needed nap.

Suddenly, the man produced a faded photograph from his wallet, his wrinkled fingers tracing the outline of a young girl's face. "This is my sweet Cindy," he said wistfully.

Sarah couldn't help but feel a pang of sympathy for the man, despite her own fatigue.

"Do you see what I mean?" The old man said with a big smile.

Sarah didn't see the resemblance except maybe for the color and length of their hair. "Yes, I do see it." Sarah lied but didn't want to hurt his feelings.

"Yes, yes." He nodded. "Are you from Portland?"

Sarah smiled. "Yes, I am. Well...a small town outside Portland. It's where I grew up."

The man nodded. His curiosity was piqued. "So, you're going home?"

"Yes, for a short while. I have a few days off from college until I have to start summer school," Sarah explained.

"Oh, I see," the man replied, an understanding glint in his eyes. "I bet your parents can't wait to see you," he added.

Sarah's face lit up with a genuine smile. "Yes, they are excited to have me back."

The man leaned back in his seat, crossing his arms over his chest. "My brother lives in Portland. It's a beautiful place, Portland."

Sarah reminisces about her childhood in the small community of Gatewood, just a short drive away from the beautiful city of Portland. Nestled east of the Cascades, Gatewood was a picturesque town with a charm all its own. The air was moist, and the scent of Ponderosa pines lingered in the breeze, painting a serene backdrop for daily life.

One couldn't help but be awestruck by the vast forests that blanketed half the state, creating a peaceful and natural oasis. The majestic presence of Mount Hood, its snowy peak visible from afar, added a touch of magic to the landscape. It was a sight that never failed to captivate visitors and locals alike.

In Gatewood, simplicity reigns supreme. The residents, with their rustic charm and laid-back demeanor, lived a life connected to nature. The town's economy thrived on timber logging and wood products, fueling a sense of camaraderie among its hardworking community.

The architecture of Gatewood mirrored its surroundings, with wooden three-story buildings dotting the streets. Each structure stood as a testament to the town's reliance on the land and its resources, a homage to the beauty of craftsmanship rooted in tradition.

As Sarah continued to reminisce, she couldn't help but smile at the memories of her childhood in Gatewood. It was a place where time seemed to stand still, where the simple pleasures of life were cherished, and where the beauty of nature was an ever-present companion. And as she thought about the possibility of living in the vibrant city of Portland one day, she couldn't help but feel grateful for the contrast of their worlds - one steeped in tranquility, the other alive with urban energy.

Yes, Portland was a beautiful place, no doubt about it. But for Sarah, Gatewood would always hold a special place in her heart, a reminder of a simpler time and a slower pace of life that she cherished more than anything.

"My brother and his wife have lived there for almost thirty years. Have you ever heard of Lake Chinook?"

"Yes, I've been there many times with my family."

"Oh, my brother wants us to take a drive up there and stay overnight in a cabin."

"It's a beautiful lake."

She thought about the lake. A number of lakes that are fed from the mountain snow-tops in the spring are only a short drive away. The winding road to Lake Chinook twisted through the large pine forests until a blue, shimmery oasis appeared. Lake Chinook was her family's favorite spot when she was a young girl. Many of her childhood memories were formed there. She and her family always looked forward to camping at Lake Chinook every year.

The day had finally come. Her body was flooded with joy as their family's car made its way up the winding road towards Lake Chinook. She couldn't help but feel a sense of nostalgia creeping in. The familiar scent of pine trees filled the air, and the sound of birds chirping echoed through the forest. It was as if her youth had been preserved in this serene place.

When they arrived at the cabin by the lake, a rush of emotions overwhelmed her. Her whole family seemed happy. The sight of the crystal-clear waters reflecting the golden hues of the setting sun brought back a flood of memories. She could hear the laughter of her family, the crackling of the campfire, roasting marshmallows, catching lightning bugs in mason jars, and the soft lapping of the waves against the shore.

As quickly as they arrived, the time to leave came too soon. The following morning, as her family packed up to leave. She knew that lake would still be there in all its beauty when they came back the following year. It was more than just a beautiful lake. It was a repository of memories and a reminder of the joy and simplicity of her childhood. Those were good times, she thought.

"Do you have any brothers or sisters?"

"I have one sister."

"Are you the oldest?"

"No, I'm not. Margaret is sixteen months older than me."

"The two of you are close in age."

"Yes."

"It's nice to be close in age. My brother is almost five years younger, and I never got the chance to grow up with him. We try to stay close, but it's not the same." The old man sighed.

"Yes, I guess you're right, but my sister and I fought a lot when we were younger. That was hard," Sarah said softly.

"Oh, I guess all brothers and sisters fight with each other, especially when it comes to getting their parents' attention. I was older so it wasn't a big deal."

"At least you are going to visit him. I'm sure he's excited to see you."

"Yes indeed." His eyes lit up.

"Is your sister as pretty as you?"

Sarah blushed. "We really don't look much alike."

If he had met Margaret, she thought to herself, he would not have asked such a question. Why couldn't she just be happy with his compliment? It made her mad. He probably wouldn't think she was as pretty like Margaret.

Margaret has always been the epitome of beauty. She was the kind of girl who made heads turn wherever she went. With her long, straight blond hair and deep blue eyes, she resembled their mother so much that people often mistaken her for her. Her tall, slender figure and soft, natural features only added to her allure.

Sarah, on the other hand, took after her father. She had his pronounced features but inherited his friendly smile that softened her appearance. Her dark blonde hair was a stark contrast to her mother's, yet she carried herself with a unique grace that was all her own. At least that's what she told herself.

Sarah couldn't help but feel a twinge of jealousy whenever Margaret effortlessly stole the spotlight. Whether it was at school, family gatherings, or even just walking down the street, Margaret had a way of shining brighter than anyone else. Sarah admired her sister's talents and beauty, but deep down, she longed to be seen and appreciated for who she was.

Despite their differences, Sarah and Margaret shared a deep bond that transcended their rivalry. They laughed together, cried together, and stood by each other's side through thick and thin. As they navigated the trials and tribulations of life, Sarah realized that her sister's light only served to illuminate her own path.

One day, as the two sisters sat beneath the old oak in their front yard, Sarah mustered up the courage to voice her feelings for Margaret. "I've always admired you, sis," she began tentatively. "But sometimes, it's hard not to feel overshadowed by your brilliance."

Margaret's eyes softened as she listened to her sister's words. "Sarah, I never meant to make you feel that way," she replied gently. "You have your own unique gifts and strengths that make you shine in your own way. You don't need to compete with me or anyone else."

Sarah never truly believed that. It always felt like a competition.

"It's annoying," Sarah said out loud.

"What's annoying, dear?" the old man asked with concern.

Sarah laughed. "I was just talking to myself." She couldn't believe she had said that out loud, she thought to herself.

"Good to know that other people do the same thing."

Sarah smirked, slightly embarrassed.

* * *

WHEN THE PLANE finally took off, Sarah closed her eyes, grateful for the chance to escape into silence. The old man's voice faded into the background, replaced by the gentle hum of the engines. Despite the delay and the stuffy air, her thoughts drifted to Charlie.

She put her headphones on to deter anyone else from talking to her. She remembered a conversation she had with Lou several months back.

Sarah and Lou were sitting in a cozy café on a lazy Sunday afternoon, sipping their iced coffees. The sun was shining brightly outside, but a cloud seemed to hang over Sarah's head.

"Do you think you and Charlie will work things out?" Lou asked, concern etched on her face.

Sarah sighed, stirring her drink absentmindedly. "I don't know. He's been acting so weird lately."

"I thought you were going to talk to him about it," Lou prodded gently.

"I know, I was, but he always cuts the conversation short. Every time I start to bring it up, he says he needs to go," Sarah explained, frustration evident in her voice.

"That does seem weird," Lou mused, trying to wrap her head around Charlie's behavior.

"Yeah, it's been bothering me a lot. I can't seem to concentrate on my work. No wonder I'm doing so badly at school," Sarah confessed, looking down at her notebook filled with half-finished assignments. "I just keep thinking about what I might have done to cause him to be so distant. Come to think of it, he never calls me anymore."

Lou reached out and squeezed Sarah's hand in a comforting gesture. "Maybe he's just busy with his job."

Sarah raised an eyebrow skeptically. "Maybe. Maybe he's mad about me having to go to summer school."

"What did he say when you told him?" Lou inquired, curious to know Charlie's reaction.

"Nothing. That's just it, he didn't say a thing," Sarah admitted, feeling a sense of heaviness settle in her chest.

As the friends sat there, pondering the mystery of Charlie's strange behavior, a sense of unease lingered in the air. Sarah couldn't shake the feeling that something wasn't right in their relationship.

* * *

SARAH HAS BEEN with Charlie for almost four and a half years now. They met when she was eighteen, and Charlie was twenty-two. From that moment, she felt like she had found her soulmate. They would spend hours talking about their future, dreaming of a life together. But there were always two obstacles standing in their way - her education and her dad.

Sarah's father insisted that she prioritize school above all else. As much as she loved Charlie, she knew that finishing her studies was important. Charlie understood this too. He knew that Sarah's father would never approve of their relationship if she neglected her education. So, he supported her decision to focus on school first.

However, when Sarah told Charlie that she had to attend summer school, he reacted differently than she expected. Instead of getting angry or causing a fight like he usually did when she had other commitments, Charlie simply said he couldn't talk any more. Sarah was taken aback by his response. She knew he struggled with sharing her time with anyone else besides him, especially because she was mostly gone during their four-and-a-half year courtship.

Sarah would somehow need to juggle her summer classes and her relationship with Charlie. She knew that something was off. She needed to have a serious conversation with him, but she was afraid of what his reaction would be this time.

The last hurdle they had turned out to be a complete disaster.

"What, you're not coming home?" Charlie's voice quivered with anger.

Sarah sighed, feeling the weight of guilt pressing down on her chest. "You know that old lady I always talk about? Well, she died last week. Lou is going to the funeral with me, and then we are going to drive down to her only daughter's house on Thanksgiving day. I volunteered to help her out with her mother's belongings."

"There's always an excuse. I'm sick and tired of this." "Please, Charlie. It's only one Thanksgiving."

Charlie's frustration was palpable over the phone. "Just one Thanksgiving," he muttered, his voice now strained with disappointment.

"I feel bad, but I think I should go. It's the right thing to do."

"So, coming home to see me isn't the right thing to do?"

"Of course, seeing you is the right thing to do, but this is different." Sarah stammered.

"This is different? I haven't seen you in months, and this is different?"

"Well, she died."

"Whatever?" Charlie hung up the phone.

Sarah snapped back to reality as she heard the old man sitting next to her speak out loud.

"Who designed these seats anyway? They never think of us old people. It's like we just don't exist."

"Well, I can see you clearly."

"I appreciate that."

The old man reached into his pocket and pulled out a white handkerchief. He wiped his forehead and shoved the cloth back into his pocket.

"This is the captain speaking. We will land in approximately fifteen minutes. It's a real nice day here in Portland, Oregon. It's 72 degrees and sunny. Again, we want to thank you for choosing American Airlines. Hope you enjoy your stay. Flight attendants please prepare for arrival."

The old man sat quietly with his eyes shut in his seat for the next fifteen minutes until it landed safely. His tense body finally relaxed.

"Hey, that wasn't so bad," Sarah said positively.

His irritated mood had suddenly changed. She smiled at him.

"No, not so bad."

"Don't like coming down."

"You don't like flying?"

"Flying is the easy part. Thinking about stopping a plane going at 350 mph kind of makes me a bit nervous."

Sarah nodded as she understood the impossibility of that. She was glad she wasn't the person designing the plane.

"You have a nice time visiting with your family. What is your name again, young lady?" he inquired.

"Sarah, Sarah Paige," she replied with a friendly smile.

"Sarah Paige? Oh... are you by any chance related to that fellow Robert Paige?" the man asked. His tone filled with intrigue.

Sarah's heart skipped a beat. She always felt a mix of pride and discomfort when others mentioned her father. Being the daughter of a successful businessman comes with its own set of challenges.

"Yes, he's my father," she replied, her voice soft.

"He is the owner of Paige Incorporated?" the man pressed on, his interest piqued.

"Yes, that's correct," Sarah confirmed, her gaze drifting downward.

The old man nodded thoughtfully, a look of admiration in his eyes.

"Your father is mighty impressive. I've read many articles about him and his company. "He knows his business," the man remarked, his voice filled with respect.

Sarah offered a shy smile, her cheeks flushing slightly at the unexpected praise.

"I suppose he does," she replied modestly.

"Well, it's been a pleasure talking to you, Sarah," the old man said, tipping his hat before turning to walk away.

As Sarah watched him leave, a sense of gratitude washed over her. Despite the assumptions and preconceptions that often came with her family's name, she knew that at the end of the day, what truly mattered was that her father had worked hard to achieve his reputation.

CHAPTER 2

Arrival

"Shit, it's an hour late."

Margaret knew she should have checked Sarah's flight status before she came to pick her up at the airport. Now she would have to kill time. She walked along the airport's corridor, going in and out of each shop. She hated airports. She hated the food, she hated the shops, and she hated all the people.

She picked up a magazine from the bookstore and studied the cover. The girl on the cover had barely anything on. She was pencil-thin, and her dark hair was long and straight. Margaret tried to imagine herself with dark hair. She closed her eyes. No, her skin would look too pale beneath its dark mass. Anyway, people would kill her for her natural blonde hair. What was she worried about anyway? As she placed the magazine back on the shelf, she noticed an art magazine. She walked toward it. "Le Art" was cleverly written on the cover, with a picture of a middle-aged woman. Margaret opened the magazine.

The article titled "The Woman of Many Palettes" caught Margaret's attention. "Emily Martin had found her true calling as a painter," the national magazine ran, praising her for coming into her own. Little did they know the journey that led her to this point.

As a little girl, Emily's heart was set on becoming a great painter. Her father, a talented artist who devoted his life to sharing his passion for art, was her greatest inspiration. He taught her everything he knew about color, brush strokes, and the magic of transforming a blank canvas into a masterpiece.

Emily would sit in awe for hours, watching her father work his magic. His hands created symphonies of color that danced across the canvas. She soaked in every lesson he imparted, every technique he shared, determined to follow in his footsteps and make her mark on the world.

Years passed, and life took Emily on a winding path with twists and turns. She embraced different careers, dabbled in various hobbies, and faced challenges that tested her strength and resilience. But deep down, the flicker of her childhood dream never faded. It beckoned her, urging her to pick up the brush and paint the world as she saw it in her soul.

And so, at sixty-one years of age, Emily Martin stood in her studio, surrounded by a palette of colors, her heart brimming with joy and gratitude. With each brushstroke, she poured her emotions onto the canvas, creating images that spoke of love, loss, hope, and the beauty of imperfection.

In a world that often overlooked the wisdom and creativity of those past their prime, Emily proved that true art knows no age. She was a living testament to the power of perseverance, passion, and the unyielding spirit of the human soul.

Margaret walked to the cashier and paid for the magazine.

* * *

As MARGARET SAT on the bench at the gate, tapping her foot impatiently, Sarah finally made her grand entrance. Despite the slight frown on her face, Margaret couldn't help but smirk - it was just so Sarah made an entrance like that. With her blue jeans and chunky black shoes, Sarah looked like she had just stepped out of a retro movie. Margaret couldn't help but appreciate her sister's unique style.

"Finally decided to join the living, huh?" Margaret teased, giving Sarah a playful nudge.

Sarah rolled her eyes. "Oh, spare me the dramatics, Marg. You act like I'm always late."

Margaret chuckled. "Well, let's just say punctuality isn't exactly your strong suit."

Sarah shot her a look before sitting down beside her, adjusting her red tank top and cardigan. "Hey, at least I made it, right?"

Margaret nodded. "True, true. Mom would be proud. You're lucky I didn't leave."

Sarah stood up after adjusting herself. She knew Margaret would do that. She was thankful that she didn't show up much later.

"You look tired?" Margaret stated, her voice filled with exhaustion as she dragged Sarah's suitcase behind her.

"You look tired too."

"What do you have in this bag anyway?"

"Just a dead body."

"Gross. You carry your own bag." The bag dropped to the floor.

Sarah leaned over and picked up her bag, groaning as she lifted it.

"So, how was the flight?"

"The flight wasn't bad... well,it was long and crowded. I met this really nice old man. He said I reminded him of his granddaughter."

"Huh...the only person you look like is dad."

"How are Mom and Dad?" Sarah asked nonchalantly, fiddling with her bag.

"Pretty much the same. Dad is as busy as usual. Mom's always off riding. I usually have the house to myself," Margaret said, scanning the airport for the right exit.

"Have you seen Charlie?" Sarah inquired, trying to catch up on the latest gossip from back home.

"Yeah, just the other day," Margaret replied.

"Did you talk to him?" Sarah asked nervously.

"No, I didn't get a chance. I just waved. I was in a hurry," Margaret replied.

"What was he doing?" Sarah probed, leaning in with curiosity.

"Sarah, how should I know?" Margaret retorted with a hint

of annoyance, her impatience showing. Margaret was walking faster.

Sarah knew she wouldn't get any real answers. She felt like she was sprinting just to keep up with Margaret.

"So, have you been waiting long?" Sarah asked, breathing hard as she realized her bag was heavy.

"What do you think? Your plane was late," Margaret pointed out, rolling her eyes.

"Sorry," Sarah mumbled, guilt creeping into her voice.

"What are sisters for?" Margaret said with a wry smile.

CHAPTER 3

Margaret

"It's always so pretty here, don't you think, Margaret?" said Sarah with a dreamy look in her eyes.

Margaret, who was lost in thought, replied, "What?"

"Pretty! The trees, the grass... you should paint this," Sarah exclaimed, nudging Margaret with a mischievous grin.

Margaret rolled her eyes and retorted, "Oh, please. Don't start that."

As they drove out onto the interstate from the airport, Sarah marveled at the lush countryside, while Margaret focused on the winding road ahead, covered in shades of pine trees. The hills rose majestically, and the trees seemed to touch the sky.

Sarah turned to Margaret, her tone light and witty, "You know, Margaret, if we ever get lost in these woods, we can just follow the scent of pine and find our way back."

Margaret chuckled, "Or we can just use Google Maps like normal people."

Sarah looked around. Margaret's once pristine white Beemer had transformed into a chaotic wasteland of clutter, a true reflection of the disarray in her life. As she navigated through the maze of magazines, coffee cups, and candy wrappers in her car, Sarah couldn't help but chuckle at the absurdity of it all.

Her dad, always the optimist, praised her for her dedication to her studies, blissfully unaware of the messy reality that resided within Margaret's car. He affectionately referred to it as her "reward," a humorous contrast to the chaos that Margaret had created.

The CDs and crumpled papers that littered her center console seemed to mock her past self - the vigilant guardian of her beloved car's squeaky-clean splendor. No longer did she forbid anyone from feasting or imbibing within, nor did she stand guard against any potential unauthorized drivers. Her once meticulous routine of weekly car washes and vacuuming had been replaced by an apathetic acceptance of the accumulating dirt and grime that now adorned her once pristine chariot.

As Margaret drove through the city streets, her car now a mobile monument to "I live in my car," she couldn't help but smile at the irony of it all. Perhaps, in the midst of her cluttered car and cluttered life, she had found a new kind of freedom - a freedom to embrace the chaos, to revel in the messiness of it all, and to find humor in the absurdity of her once meticulously orderly existence.

"So, you want me to help you clean your car while I'm home?" Margaret gave Sarah the evil eye.

"What's that?" Sarah asked, feigning innocence.

"What's what?" Margaret replied, playing along.

"That magazine? It's a picture of Emily." Sarah pointed out, a hint of excitement in her voice.

"No duh." Margaret retorted, rolling her eyes.

Sarah's excitement continued. "This is great. It talks about her life. Where did you find this? I've never heard of this magazine."

"I bought it at the airport," Margaret explained, a mischievous grin creeping across her face.

"When?"

"Just now when I was waiting for you."

"I didn't see it."

"I had it under my jacket."

"So, you were hiding it?"

"No." Margaret said it sarcastically.

"Are you going to tell mom and dad about this?" Sarah asked, her tone dripping with false concern.

Margaret's face was red from boiling frustration. She shot a sharp glance at Sarah, who was sitting next to her, oblivious to the storm brewing inside Margaret.

"Absolutely not, and you're not going to say anything about it. Is that clear? I don't need them nagging me any more than they already are."

"Your secret is safe with me."

"It better be."

"Geez," Margaret muttered under her breath, struggling to keep her cool.

"It's still impressive. I'm glad for Emily. You don't seem happy for her."

"So, I should be happy?"

Sarah, always the instigator, had somehow managed to steer the conversation towards Emily's recent art exhibition – a topic that Margaret had been avoiding like the plague. As the conversation veered towards discussing Emily's success, Margaret felt a pang of inadequacy creeping in. Emily's recent achievements had cast a long shadow over Margaret's own artistic journey.

Attempting to distract herself from the overwhelming wave of emotions, Margaret reached over and cranked up the music playing in the background. The loud beats filled the small car space, momentarily drowning out the noise in her head.

"Sorry, Margaret. I wasn't trying to make you mad."

"Yeah, whatever."

"I was just surprised. Why did you buy the magazine if it made you so mad?"

"I don't know.”

“Do we have to talk about this?"

Sarah shifted her body and changed the subject: "No... So, what was Charlie doing when you saw him?"

"Um... I think he was in his truck."

"You think?"

"No, he was in his truck."

"Oh."

"Don't you talk to Charlie? He is your boyfriend?"

"Yeah, we talked. I'm just excited to see him."

Sarah suddenly felt nervous. She hoped that he was looking forward to seeing her, but she doubted it after the way he had been acting towards her.

"Are you seeing Charlie tonight after Dad gives you one of his lectures?"

"Is Dad pissed?"

"I try not to talk to him. He's always mad at me."

"Really?"

"You and Charlie should go out so you don't have to deal with him."

"I know, but I really just feel like staying home. I thought I'd invite him over after dinner. If he calls."

"If he calls?"

Sarah couldn't help but smirk as she remembered the buzz that had surrounded Charlie when he first arrived at Gatewood. It was as if a tornado of curiosity had swept through the small town, leaving everyone gossiping about the enigmatic new boy with a charming smile.

Margaret and Sarah, being the curious souls that they were, had made it their mission to find out everything they could about Charlie. They had scoped him out from a distance, observing his every move with a mixture of fascination and amusement.

"I mean, when he calls..." Sarah trailed off, her tone tinged with a hint of frustration.

Margaret raised an eyebrow, a mischievous glint in her eyes as she echoed Sarah's words, "Oh, when he calls, indeed."

* * *

ONE DAY, Margaret and Sarah took their mom's car to the shop to get the brakes fixed. Their mom noticed that, when she tried to stop the other night in the rain, the brakes had slipped, and for a moment, she lost control. The girls had volunteered to take the car in to get the brakes checked out. This would be the perfect time to get a closer view of Charlie.

Once Charlie Parker straightened up and turned to face Margaret and Sarah, a sly grin played across his lips. His eyes twinkled mischievously, as if he knew a secret that he was dying to share.

"Hey there ladies. What can I do for you today? Brakes feeling a little wonky?" he quipped in a smooth, confident voice that made them both blush.

Margaret, always quick-witted, replied, "Wow, you must be some kind of brake whisperer to have sensed that just by the sound of our arrival. Or are you just psychic?"

Charlie chuckled, a deep, melodious sound that seemed to fill the garage with warmth. "Well, I do have a knack for foreseeing car troubles, but my psychic abilities might be pushing it. Let's see what's going on with that trusty old chariot, shall we?"

Margaret got straight to the point. "So, you're working for Mitch Connors?"

"Yeah, I just started here a few weeks ago," he said.

"How did you get the job?" she asked.

"He's my uncle," he replied.

"I see. Are you staying in town for a while?"

"You could say that. I have nowhere else to go."

"What about the two of you?" Charlie asked nonchalantly.

"We live up the street, at the Paige house. You know... the house with all the horses," she explained.

"Oh yeah. Nice house. My uncle pointed it out to me," he said.

As he inspected the car with expert precision, Margaret and Sarah couldn't help but be captivated by his easy charm and rugged good looks. There was something undeniably magnetic about him.

After a few moments of tinkering and testing, Charlie straightened up and flashed them a winning smile. "All fixed and good to go. You can trust me, I'm practically a car magician," he boasted, his tone playful and laced with a hint of flirtation.

Margaret and Sarah exchanged knowing glances, unable to deny the sparks of attraction that Charlie had ignited within them. As they drove away from the shop, the image of the mysterious mechanic lingered in Sarah's mind, leaving her to wonder if this chance encounter was just the beginning of an unexpected and thrilling adventure.

When Sarah and Margaret got home, Sarah had a mischievous glint in her eye. "I swear, Margaret, Charlie was staring at me the whole time," she exclaimed with a coy smile.

Margaret rolled her eyes, not bothering to look up from her phone. "Oh, please, Sarah. Not everything revolves around you and your fanciful crushes," she scoffed playfully.

Sarah pouted, feeling slightly deflated. She had hoped that

Charlie would notice her, but it seemed like he was more interested in his tools than in her.

Two days later, Sarah, Margaret, and their mother were gathered in the kitchen, enjoying a delicious snack of strawberries and cream. Their mom was washing the dishes in the sink when the doorbell rang. Their mom excused herself to answer the door, expecting a long-awaited package. But to everyone's surprise, standing on the doorstep was none other than Charlie, with a sheepish smile playing on his lips.

"Well, well, if it isn't the tool-tinkering mechanic himself," their mom chimed, a mischievous glint in her eye. "To what do we owe this unexpected pleasure, Charlie?"

"Uh, hello there," he said, scratching the back of his head nervously. "I, uh, was wondering if Sarah was around."

Sarah's mom laughed. "Follow me."

Sarah's eyes widened in disbelief as Charlie entered the kitchen, while Margaret smirked knowingly from the corner by the refrigerator.

"What are you doing here?" Margaret asked inquisitively.

"Nice place," he replied.

"You came by to check out the kitchen?" Margaret retorted.

"I'm here to see her," he said, his finger pointing at Sarah.

Margaret went silent.

"Would you like to go to the movies sometime?" he asked.

It seemed that fate had a way of turning the tables when you least expected it. But it was too much for Margaret, and she stomped out of the room.

"What's up with her?" Charlie snickered.

"Usually, the guys come over for her."

"Nah, she's way too uptight for me."

As they sat down to enjoy their strawberries and cream once more, Sarah couldn't help but feel a spark of nervous excitement in her heart. And so, in a twist of fate, Sarah learned that sometimes, the best things in life come when you least expected it.

* * *

As Margaret's car navigated the long and winding driveway toward their house in Gatewood, Sarah couldn't help but feel as though she was entering a magical realm straight out of a fairy tale. The afternoon sun cast a golden glow over the landscape, painting the skies with hues of mango and orange, as if the heavens themselves were putting on a show just for her.

"Ah, what a splendid sight!" Sarah exclaimed, leaning back in her seat and taking in the beauty that surrounded her. The crackling of gravel beneath the tires added a rhythmic beat to the peaceful atmosphere, while the gentle slope of the driveway seemed to beckon her closer to the enchanting house perched atop the hill.

As they pulled up to the house, their stunningly grand rustic cabin-meets- contemporary abode, Sarah couldn't help but marvel at the sight before her. The facade, a beautiful blend of wood in a rich golden tan hue, was accented with ivory stones and large floor-to-ceiling windows.

Their house stood in stark contrast to the simplicity of the nearby barn - each structure a testament to the unique personalities of their parents. Their father's car was already parked nearby, blending in seamlessly with the overall picturesque scene.

Sarah glanced over at Margaret, her usually chatty sister, who had been surprisingly quiet throughout the journey. It seemed like her thoughts were miles away, lost in some deep pondering. Sarah couldn't help but wonder what could be bothering her usually chatty sibling.

As Margaret and Sarah parked next to their father's car, the tension between them was as thick as fog. Their mother had mentioned that Margaret had been acting strange lately, always lost in her thoughts and constantly keeping to herself.

"Wow, Margaret, it's like we're not even related anymore. Are you training to become a hermit or something?" Sarah teased, trying to break the ice.

Margaret shot her a look that could freeze boiling water. "Very funny, Sarah. Maybe I just enjoy the peace and quiet away from your constant chatter."

Sarah raised an eyebrow. "Well, excuse me for trying to be a loving sister. Unlike someone here who's been MIA in the family drama."

Margaret sighed, her shoulders slumping. "I'm sorry, Sarah. I've just been dealing with a lot lately. You know, adulting and all that jazz. I promise I'm still the fabulous sister you once knew."

Margaret opened her trunk and took out Sarah's heavy bag. "I'm pretty sure there's a dead body in your bag."

Sarah laughed. "No, just a bunch of textbooks for summer." Sarah quickly remembered she would have to face her father. "Ugh, I don't want a lecture from dad. Maybe this is good therapy for Mom and Dad. Keeping them in constant fear of their daughter not graduating."

Margaret laughed. "Yeah, they probably can't sleep at night knowing you just might be the next child not to graduate. Two deadbeat kids. Oh, what will the neighbors think?"

"I guess Mom and Dad are really mad at me."

"Don't worry about it. What can they do to you anyway?"

"Disown me?"

"Maybe that wouldn't be so bad," Margaret said quietly under her breath.

They walked up to the grand door and Margaret punched in the passcode. Sarah was trying to lift her heavy bag over the threshold.

"Mom, we're home."

"I'm in the kitchen."

Their mom rolled meatballs in her hands. She looked up as they entered the room. Her eyes twinkled as she looked at Sarah.

"Hey, sweetie. Glad you're home."

"Me too, Mom.”

She walked over and hugged Sarah with her greasy hands. Maybe she's not mad at me, Sarah thought.

“Where's Dad?"

"He's in the study finishing up a business call."

"How was your flight?"

"Good. Except for the delay."

"What are you cooking? I'm starving?"

"Swedish meatballs," her mom said excitedly.

Her mom always made the best Swedish meatballs. Sarah was determined to whip up some delectable Swedish meatballs for her father's birthday a few years back. As she mixed the ingredients with determination and a dash of optimism, Sarah couldn't help but feel a twinge of doubt. Her mom made it look so effortless, gliding around the kitchen with the finesse of a master chef. Meanwhile, Sarah was battling to keep the meatballs round and her apron pristine.

After hours of slaving away and a few trips to the grocery store for forgotten items (parsley, where did you hide?), Sarah presented her culinary creation to her dad with a hopeful smile. His face lit up with enthusiasm as he took a bite, but she couldn't help but notice the slight twitch in his eyebrows - a telltale sign that her masterpiece might not be as flawless as she'd hoped.

"Dad, do you like it?" she asked, trying to gauge his reaction.

Her dad, ever the diplomat, nodded and said, "It's...interesting." The dreaded "interesting," the polite code for "bless your heart, but this tastes like a shoe."

"Sarah," her mom broke her trance, "why don't you go and unpack? Your father should be off the phone shortly, and we can all eat and catch up on everything."

"I'm not eating here tonight. I already have plans."

Her mom looked at Margaret with disappointment.

"Look, Margaret, I'm sick of your selfishness. Sarah just got home, and..."

"Mom, it's okay."

"See, Mom? Sarah is fine with it. You always make such a big deal of everything."

"It's not okay, Margaret. You knew Sarah was coming home tonight."

"I forgot when I made the plans, and I'm not breaking them."

"Your father is going to be mad."

"Whatever. He'll get over it."

"Just leave, Margaret, before I say something I'll regret."

Margaret snatched up her keys and strode out the kitchen door, leaving behind a bewildered Sarah who watched her in utter confusion. Her mom, wearing a deadpan expression, simply stared at the glass pot of meatballs, as if trying to calm her internal frustration before saying something she might regret.

CHAPTER 4

Charlie

SARAH GLANCED AT HER WRISTWATCH. It was nearing eight o'clock. The trio had just finished their meal. Her parents were debating Margaret's conduct.

"Gwen, you should have informed her that she couldn't go out."

"And pray tell, Robert, how do you suggest I do that? She refuses to listen to me."

"You cave in far too easily, my dear."

Gwen's face was flushed crimson.

"I'm utterly exasperated with her impudence. Something simply must be done," Robert huffed.

"We've discussed this a million times, and nothing seems to work. I'm tired of thinking about it. Perhaps we should give her some space."

"Really Gwen. You amaze me. She is our daughter, and she needs to be taught a lesson or two."

Sarah sat quietly, not daring to utter a word. She knew her father was also angry with her, and he was waiting for the chance to lecture her, but tonight, his mind was on Margaret, and Sarah was more than content to stay under the radar.

As her parents continued their heated discussion, Sarah couldn't help but think about Margaret's rebellious nature. She had always been the one to push the boundaries, to test her parents' patience.

Sarah looked around her parents' impeccably designed kitchen. She glanced around the room in a mixture of awe and amusement. The kitchen was a large rectangle, probably big enough to host a fancy cooking show.

The countertops sparkled with luxurious white quartz that made Sarah wonder if they were worth more than her entire college apartment. A floating island proudly displayed itself in the middle of the room, adorned with four industrial, farmhouse, rustic, and wood barstools that looked like they had never been touched.

The appliances stood proudly in stainless steel, as if daring any spills or stains to mar their sleek surface. Sarah couldn't help but think they were like the Avengers, high-tech, ready to save the day with their culinary powers.

The high ceiling made her feel like she was in a regal banquet hall, and the walls, textured with greige colored paint, whispered tales of exotic destinations. The breakfast nook where Sarah sat felt like a cozy oasis amidst all this grandeur.

"Welcome back to Sarah's Spectacular Kitchen!" she would announce to the empty room, brandishing a spatula like a sword. "Today, we're making a five-star meal with leftovers and a dollop of creativity! "The setting sun filters in through the windows, casting a warm glow over the room.

"Sarah, I asked you a question."

"What?" Sarah was immediately pulled back to reality.

"When can the two of us sit down and talk about your grades?"

Sarah was startled. She had not realized the conversation had turned to her. Her father's eyes stared into hers as he awaited her answer.

"Uhh," is all Sarah could utter.

Sarah had imagined how the conversation would go when she spoke with her father. She wasn't going to be able to graduate with her classmates. As hard as she tried, she didn't make it. Her father's words would hurt. But Sarah, using her imagination and being the witty daughter that she was, would spin the situation around.

With a mischievous glint in her eye, she began, "Well, Dad, who needs a graduation cap when you've got a top hat full of extraordinary ideas, right?"

Her father's stern expression would waver as a small smile tugged at the corners of his lips.

Sarah had him intrigued. "I may not be walking across the stage in a cap and gown, but mark my words, Dad, I'll be waltzing into the world with my own unique flair."

* * *

SHE HAD FAILED one of her core classes, and her teacher would not pass her. Her teacher wasn't going to budge.

"Please, I'll take a D, but please don't fail me."

"I'm sorry, Sarah. What about all those other students who worked hard to pass?"

"I tried. I really did."

"Then the class should be easier next time."

Sarah had known for three days before she had called her father. The weight of her secret had been crushing her spirit, making her feel sick to her stomach. With trembling hands, she dialed his number, her heart pounding in her chest.

Her father's voice answered at the other end of the line, his tone quiet and steady. She hesitated for a moment, feeling the weight of her mistake heavy on her shoulders. As she poured out the truth, she could sense his silence on the other end of the line, wondering if he had hung up the phone in disbelief.

"Dad, are you still there? Say something," Sarah finally broke the tense silence, her voice quivering with emotion.

His sigh was heavy, his disappointment palpable even through the phone line. His next words, filled with anger and hurt, cut through her like a knife.

"It's absolutely unbelievable," he said.

"I'm sorry," she whispered, her voice laced with deep remorse. But her father's response was sharp, his tone filled with a mix of anger and disappointment.

"Sorry. Don't tell me you're sorry," he snapped, the words hanging heavy in the air between them.

Sarah felt her heart shatter into a million pieces, realizing the depth of the pain she had caused. As the weight of her actions sank in, she knew that rebuilding trust with her father would be an uphill battle.

"I don't understand you. You knew what was expected of you to finish these classes. What happened?" His words cut through her like a knife.

Tears welled up in Sarah's eyes as she remembered the countless hours she had spent studying, the late nights she had sacrificed to keep up with her coursework. She had tried her best, she really had.

"I don't know."

"Sarah, we've talked about focus," her father's tone was stern and uncompromising.

"I know, Dad. All my classes this semester were hard," Sarah explained, her voice pleading.

"You obviously weren't applying yourself enough," her father's accusation stung.

The silence that followed was heavy and suffocating. Sarah felt the weight of her father's disappointment pressing down on her.

"Dad, can I come home for a couple of days? I'm exhausted?" Sarah finally mustered the courage to ask.

"Sarah, maybe you should stay there and think about how you plan on finishing," her father replied.

"Please let me come home," Sarah's voice trembled with emotion.

Her father hesitated, the sound of his ragged breath the only response on the other end of the line. Sarah held her breath, waiting for his decision.

"Come home and rest. After that, I want you back on track," her father's voice was strained, weary.

"Okay," Sarah whispered, a mix of relief and worry.

* * *

"WELL, SARAH?"

Sarah quietly snapped back to reality. "What was the question?"

"Your grades. We need to talk about this."

Sarah's prayer had been answered. Her phone rang. She reached into her pocket to answer it before it stopped ringing.

"Hello? Hey, Charlie."

"You're still talking to that punk?" her dad asked sternly.

Sarah shushed her father. She put her finger in her mouth.

Ignoring Sarah's gestures, her father replied, "We will talk first thing tomorrow."

Sarah's heart sank at her father's disapproval of Charlie. She knew her parents always had high expectations for her, but she never expected such a blatant dislike of Charlie. All she wanted was a chance to follow her heart, even if that meant being with someone from a different background.

As she walked out of the room, Sarah could feel the weight of her father's disapproving gaze on her back. She pulled her phone to her ear again, hoping Charlie was still on the line.

"Hey, Charlie. I'm sorry," Sarah said, trying to mask the unease in her voice.

"Hey, babe. Is everything okay?" Charlie's warm voice instantly brought a sense of comfort to Sarah.

Sarah hesitated for a moment before responding, "Yeah, everything's fine. My dad just... he's mad at me."

Charlie's tone softens. "Don't worry about it, Sarah."

"I'm so glad you called."

"Of course, Sarah. I've been waiting for you to come home."

"Thank you, Charlie. I'll see you soon, okay?" Sarah said, her voice filled with determination.

As she hung up the phone, Sarah felt increased excitement to see Charlie.

* * *

CHARLIE FINALLY SHOWED up at Sarah's house around a quarter to nine. He looked like he had been through a storm, with his tousled hair and tired eyes. His usual pulled-back hair was now hanging freely around his face, giving him a rugged yet charming appearance. Dressed in dark-colored jeans and a light blue, long-sleeved shirt, he seemed like he had rushed over without much thought to his outfit.

Sarah was taken aback by the cut on the side of his face, still red and puffy. Despite his weary appearance, there was a hint of reluctance in his expression as he looked at her. Sarah leaned in and kissed him, making him crack a small smile.

"I've missed you," she said, trying to break the awkward silence. She squeezed him hard.

Charlie remained silent, his eyes scanning the room as he followed Sarah towards the family room.

A broad grin came over his face. "Where is everyone?" he asked.

"I think Dad's in his study, and Mom went up to her room," Sarah replied, glancing around.

"Where's your sister?"

"I don't know. She had plans tonight, but she didn't say where she was going,"

Charlie nodded.

Sarah couldn't help but tease him. "Wow, you're really on top of things tonight, aren't you?"

"I like that we are alone," Charlie chuckled, his tired demeanor slowly melting away in Sarah's presence.

Charlie and Sarah sat on the sofa, surrounded by the cozy ambiance of the room that felt like a warm hug on a chilly winter evening. Sarah couldn't help but admire the way her father had borrowed design elements from an Austrian ski lodge to create this enchanting space.

As she gazed at the floor-to-ceiling stone fireplace, she imagined the crackling flames dancing merrily, casting a soft glow across the room. The oversized rustic furniture seemed to beckon them to sink into its plush cushions and never leave. An equestrian motif filled the room, including pictures of her mom during her competitions as a rider. In one picture, she was holding up a silver cup, standing next to her father. She was younger then, only eighteen years old, but she hadn't changed much in all those years.

Sarah raised an eyebrow, looking at Charlie curiously. "What are you thinking about?" she asked, breaking the comfortable silence that had settled between them.

Charlie stayed silent. He was gazing at the fire.

"I love this room," Sarah said.

"It's nice," Charlie replied.

Sarah looked around the room. "I've always wondered why my mom stopped competing," she confessed, her brows furrowed in thought.

Charlie cocked his head to the side, considering Sarah's words. "She got married and had two kids," he pointed out matter-of-factly.

Sarah nodded slowly. "Yeah, maybe. But she could have always gone back after we got a little older," she mused, her mind drifting to the past.

Charlie raised an eyebrow. "Maybe she didn't have the desire anymore, just like Margaret," he teased.

Sarah's eyes widened in protest. "No, my mom's different from Margaret," she defended her mother's honor, a hint of pride in her voice.

Charlie leaned back, a sly smile playing on his lips. "Maybe not. In some ways, they're a lot alike," he countered, enjoying the banter between them.

Sarah shook her head adamantly. "But my mom would never just give up," she insisted, her voice filled with admiration.

Charlie chuckled. "I guess your mom didn't completely give up on it. She still has a barn full of horses that she rides and takes care of," he pointed out, gesturing towards the stables in the distance.

Sarah smiled wistfully, her eyes softening. "Yeah, she loves horses. She's out with them all the time. But if I were a champion like her, I wouldn't have given that up," she confessed.

Charlie nudged her playfully. "You don't know that," he teased, nudging Sarah's shoulder with his own.

Sarah turned to Charlie, a soft smile on her face.

"You wouldn't give it up for me, would you?" he demanded, his eyes blazing with an intensity that sent shivers down her spine.

Sarah's heart raced as Charlie's piercing gaze bore into her. She knew that look. With a heavy sigh, she lowered her gaze, unable to meet his eyes any longer. The disappointment in Charlie's voice cut through her like a knife, leaving her feeling exposed and vulnerable.

"I'm sorry, Charlie," Sarah whispered, her voice barely audible in the tense silence that enveloped them.

"You would never give up anything for me." He paused. His foot was moving up and down. "It's always about you. Your father is constantly judging me."

Sarah bit her lip, struggling to find the right words to say. She knew that Charlie was mad because he felt like he could never be good enough for her father and that her father expected Sarah to feel the same way. Her sights were set on something much higher than Charlie. She would never have enough time for him.

"Charlie..."

But he interrupted her, his anger palpable in the air between them.

"Don't say anything else," he snapped, turning away from her with a look of disdain.

Sarah reached for Charlie's arm. He turned around. Out of nowhere, Charlie's mood suddenly shifted. His hands tenderly caressed Sarah's face, fingers intertwining with her hair in a moment of sheer intimacy.

Drawing closer to her, Charlie's eyes held a mesmerizing gaze as they traced her delicate figure. Sarah recognized that familiar look that always sent shivers down her spine. As his touch grazed her skin, a wave of warmth washed over her, heightening her senses. With flushed cheeks and tousled dark hair cascading forward, Charlie's intensity only deepened Sarah's longing for him.

Their gazes were locked, their blue eyes meeting hers in a silent exchange of unspoken desires. In that moment, Sarah knew how much she had missed him, missed this fiery connection that bound them together. They fell into each other's embrace, breathing hard and producing droplets of sweat. Suddenly, a loud bang shattered the tranquil moment, jolting them from their intimacy.

"What was that?" Sarah's voice rang out, laced with a hint of curiosity.

"I'm not sure," Charlie replied, his tone tinged with a touch of wit despite the interruption, feeling relaxed and satisfied.

She pulled away, straightening out her clothes. "We can't get caught," Sarah said, combing her hair with her fingers.

The noise now sounded closer. As they both glanced towards the source of the disturbance, a mix of intrigue and anticipation filled the air, unsure of what awaited them beyond the threshold.

"Who is that?" Sarah whispered.

Charlie nodded, equally intrigued. "Well, there are only two choices unless your mom got a dog," he joked, trying to diffuse the tension with a hint of humor.

"I wish we could get a dog. My dad never lets us."

The shadow slunk its way down the hallway, towards the kitchen, its movements accompanied by the distinct tap-tap-tap of footsteps against the unforgiving wood floor. Sarah and Charlie exchanged glances.

"Do you think whoever it is knows we're in here?"

"I didn't tell anyone you were coming over... well, Margaret knows."

Charlie laughed. "Maybe it's your new dog you're not telling me about."

"I wish."

Just as they thought the shadow had vanished into thin air, it reappeared in the hallway, its contorted shape dancing playfully on the walls. The sound of footsteps grew louder, echoing through the house as they followed the mysterious figure into the foyer, only to be met with a sudden silence that hung heavy in the air.

Charlie chuckled, though his eyes betrayed a hint of apprehension. "Well, it looks like we've got ourselves a houseguest. Unfortunately, it's not a dog. It looks like Margaret's shadow."

"It does look like her."

"Hopefully, it's not your dad."

"Let's hope not. It didn't go well last time when he caught us being intimate."

"Who cares?" Charlie was getting aroused again. He pulled Sarah close to him again. He tried to kiss her.

"Charlie, stop. We can't get caught, besides, we need to talk." Charlie's body stiffened.

"Why have you ignored me?"

"I don't want to talk about it."

"No, Charlie, we need to talk about it," Sarah said firmly, her voice tinged with frustration.

He quickly dropped his hands and leaned back on the sofa. He crossed his legs and looked at his hand, absentmindedly playing with his silver pinky ring. "What do you mean?" he asked, trying to keep his voice steady.

"Come on, Charlie, you know what I mean. Why have you been avoiding me? I've left messages, and you never called me back," Sarah pressed, her tone insistent.

"I've been busy lately, working a lot in the shop," Charlie replied, his voice slightly defensive.

"Really? I've called you there too, and Mitch never knows where you are. He's mad about it too. "He started yelling at me about you the last time I called," Sarah explained, her eyes searching for answers.

"Look, Sarah, Mitch is an asshole. He's just like my father, a freaking jerk," Charlie retorted, his tone turning angry as he defended his actions.

The room fell into heavy silence as the weight of their unspoken feelings hung in the air. It was clear that there were deeper issues at play, ones that needed to be confronted and addressed.

"Why are you calling me there anyway? Are you trying to get me into trouble?"

Sarah's voice deepened. "No, of course not. You can be such a jerk sometimes. I just want to talk to you."

He ran his fingers through his hair.

"I've called you plenty of times too," Charlie stated. "Either the phone is on silent or you're avoiding me."

"You don't answer my calls either." Charlie retorted.

"That's a lie, and you know it. I don't have any missed calls from you or texts."

Charlie rolled his eyes.

"Stop doing that. I hate it when you do that."

"Do what?"

"When you roll your eyes."

"Huh... You're probably out with some douchebag behind my back and you don't think I'll find out. Poor stupid Charlie," he said sarcastically.

"Charlie, I have lots of studying to do, and that's what I've been doing. You could come to visit me at any time. I have nothing to hide from you. In fact, I have no choice in the matter but to get through school, which means I work my ass off. My father is really upset about me right now."

"It seems your father is more important to you than I am."

"What's your problem? You know that's not true." Sarah was frustrated.

"God, haven't we talked about this a million times? We, that's you and me, agreed that we would have to be patient until I could get through college."

"Well, I have been more than patient and I'm fed up with this whole relationship."

Sarah flinched. "What do you mean, Charlie?"

Charlie seemed pleased that he had hurt Sarah. "Who's Jake?"

Sarah was surprised. "Jake, um... how do you know about Jake?"

"I called your roommate Lou. She said you were out with Jake."

"Why are you calling Lou?"

"Are you spying on me?"

"Well... your phone always goes straight to voicemail."

"He's just a friend of mine from class."

Charlie looked at her. She could see from his demeanor that he didn't believe in her.

"He doesn't have many friends. He's kind of shy. I said I would go get a bite to eat with him." She paused. "What? Why are you looking at me like that? He knows all about you Charlie. That's all I ever talk about. That's it."

Charlie laughed obnoxiously. "You're such a liar."

"It's true."

Charlie's face was bright red. "How convenient for you that I'm not around! You're probably dating a bunch of guys behind my back."

"What? Fine, don't believe me?"

"Tell me, why would you want to date a mechanic when you have the choice of all those other rich guys?"

"Stop it, Charlie. You know I don't care about that. I want to marry you."

"Oh, that's funny," he laughed and snickered. "You want to marry me?"

"No, I'll take it back. I definitely don't want to marry you when you're acting like this," Sarah said firmly.

"You are having doubts about us. Maybe it's that Jake guy." His voice was loud now. I'm just your fucking backup plan until you find Mr. Rich guy. You're probably planning on dumping me for him, aren't you?"

"What is all this about? You're acting crazy."

"You're right, I am acting crazy. Are you sleeping with him too?"

Out of nowhere, Sarah's hand landed on his face, leaving a red outline of her hand.

"You fucking bitch!"

It happened so quickly. His fist landed on her head. Sarah fell back hard, and the side of her body crashed against the coffee table. Sarah's t-shirt caught the edge, and it ripped. Blood dripped down the side of her face. It felt oddly warm. Her head was throbbing from the blow. Charlie was now hovering over her, breathing loudly. Her eyes were wide open, staring at his clenched fist. His hand was in the air, ready to punch her again.

Sarah's heart raced with fear and anger. How did things escalate to this point? She never imagined she would find herself in a situation like this. Betrayal and hurt filled her mind, fueling a fire of defiance within her. She refused to cower before him, despite fear bubbling in her chest.

As Charlie's fist hung in the air, Sarah's survival instincts kicked in. She pushed herself up, ignoring the pain shooting through her body. With a swift motion, she kicked Charlie in the stomach, causing him to stagger backwards. Adrenaline coursed through her veins as she scrambled to her feet.

"Enough!" Robert's voice cut through the tension in the room, laced with anger and determination.

"Don't touch her again!" Her dad was holding a bat, and it took all his strength not to use it.

CHAPTER 5
Contempt

Sᴀʀᴀʜ's ᴍɪɴᴅ was racing at a thousand miles per second. What had just happened? Did Charlie really just hit her? All she could hear amidst the chaos were the deafening shouts reverberating through the room like a poorly tuned speaker.

She tried to focus, to make sense of the mayhem unfolding before her eyes. The shouting was like a hurricane of fury, and its epicenter was her father. Sarah had never witnessed her father in such a state of wrath. It was like watching a volcano reach its boiling point, ready to erupt at any moment. Charlie stood motionless as a statue, as if time had come to a screeching halt.

"Leave now!" Her father bellowed, the weight of his words heavy in the air as he brandished a threatening baseball bat.

But Charlie remained rooted to the spot, his eyes finally meeting Sarah's in a moment of remorse.

"I'm... sorry," he managed to murmur, his voice a mere whisper in the storm of anger.

Sarah's father trembled with a ferocity that could make a hurricane seem like a mild breeze. It was as though he was single-handedly trying to halt a runaway train, with his rage as the only brake in sight.

"Charlie, if you don't leave this instant, I swear I'll rearrange your face!" Her father warned. His face flushed a vivid crimson, and spittle flew with each vehement syllable. "You will never lay a finger on her again," he started, his words interrupted by the sudden tense silence that fell over the room. In that moment, the room seemed to hold its breath, as the standoff between father and Charlie hung in the air like a silent thunderstorm, awaiting the spark that would ignite the chaos once again.

"You're right, Mr. Paige. I was wrong. I don't know what's come over me," Charlie stammered, his demeanor softening into that of a contrite child pleading for forgiveness. He rubbed his forehead in frustration, his voice laced with anxiety. "Fuck... I've been under a lot of stress lately. Mitch...he's been an asshole."

Sarah studied the cut on Charlie's face, connecting the dots in her mind. What was brewing between Charlie and Mitch that led to this erratic behavior? It seemed like Charlie was constantly embroiled in battles, now including herself, and now her father was in the mix.

Robert's eyes flashed with warning, his patience wearing thin. "Don't you push that crap on me, mister! You're walking on thin ice. I could ruin your life with one phone call."

Charlie's voice shook as he promised, "I know. I'll never hurt her again."

"Charlie, leave!"

Charlie turned and headed through the door. The door slammed behind him.

* * *

As Charlie marched towards his truck, he couldn't help but curse under his breath. "Fuck," he muttered to himself. His heart was pounding in his chest, matching the rapid beat of his pulsating blood. In a moment of reflection, he couldn't help but think, "Fuck, now I've turned into my old man. What a horrific turn of events?"

The image of Sarah's shocked expression as he raised his voice at her flashed in his mind, and he winced. "What the fuck?" He scolded himself silently. He could practically feel Robert's disapproving gaze boring into his back through the window. It was clear that he had overstayed his welcome.

Shaking his head in bewilderment, Charlie tried to make sense of the chaos that seemed to have taken over his life. "Is it stress? The pressure? Nah, it's probably just that obnoxious asshole Mitch getting under my skin," he reasoned. Mitch was starting to resemble his old man more and more with each passing day.

Charlie had blamed booze for his father's less-than-stellar behavior, but deep down, he knew the man was just plain insane.

Charlie slammed his fist against the steering wheel as he navigated down the dusty road, his resolve as firm as the grip he had on the wheel. "No way, there's no way I'm going to end up like my dad," he muttered to himself, the words echoing in the confines of the truck.

His reckless actions had led him to a crossroads where he had to make a choice – either straighten up and fly right, or spiral down the same dark path his father had trodden. And damn it, he was not about to let history repeat itself.

The wheels of his truck squealed over the gravel road as if protesting against his newfound determination. "Come on, old girl, we've got places to be," he said, urging his faithful truck to carry him away from his past mistakes. As he drove on, in the blackness of the night, beneath the towering ponderosa pines, the realization hit him like a ton of bricks – he needed to make a change, to break free from the cycle that had ensnared his family for generations.

* * *

Sarah huffed out a deep breath of air, stammering her words while trying to explain the situation to her father in a casual tone.

"Please, Dad. It was stupid, really. We were arguing about something silly, and I just lost my temper."

Her father's expression softened as he listened to Sarah's explanation. He knew his daughter well enough to understand that she was not one to start fights needlessly.

"I'm sorry, Sarah," her father's voice was firm. "Charlie should have known better than to react violently."

Sarah nodded, feeling confused. She understood her father's concern, but she knew she was to blame too for her actions as well.

"Sarah, I don't want you to see Charlie again."

"Dad, that's not fair."

"I don't want you to say another word."

Sarah's heart felt heavy as she stormed up the stairs, her father's words echoing in her mind. Nothing made sense. She couldn't believe he had told her she couldn't see Charlie again. Charlie, her best friend and the love of her life, was the one person who truly understood her. As she reached her room, tears streamed down her cheeks, a mix of sadness and frustration.

She paced back and forth, trying to make sense of her father's lack of understanding. How could he not see that Charlie wasn't himself and needed help? How could he ask her to turn her back on someone she cared so deeply about? There was more to the story. As Sarah lay on her bed, her tears flowing freely, she couldn't shake the overwhelming feeling of helplessness. Mitch was somehow involved, but Sarah couldn't quite piece together the details. Lost in her thoughts, Sarah felt a presence in the room with her. Opening her wet eyes, she saw her mom standing in the doorway.

"Are you okay Sarah?"

Her mom looked like an angel in the doorway.

"I'm okay, mom," Sarah forced a weak smile, trying to reassure her mother despite the turmoil inside her.

Her mother's worried expression deepened as she gently prodded, "What happened, Sarah? Your father is beside himself?"

Sarah took a deep breath, her voice trembling as she recounted the heated argument with Charlie that had spiraled out of control.

"Charlie accused me of seeing someone else, Mom," Sarah confessed, her heart heavy with the weight of misunderstanding. "I lost my temper. And then," Sarah stammered. "Then he just snapped, like his father did to him."

Her mother's eyes widened in shock.

"Your father said that he hit you," her mother whispered, the worry lines on her face deepening with every word. "Is that true?"

Sarah nodded, her voice barely a whisper, "Yes."

"Do you think he's drinking or taking any drugs?" Her mother's voice was laced with concern, her eyes fixed on Sarah, searching for answers.

Sarah's heart was heavy with worry as she sat across from her mother, their voices hushed in her dimly lit bedroom. The mention of drugs and alcohol sent a shiver down her spine, as memories of Charlie's father's struggles with addiction flashed before her eyes.

"No, absolutely not," Sarah replied, her voice firm but tinged with doubt. She believed in Charlie, in his strength and resolve to be different from his father. But fear lingered in the back of her mind, threatening to consume her.

Her mother reached out, placing a reassuring hand on Sarah's trembling one. "Sarah, something's wrong. If it's not drugs, then I don't know what it could be. If he shows any signs of abuse, he could be very dangerous like his father."

The weight of her mother's words pressed down on Sarah, filling her with a sense of dread. She tried to push away the nagging doubts, the possibility that Charlie could be spiraling down a dark path.

"But Mom, he's not that way. He's never done this before," Sarah pleaded, her voice cracking with emotion.

Her mother's gaze softened, mirroring Sarah's own turmoil. "But that doesn't mean it can't happen. We need to be prepared, just in case."

Sarah's mind swirled with anxiety, her thoughts racing as she grappled with the uncertainty of the situation. What if her worst fears were realized? What if Charlie was in trouble, lost to a shadow that mirrored his father's demons?

"God, mom, what am I going to do?" Sarah whispered, her voice filled with desperation and fear.

As the room fell into heavy silence, Sarah and her mother remained locked in a shared moment of fear and uncertainty, bound by a love that stood firm in the face of looming shadows. The darkness outside seemed to press against the windows, a reminder of the unknown dangers that lurked beyond their safe haven.

* * *

"GOD DAMN IT, Gwen. What am I supposed to do? Who is supposed to pay for all of this?" Robert exclaimed, frustration evident in his voice as he picked up Gwen's necklace and dangled it in his hand.

"All this stuff that you're always buying costs a hell of a lot of money. That's the price we pay when you can't stop spending," he continued, a tinge of sarcasm lacing his words.

Gwen, her eyes reflecting a mix of defiance and regret, replied, "I don't want it, not anymore."

"Be careful what you wish for," Robert warned, rubbing the necklace back and forth in his hands with a thoughtful expression.

"You're never home, and I can't take it," Gwen continued, brushing her hair.

Robert sighed, a hint of resignation seeping into his tone. "When you married me, you knew what my work meant to me. We agreed on this together."

Gwen sighed, her voice hoarse with a sense of defense. "I was young then, and you took advantage of me," she added, attempting to shift the blame.

"Gwen, don't put this on me. You like money more than I do. You had to have a horse farm. That alone costs us thousands of dollars a month. Would you be happy to give that up?" Robert shot back, his frustration reaching a boiling point.

"No, Robert, please, that's all I have," Gwen pleaded. Her voice was tinged with a hint of desperation.

Gwen wiped away her tears, her eyes still watery from the memories that flooded her mind. Ah, her beloved horses. She could recall the day her father surprised her with Stan Miller's old horse as if it were yesterday. Stan, a longtime family friend, had gifted them the horse, knowing Gwen's enthusiasm for horses and her desire to help and ride them.

From a young age, Gwen's affinity for horses was evident. Her father and Stan had seen the spark in her eyes, the determination in her spirit. She vowed to become a champion rider one day, and nothing could stand in her way. The day she clinched her first victory at the age of thirteen, her trophy gleaming proudly on the mantel, was etched in her memory.

Her father's gaze was brimming with pride, the townsfolk showering her with congratulations – she was the local sensation, the star of the equestrian world. With a national title under her belt, Gwen set her sights on competing with the best riders in the nation. Her unwavering belief that she was destined to be the best equestrian in the world.

As Gwen reminisced about her journey from a small-town prodigy to a house-hold name, a mischievous glint danced in her eyes. The trials, the triumphs, the road to glory – it had been a rollercoaster ride. But through it all, Gwen's wit and tenacity shone brighter than any trophy. Now she didn't recognize herself.

"Robert, please. Both of our girls will be leaving soon to start their lives. I'll be all alone," Gwen pleaded, her voice tinged with worry.

"That's another thing. What's Margaret going to do with her life? "She's using you, and you're letting her," Robert shot back, his tone firm and resolute.

Gwen's eyes widened in disbelief. "That's not true."

"Yes, it is, Gwen. You don't want her to leave because you're afraid of being alone. She needs a good kick in the pants. She's lazy. She's so certain that the money is hers. "Well, frankly, I'm fed up with it," Robert declared, his frustration palpable.

As the tension in the room escalated, Robert reached for the gold necklace again, one of the three necklaces he had bought for the women in his life, each one with their unique birthstone. The way his fingers closed around it conveyed both a sense of protectiveness and weariness.

"We've been too hard on her, Robert. She's not been herself lately," Gwen interjected, her voice tinged with concern.

"She's a spoiled brat. My father made sure that I learned how to work hard and be responsible. Sometimes things happen when you least expect them. You can't always expect other people to come through for you," Robert responded, his tone laced with wisdom.

Gwen sighed, realizing the truth in Robert's words. "Not everyone is like you, destined to be..." she trailed off, unable to find the right words to convey her admiration for her husband.

Robert moved about the room, his socks whispering quietly against the floor. At only 27, he had already amassed his first million. His mother's words echoed in his mind, urging him on to success. "Robert, you can do anything you put your mind to. You're a smart, young go-getter. Find something you like and stick with it. Work hard, harder than everyone else if you need to. Complaining won't get you anywhere. Someday, it will all pay off."

Those words had become his mantra, driving him to push through challenges and strive for greatness. But as he looked at his daughters, he couldn't help but wonder how they could be so oblivious to the opportunities before them. They had the world at their feet. Yet, they seemed content to simply float through life.

"When my father died unexpectedly, I thought our whole world would crumble," Robert said emotionally. "It was hard selling our house. My father built that house. When my family came across the country in covered wagons, they finally stopped and planted their roots in Bend, Oregon."

"Yes, Robert. I've heard this story many times," Gwen reminisced, a hint of nostalgia in her voice. "It was by a running creek."

"That land had been in our family for almost a hundred years," Gwen sighed at Robert's words, her gaze fixed on the distant horizon.

"My father worked so hard. Not once did he ever complain."

Gwen leaned against the counter, the weight of the world seemingly on her shoulders. Gwen knew how much pride and respect Robert's father had.

"I promised my father I would go to college, and I finished. Is that too much for a father to ask?"

"No, Robert, but you're different," Gwen replied.

"How? They are made of me," Robert retorted, a mischievous twinkle in his eye.

"And me," Gwen added with a smirk.

"Well, I won't let her take advantage of me anymore. My father taught me to count on myself. How can we just give her everything? What kind of parent would I be if I didn't bring her up to be able to support herself?" Robert exclaimed. His voice was tinged with frustration.

Gwen, ever the peacemaker, tried to reason with him. "Robert, sometimes you're too hard on them but you're a good father."

But Robert wasn't having it. "No, Gwen. Obviously, I'm not hard enough. We need to make some changes. I'm not giving her any more money. I'm through with this."

Robert paused. He seemed a million miles away.

"Ugh, and another thing earlier tonight. I don't want Sarah to see him anymore. You should have seen the look in his eyes. I swear, if I hadn't come just then, I think he would have punched Sarah a second time," Robert exclaimed, his frustration evident.

"So, you're planning on destroying both your daughters' lives," Gwen retorted, her tone sharp and unyielding.

"I've made up my mind. It's time someone took charge around here," Robert insisted, his voice resolute.

"No. I'm not going to let you ruin their lives like you have mine," Gwen shot back, her eyes flashing with a mixture of anger and hurt.

"Ruined your life? Look at you, you have everything. You're not going to change my mind about Margaret, Sarah or Charlie," Robert declared, his words cutting deep. Robert's voice reverberated through the room, the tension between them reaching a breaking point.

"You're such an asshole, Robert," Gwen spat out, her frustration boiling over.

"Maybe I've earned that right. You don't think I know? Please, Gwen, give me more credit than that," Robert retorted, his voice tinged with regret.

"What are you talking about now? I can't even keep up." Gwen continued her night-time routine.

Robert recalled his conversation as clearly as the back of his hand.

"I finally got to meet your wife."

"Huh... Oh, you mean when you stopped by the house the other day? I had forgotten you hadn't met her yet." Robert responded to his colleague.

"Yeah, the three of us had a glass of lemonade."

Gwen always made her own lemonade with fresh lemons.

"Oh... You met Margaret? She's usually not around," Robert chuckled.

"No, your friend... uh, I forget his name. Joe or something... the guy working in your barn."

Who was Joe? They didn't have a friend named Joe. It was all starting to make sense. Robert's coworker had stopped by there because Robert had asked him to, and he had forgotten to mention it to Gwen. Gwen introduced Joe to his coworker as their friend, the guy working on their barn. That was the first he had heard of any work being done to the barn. Robert sighed. His ego was crushed. He had hoped that he was wrong, but now the truth was out. His blood boiled. Another night of no sleep.

The mirror reflected his troubled eyes, revealing a storm brewing beneath the surface of his calm demeanor. Gwen was finishing up taking off her makeup. Robert couldn't shake off the feeling that something had shifted in his relationship with Gwen. Her once vibrant spirit was now cloaked in shadows of mystery, leaving Robert to navigate through the fog of insecurity that had settled in his heart.

With each restless pace across the room, Robert's thoughts danced around the figure of Sally, a name that echoed with a sense of unease. Sally, the elusive enigma who seemed to drift in and out of Gwen's world like a shadowy specter, casting doubt on the foundation of trust that Robert had painstakingly built.

The mention of late-night dinners and secret rendezvous with Sally left a bitter taste in Robert's mouth, like a cocktail of betrayal and deception. As he confronted Gwen about her elusive escapades, the air between them crackled with tension, an invisible thread ready to snap under the weight of unspoken truths.

He remembered their past discussions that never sat right with him. "Where were you?"

"I went out with Sally."

"Great, Sally," Robert muttered to himself, his words dripping with sarcasm and disdain for the woman. Sally, with her reckless abandon and insatiable thirst for adventure, was a stark contrast to the stability and comfort that Robert had sought in his life.

"Where did you two go?"

"Al Forno."

"What did you get?"

"Lasagna."

"How was it?"

"It tastes like lasagna."

Robert knew there was more, but she refused to talk about it. It was like a mysterious shadow looming over their marriage, casting an eerie silence between them. Gwen, his once vivacious and inquisitive wife, now seemed disinterested in his comings and goings.

Robert's brain was pulled back to reality as Gwen's voice raised a full octave. "May I have my necklace?" Gwen demanded.

Robert hadn't realized he was still holding it. He handed it back to her. His voice was soft as he spoke. "Who's Joe? How did it happen, Gwen?"

Gwen just stared at him. Her eyes fixed on Robert's accusing gaze. The air between them crackled with tension as she struggled to find her words. Her mind raced, trying to make sense of the situation. How could he know about her late-night escape to another man's bed? What did he know? Instead of being on the defensive, she shifted her stance.

"I can't believe you're throwing stones, Robert," Gwen retorted, her voice dripping with sarcasm.

"The whole household is falling apart." Robert's frustration was apparent.

"Well, maybe if you showed up once in a while instead of burying yourself in work, things wouldn't crumble around us." Gwen's tone turned mocking. "Always jetting off whenever things get tough, leaving me to pick up the pieces. Your real mistress is that job of yours, isn't it?"

"Don't you dare try to paint me as the villain here?"

Gwen's eyes flashed with defiance as she continued, her wit cutting through the tension like a knife. "So, before you start casting blame, take a good look in the mirror, Robert. Maybe it's not just the household that's falling apart—it's us."

Robert's jaw clenched as he listened to her cutting words. It was true; he had let his career consume him, neglecting the bond they once shared. But now, faced with Gwen's revelations, he felt a pang of regret.

"Who is supposed to pay for all of this? And what do you mean we are falling apart?"

"You're a smart guy. You figured it out?"

With that, Gwen turned on her heels and walked away, leaving Robert standing there, speechless and filled with a newfound sense of introspection. As her footsteps faded into the distance, he knew that their relationship could never be the same again.

* * *

AFTER THEIR FIGHT, not being able to relax, Robert rolled over in bed. He tossed and turned.

Trying to find a comfortable position. He hated these pillows, stuffed with lumpy feathers that poked him in the face from time to time. The comforter was too hot, yet he felt cold with it off. Lately, he couldn't sleep. He thought about when he first met Gwen.

Gwen was different. She was a puzzle wrapped in an enigma, with a quirky charm and fierce independence that made her stand out from the rest. Her passion for horses added another layer of complexity to her character, one that Robert found incredibly fascinating.

Despite his usual charm and confidence, Gwen seemed unfazed by his advances. She rebuffed his attempts with a nonchalant smile, her focus firmly fixed on her equestrian pursuits. This rejection only fueled Robert's desire further. How could she resist his charm? Wasn't he irresistible to any woman he set his sights on?

As the days turned into weeks and the weeks into months, Robert's initial interest in Gwen blossomed into something more profound. He found himself drawn to her wit, her silliness, her wild streak, and her unwavering independence. He admired her strength and determination, qualities that were rare to find in the shallow world he inhabited.

Yet, no matter how hard he tried, Gwen remained unattainable, like a beautiful mirage shimmering on the horizon. She was the one challenge he couldn't conquer, the one prize that eluded his grasp. And strangely enough, that excited him more than anything else. He wouldn't give up until he won her over. They fell in love. They were inseparable. What had happened to them?

Now fighting seemed to be the only thing the two of them had in common anymore. It was exhausting. Robert knew his work was demanding and it was a major contributor to their disagreements. Sometimes he was gone for two weeks at a time. Gwen hated being by herself, but Robert always thought that she would somehow get used to their lifestyle. She hadn't yet. She always complained and Robert said he would try harder. Robert's work still pulled him away.

* * *

ONCE AGAIN, Mitch found himself facing the mirror in a state of self-advancement. His reflection stared back at him with the confidence of a man who knew he had it all - looks, charm, and, of course, the ability to look effortlessly rugged at any given moment.

As he ran his fingers through his unkempt hair, feeling the coarse texture that added to his mysterious allure, Mitch couldn't help but smirk at himself. "I must be the most handsome man to have ever existed," he thought with a chuckle, reveling in his own cheeky self-assurance.

It didn't matter that he couldn't recall if he had skipped shaving yesterday. What mattered was the fact that he owned his imperfections, turning them into a part of his undeniable charm. With a wink at his reflection, Mitch sauntered out of the bathroom, ready to conquer the day with his trademark blend of charisma and disheveled appeal.

Mitch grimaced as he replayed last night's events in his mind. That goddamn Charlie just had to stick his nose where it didn't belong. Who does he think he is, the morality police? Mitch scoffed at the thought, muttering under his breath about the prick.

After a heated argument with Charlie, Mitch stormed out and met up with his buddies for a night out. They ended up in a crowded bar where drinks flowed freely and their inhibitions were left at the door. It didn't take long for Mitch to catch the eye of the beautiful woman across the room. With a confident swagger, he sauntered over, and soon enough, they were wrapped up in each other's arms.

As they stumbled back to her place in the early hours of the morning, Mitch's mind was clouded with anger and desire. The adrenaline from the fight with Charlie still pulsed through his veins, mixing with the alcohol coursing through his system. Mitch needed an escape, a release from the tension that gripped him.

And she did just the job. As they tumbled into her bed, Mitch felt the weight of the world slip away. In that moment of raw passion and pleasure, he forgot about Charlie, about his troubles, about everything except the woman beneath him. With each touch, each kiss, each whispered breath, Mitch felt his body relax, his mind clear.

In the aftermath, as he lay tangled in the sheets, Mitch couldn't help but smirk. He'll deal with Charlie later, but for now, Mitch was content to bask in the afterglow of the night before. She was damn hot, and he felt himself getting aroused again just thinking about their sex last night.

He had left her place without saying goodbye and raced to the mechanic's shop to get cleaned up. He shifted himself. He had too much to do and forced himself to focus.

As Mitch walked out into the hallway, he found Fred leaning against the wall, looking nonchalant.

"Hey, what were you doing in there anyway?" Fred inquired.

Mitch, with a sly grin, retorted, "Fred, mind your own damn business."

"Hey, buddy. You look like you had a long night."

"That's not your concern, Fred, now is it?"

"Just checking to see if you're okay."

"I'm dandy."

Interrupting their banter, a voice called out, "Mrs. Jones is here to pick up her Bronco, but we have a slight problem. Um...she says she didn't agree to the alignment."

Mitch rolled his eyes. "She smashes up the front end of her car and she doesn't want an alignment?"

Fred nodded. "That's right."

With a shake of his head, Mitch scoffed, "Geez, women, all the same."

"She refuses to pay. She's causing a scene," Fred added, his expression exasperated.

Looking around, Mitch asked, "Where's Charlie?"

"He hasn't come in yet. Shit. Look at all those cars. We're swamped," Fred replied, gesturing towards the busy garage.

"Let me know as soon as he comes in," Mitch instructed before turning on his heel to attend to other matters.

* * *

SARAH WOKE up to the sound of raised voices echoing through the house. Groaning, she realized she would have slept in if it weren't for the incessant fighting. Glancing at the clock, she was surprised to see it was already 10:45 am. "Oh. I did sleep in, but I don't feel rested" She thought to herself. Then came her next thought. The events of the previous night flooded back into her mind - the argument with Charlie, the pain, the fear.

"Oh my god... Charlie hit me!" Sarah thought, disbelief mingling with residual shock. The pit in her stomach was still there. It all seemed like a terrible dream she desperately wanted to wake up from. Rubbing her sore head, she felt the lump where she had collided with the coffee table, a stark reminder that the nightmare was real.

As she strained to hear her parents' muffled voices drifting down the hallway, she couldn't make out much of what they were saying. Her mother's tone was heavy with anger and frustration, a mirror of the tension that seemed to suffuse the house lately. Margaret had warned her that things were getting worse between her parents, but Sarah had never imagined it would escalate to this.

Feeling a mix of exhaustion and dread, Sarah slowly got out of bed and made her way to the mirror, her mind racing with uncertainty about what the day would bring. The casual tone she tried to maintain belied the storm of emotions swirling within her, unsure of how to navigate the turbulent waters ahead.

As she stared at herself in the mirror, thoughts of school and Charlie were all she could think of. Her eyes looked tired and glossy. She would have to go back to summer school soon. Her father's ultimatum about her never seeing Charlie again felt like a knife stabbing her in the heart. "He hit me," she thought again to herself. The pit grew larger in her stomach, an aching darkness. Sarah's heart sank further as she remembered the look of regret in Charlie's eyes.

Determined to change her father's mind, Sarah pondered her options. Maybe if she could just explain to him how sorry Charlie was, he would understand. But deep down, she knew it wouldn't be that easy. Her father was a stubborn man, set by his beliefs.

As she made her way downstairs, her heart raced with anticipation. The moment of truth has arrived. With a mix of nervousness and determination, Sarah prepared herself for the difficult conversation that awaited her.

As she entered her father's study, she found him sitting behind his desk, his face etched with a look of stern disapproval. She braced herself for the impending storm, ready to defend her choices and plead her case.

"Hey, Dad. Was that you and mom fighting?"

He looked up from his paperwork, his brow furrowed in concentration.

"Sarah...that's not your concern."

Sarah cleared her throat. "I thought we could talk."

He took off his reading glasses. A look of concern crossed his face.

"Did you sleep okay?"

"Not at the beginning, but I must have finally fallen asleep."

"How's your head?"

She reached up and touched it, wincing slightly. "It's fine."

"It doesn't look too bad. I've been thinking about it all morning. I can't get the scene out of my head. I should have called the police."

"Dad."

"Sarah. He concerns me. I don't know what it is, but I will not let you see him anymore."

"Dad, you're being unreasonable."

"No, Sarah, I'm not."

"I know you've never really liked him. It's because he's poor."

Sarah thought about how Charlie had described his life to her. He grew up in poverty. His father was a heavy drinker and couldn't hold down a job for long due to his habits.

"Damn right he's poor," Sarah's father said.

With a touch of wit in her voice, Sarah retorted, "Well, Dad, if it makes you feel any better, he's rich in spirit."

* * *

CHARLIE HAD A ROUGH UPBRINGING. His father was a dedicated member of the drinking team and a professional job quitter. On the other hand, his mother struggled to make ends meet with her limited income and lack of education. The little money she made was mostly poured down the bottomless pit of her husband's binge drinking.

At the age of ten, Charlie decided to take matters into his own hands and started doing odd jobs to help his mother out. From mowing lawns to washing cars, there was no job too small or too big for the determined young lad.

As Sarah listened to Charlie's story, she couldn't help but be amazed by his strength and resilience despite the challenges he faced. She admired his determination to make life better for himself and his family, even at such a young age.

Charlie's childhood home was nothing more than a broken-down building. The exterior of their building was a true eyesore, with chipped paint, broken windows, and a collapsed front step that acted as a constant reminder of the uphill battle they faced each day. Navigating the overgrown grass and debris-strewn sidewalks felt like wading through a jungle of neglect, with a rusted car serving as a not-so-subtle ornament to the scene.

Inside, living conditions were equally as challenging. They had a small kitchen, a family room, two bedrooms, and a bathroom upstairs. Most of the rooms had little furniture, and the furniture they did have was old and falling apart.

Upstairs, the two bedrooms were havens of chaos and makeshift, with creaky floors and memories etched into every corner. The bathroom, with its leaky sink that provided a constant soundtrack to their mundane moments, was a testament to their ability to find humor in the face of adversity.

Charlie's room was modest. His furniture was a mismatched assortment of hand-me-downs, topped off with a twin bed that had seen its fair share of spills and stains. His three-drawer dresser held his meager collection of clothes and shoes, each item carefully placed to maximize the limited space in his cramped abode.

Despite the humble state of his room, Charlie was content. He saw his room not as a limitation, but as a reminder of how far he had come. Working hard day in and day out, he saved every penny he could to afford small luxuries, like a new shirt or a pair of shoes that weren't worn out at the soles.

But the ultimate dream that kept Charlie going was owning his own truck. He imagined the freedom of hitting the open road, wind in his hair, with no destination in mind but the promise of adventure.

* * *

"SARAH, ARE YOU LISTENING TO ME?"

"Huh?" Sarah hadn't heard what her father had said.

"His growing up poor has nothing to do with me not wanting you to date him."

"It does have to do with that, and now that he has hit me, you're certain that he's just like his father."

"Well, isn't he? He hit you just like his father did to him?"

"I wish you didn't know about all those things... then maybe he would have a fair chance."

"I do know, Sarah. It's a small town, and everything gets around. After Mitch took him in, news about his parents' car accident spread through the town, not to mention his childhood and his father's alcoholism."

"It's not fair."

"So, doesn't it bother you that he hit you? It even looked like he was about to hit you again."

"What?"

"When I came into the room."

"No dad, you're wrong," but Sarah knew that was true.

"Well, once is plenty for me."

She wasn't getting anywhere with her father. He was as stubborn as ever. She thought about the first time her father met Charlie. She had been seeing him for a few months and she had finally decided to invite Charlie over to dinner to meet her dad. Her father just sat in silence. He hardly said a word. He just moved the food around on his plate. Her mom, on the other hand, didn't stop talking. Margaret occasionally intervened. Her father had disapproved of that very night, she thought. She had not realized that until this moment.

"This is your last chance," he said, his tone laced with a mix of disappointment and hope. She couldn't help but roll her eyes internally at his dramatic flair.

Raising an eyebrow, Sarah tilted her head and replied, "Your last chance?" Dad, come on. You sound like the protagonist of a cheesy movie. Really?" She knew how to play the game of wit and sarcasm, a trait she had undoubtedly inherited from her father.

Her father sighed and leaned back in his leather chair. "Sarah, I'm serious. You've got two more months left until graduation. I've guided you as much as I could, and now it's up to you to shine. Your mother and I have high hopes for you."

Sarah couldn't help but smirk. "So, you're telling me I have two months to dazzle you both before I become a disgrace to the family name?"

Her father exhaled a chuckle, a smile tugging at the corners of his lips. "Something like that, yes."

"Well, no pressure then," Sarah said, wagging her finger

teasingly. "But don't worry, pops. I'll graduate, make you proud, and prove that Margaret was just a warm-up act."

Her father nodded firmly, a glimmer of pride evident in his eyes. "After Margaret, I had high hopes for you. I hope it's not too late."

Sarah stood up, her playfulness momentarily giving way to a sense of determination. "Dad, trust me. I've got this. Two months is all I need to show you what I'm made of."

As she walked out of the study, Sarah couldn't help but feel a surge of motivation. Her father's words lingered in her mind, but instead of weighing her down, they fueled her drive to succeed.

CHAPTER 6
Sisters

Margaret was sitting in the kitchen when Sarah entered the room. She was eating a bagel with cream cheese.

"Hey. When did you get home last night?"

She took a bite of her bagel. She spoke with her mouth full. "I got home a little after 1:00, I think."

Sarah couldn't remember hearing her come into the house.

"How was your night?"

"Average," Margaret said, taking another bite of her bagel.

"Did you have a nice visit with Mom and Dad?" Margaret chuckled with her mouth full.

"Hell no. Two months."

Margaret raised an eyebrow, staring at Sarah as if she had just announced she was joining a circus. "Two months...for what?

"Dad gave me two months."

"What are you going to do if you don't?" she quipped, a smirk playing on her lips. "Come here and live with Mom and Dad and me?"

Sarah rolled her eyes in response. "Ha, ha. Well, if I don't graduate, I'm thinking of starting my own business."

Margaret leaned back in her chair, looking intrigued. "Oh, so Sarah's going to be the next big entrepreneur, huh? What's the genius plan then?"

Sarah grinned, knowing Margaret couldn't resist a juicy story. "Well, you know how I've always loved baking, right? I'm thinking of opening a little bakery. Homemade cookies, cakes, the whole shebang."

Margaret's eyes widened in surprise. "A bakery?" That sounds pretty cool. And here I was thinking you were just going to mooch off Dad forever."

Sarah playfully swatted at her sister. "Hey, I have dreams too, you know. Plus, I can't rely on Dad forever. I need to make my own path."

Margaret nodded, a hint of pride in her eyes. "I hear you, sis. Well, if anyone can turn baking into a successful business, it's you. Just promise me free cookies for life, okay?"

"Deal."

She pulled out the chair next to Margaret. Sarah grabbed a piece of Margaret's bagel.

"Hey!"

"Thanks," Sarah smiled.

"I heard Mom and Dad fighting again this morning." Sarah "paused. "Well, I guess it's not just me that's fighting."

"Oh yeah?"

"Charlie and I had a really bad fight last night."

Sarah slumped in her chair.

"About what?"

Margaret was now smearing strawberry jam on top of her cream cheese.

"I'm not really sure. We were fighting about everything. He accused me of seeing this guy, Jake, at school... who is just a friend."

"Really? So, are you?"

"No, of course not."

"So, what's the problem?"

"He doesn't believe me. Can you believe he called me a liar?"

"Yeah."

Sarah gave Margaret a look. "He thinks I'm cheating on him behind his back."

Margaret chewed her food and swallowed. "Something seems to be stuck in his butt."

"I know, but what? How can you eat it like that? Gross."

Margaret took another bite of her bagel. "Like this," Margaret said as she chewed the piece in her mouth. "Maybe Charlie is having doubts about you?" Margaret said nonchalantly.

Sarah felt herself getting mad. "What's that supposed to mean?"

What was it that Charlie said, Sarah thought to herself? He was fed up with their relationship. Sarah felt her stomach turn.

"Do you know something, Margaret?" Sarah asked.

"Nope," Margaret said as her bagel dripped jelly onto her white shirt. "Shit, look at this." Margaret pointed to the jelly stuck to her shirt, a look of mild annoyance on her face. Without much thought, she dabbed the sticky spot with her finger and licked it off with a slurp. "Well, at least it's tasty," she muttered to herself. Leaping up from her chair, she made her way to the refrigerator. Opening the door, she rummaged around until she found what she was looking for - an ice cube. Grabbing it, she closed the door with her foot and made her way back to her seat.

Sitting back down, she pressed the cold cube against the red stain left behind by the jelly. The sudden chill made her shiver, but she persevered, rubbing the ice over the fabric in small circles. Slowly but surely, the redness faded away almost to the icy touch.

"There, good as new," Margaret declared triumphantly, tossing the melted ice cube into the sink.

"You might need to put some stain remover on it," Sarah chuckled.

Margaret took another large bite out of her bagel. The side of her mouth was stuffed with a wad of cream cheese and jelly. She reminded Sarah of a gerbil.

"Maybe he's sick of waiting for you... and I know I wouldn't wait."

"Of course you wouldn't wait, Margaret, because you have no idea what a relationship means."

Margaret laughed. "Did I hit a sore spot?"

"Yeah, I'm mad and stop laughing. Did you know, Mom and Dad are fighting because of you?" Trying to push Margaret's buttons.

"I'm sure," Margaret looked back down at her shirt. "Oh, man."

"I really don't get you, Margaret. You have so much going for yourself, and you choose to do nothing. So many people dream of being as gifted and smart as you. I wish I had your talent. Does that ever occur to you?"

She was now rubbing her shirt with her napkin. "Does what occur to me?"

"God, Margaret, aren't you listening?"

"Um, no, not really. I was thinking about this stupid stain. Do you know of a way to get it out?"

"God, Margaret. Use a stain remover."

Sarah was frustrated, but she knew that fighting wasn't going to get them anywhere. There was already too much fighting going on at this place. Margaret definitely had an attitude problem, but maybe it was more than that. Her whole life people have constantly expected something from her. Since the time their parents discovered that she could paint she has never been able to decide on her own. Margaret had never seen herself as an individual, capable of making choices, but now something seemed different about her. All their parents' push-back fired back on them.

Sarah looked at her sister. She was now scrolling through her phone. Sarah could feel her anger subsiding. She had no reason to be mad at Margaret. Margaret had simply told her what she didn't want to hear.

"Hey, I thought I would help you wash your car this morning," Sarah said. Margaret looked up from her phone.

"It's a nice day, and it would be kind of fun. What do you think?" Sarah asked.

"Yeah, okay," Margaret replied.

* * *

IT WAS A BEAUTIFUL DAY OUTSIDE. The sun felt warm and calming against Sarah's back. The trees were slightly swaying in the breeze, and birds were chirping in the distance. Sarah noticed the layers of wildflowers that surrounded their nearby barn. The temperature was a nice break from the hot, sticky heat of where she went to school. The sun was high, so her shadow was close and squat to her body. She had gotten the red bucket from the barn. It was filled with towels and soap. Margaret's tan legs were long and lean. She was wearing short shorts. Her blonde hair hung free and blew across the soft features of her face.

"When was the last time you saw the sun?"

Sarah looked at her pale legs. "Didn't you hear? Tan is out?"

"Yeah, right?"

Margaret's car was covered in a layer of caked-on dirt. Her white car now looked like a dirty gray color.

"Hey, did you see this? Someone wrote 'wash me' on my car."

"Yeah, I wrote that," Sarah laughed.

"You're weird."

Margaret had stretched the hose from the water spigot to the car. Margaret handed it to Sarah. "Here you go."

The water felt ice cold as it spurted out of the hose. The brown gunk dripped slowly down the side of the white car.

"Whoa. When was the last time you washed this thing?"

"Uh..." Margaret looked like she was straining to remember.

Sarah changed the subject. "Do you ever think about what you want to do?" Margaret gave Sarah a "why did you have to bring that up?" look.

"I mean, I'll be graduating in a couple of months. I still don't know exactly what I want to do. What if, after all that money and time at school, I don't get a job?"

"I thought you wanted to start a bakery?"

"What? I was being sarcastic?"

"I don't think you're asking the right person about all of this. Remember I'm a quitter?"

"What if I can't figure out what to do?"

"God, Sarah... stop stressing yourself out. You're making my head pound."

Margaret said as she was rubbing soap across the hood of her car. "Maybe you don't need to know just yet. Just finish school. You can decide later what to do."

"Why didn't you finish with Emily?"

Margaret threw the rag at Sarah. Sarah screamed and jumped out of the way. "Stop it!"

"Hey, butthead. That's what you get for asking all these stupid questions. Maybe I didn't want to end up in a crazy hospital," Margaret replied, crossing her eyes and sticking out her tongue at Sarah.

"You're actually the weird one," Sarah said playfully.

"Yeah, so." Margaret adjusted her hair from getting wet. "Sarah, don't you ever feel like you could go crazy?"

"I don't know. I don't think so."

Sarah thought about how hard Margaret worked on her paintings. There wasn't much time for fun in her life. Margaret never thought her paintings were good enough. Like her parents and teachers, she was too hard on herself. Margaret expected perfection and wanted everyone to approve of her. This gave her a sense of self-worth. With each approval, Margaret tried to outdo the last. But Margaret couldn't keep up with the escalating demands.

Sarah and her parents didn't see the frustrations that Margaret was dealing with. Margaret thought her limitations were her weaknesses. She was trying to do what they expected of her because that's all she knew. She assumed happiness would follow, but she wasn't happy. Her inner frustrations turned into anger, blaming everyone and everything around her. She started hating the gift she was given. No wonder she felt like she was going crazy.

"You were discovered, Margaret. Most people never come close to that."

It all started when Emily made that life-changing call to Robert. Margaret Paige was about to become a household name, a sensation that would rock the art industry to its core. Robert and Gwen Paige placed their trust in Emily as if she held the key to their daughter's destiny.

She had chosen Margaret over thousands of students to be her young apprentice. Emily Martin's goal would be to teach and show Margaret, her new pupil, the glorious world of art. She would work with her hour after hour, day after day, year after year, for as long as it would take.

Sarah remembered the initial fear that gripped Margaret as she embarked on this fabulous journey. Doubts lingered in Margaret's mind - what if she wasn't good enough? What if she disappointed her parents who had unwavering faith in her talent? But Emily was determined to guide Margaret towards greatness, to showcase her inner brilliance to the world.

As Sarah reflected on Margaret's rise to success, she couldn't help but feel a sense of sadness that the road was so difficult. Margaret had blossomed into a star under Emily's expert guidance, gracing the walls of galleries in cities like London and Paris. Emily knew she had played a crucial role in Margaret's transformation, a fact that filled her heart with joy.

Sarah and her parents, in their obliviousness, failed to see Margaret's inner turmoil. Margaret, burdened by her perceived limitations, believed that she needed to meet the expectations set by others to find happiness. However, despite her efforts, she found herself feeling empty and lost.

As time went by, Margaret's inner frustrations festered and transformed into a simmering pot of anger. She began to blame everyone and everything around her for her unhappiness. The once cherished gift of life felt like a heavy burden on her shoulders, suffocating her with each passing day.

Margaret's mind became a whirlwind of chaos, making her question her sanity. She couldn't understand why she was feeling this way and why happiness seemed to elude her grasp. The weight of her emotions threatened to consume her, leaving her feeling like she was on the brink of madness. In her darkest moments, Margaret found solace in the absence of painting. Slowly but surely, time helped lift the veil of despair that clouded Margaret's mind.

"The pressure was so intense. Shit, I felt like my chest was caving in. I wasn't sleeping or eating. I was a wreck. I had let them control so much of my life."

"Why did you go if you knew that's not what you really wanted?" Sarah said, as if she was really trying to understand.

"I don't know."

"What if you start painting again?"

"No way."

"You're going to paint again someday. I just know it."

"Yeah, wanna bet?" Margaret said slyly.

"You were born with a gift."

"Some gift. I'll bet you fifty bucks."

They continued washing the car. A brown soapy mixture continued to drip down the car to the ground.

"God, Margaret, that must have been awful." "Nah, look at me, I'm as good as new."

"Where's my fifty bucks?"

Sarah pulled out a wet, soggy ten-dollar bill. "This is all I've got."

"Give it to me. I could use a venti coffee."

Margaret turned up her car radio and started dancing around the car. Sarah was now the one scrubbing the grimy dirt.

Margaret had become resentful towards everyone who cared for her, and for good reason. For almost twelve years of her life, she had lived her parents' dream. It was their fault that she had not succeeded. She never asked for it. What did they expect? She was just a young girl who thought her parents knew what was best for her. They were wrong, and now they are having to deal with the consequences of it.

Sarah knew Margaret was making some sort of statement. It seemed to work. Their parents were mad. No one was going to tell her what to do. This was a new side of Margaret, and it seemed that she was enjoying it. Sarah wondered if Margaret would ever do much with her life, but in some ways, it seemed good that she was taking control of her life. It was time that her parents let go.

CHAPTER 7

Charlie's Old Man

CHARLIE WOKE UP SUDDENLY, his head throbbing like a bass drum. He squinted at the blinding sun peeking through the half-open window, feeling like he had gone twelve rounds with a beer and lost spectacularly. Sweat trickled down his forehead, mixing with the tiny blood spots on his shirt.

With a groan, he tried to shake off the remnants of the nightmare that lingered. It was something about Sarah and her dad, a scene replaying in his head like a broken record. As if to add insult to injury, his neck screamed in protest as he tried to turn his head, a painful reminder of the lump on the left side of his face where Mitch had struck him.

Considering his current state, resembling a drunken sloth, it dawned on him that he must have pulled over during his nocturnal escapade. He vaguely remembered parking his truck on the side of the road, finding solace in the uncomfortable embrace of the steering wheel.

"Ah, what time is it?" he muttered sarcastically to no one in particular, his voice raspy from hours of restless sleep.

He wondered what cosmic joke had landed him in this sorry state. Charlie couldn't help but feel the knots of anger tightening within him. Last night was a disaster. He was suddenly triggered by thoughts about his old man.

His father, a towering figure with a voice that boomed like thunder, had cast a dark shadow over their household for far too long. His bubbly mom's nature had long gone into hiding, masked behind large, oversized clothes and a perpetually tight bun. Makeup was a foreign concept to her, and her dark, streaked hair told silent tales of battles fought and buried deep within.

Every day, Charlie's mom walked on eggshells within the confines of her own home, trying desperately to keep the turbulent waters calm. Her husband, a tempestuous storm with a penchant for whiskey, would often erupt in fits of rage that shook the very foundation of their fragile existence.

One such evening, as the shadows crept longer and the air grew heavy with unspoken tension, his mother found herself faced with the fury of a man drowning in his own vices. The metallic tang of whiskey filled the air as he hurled accusations and obscenities, his eyes clouded with the haze of intoxication.

"Fucking bitch, where did you hide my goddamn whiskey?" he bellowed, his voice a thunderous symphony of anger and entitlement.

Meanwhile, Charlie, ten at the time, sat quietly in the corner of the room, his innocent eyes fixed on the flickering glow of the old TV set. He had grown accustomed to these nightly rituals of chaos, and destruction, the turmoil of his father's drunken outbursts etched into his young mind.

As the echoes of his father's demands reverberated through the stale air, his mom felt a flicker of defiance ignite within her. With a steely resolve, she met his gaze with unwavering eyes and spoke in a voice laced with calmness.

"Where you left it, my love. Where you always leave it," she replied, her words a soft gentleness in the face of a raging storm.

Her calmness wasn't enough. He had already been triggered. Little Charlie blinked rapidly, fearing what was about to happen, trying to process the chaos unfolding before him. His father's tirade was like a storm. Charlie felt like a tiny boat being tossed around in its wake.

"Where is it?" His father opened and slammed the cabinet. "Where did you hide it?" As his father continued his tirade, Charlie noticed a glint of metal peeking out from underneath the old armchair. Could it be? Was that the precious bottle his father sought with such desperation?

Charlie glanced at his mother, her eyes wide with fear, before he made a split-second decision. With all the stealth he could muster, he lunged forward, snatching the bottle from its hiding place and pocketing it in one swift motion.

Just as his father turned towards him, his expression a mix of confusion and rage, Charlie grinned mischievously.

"Well, well, well, look what I've found," young Charlie said, holding up the bottle with a sense of mischief. "I guess the party's back on, huh?"

His father's face contorted in a mix of shock and disbelief as Charlie took a triumphant sip of the stolen whiskey.

"Cheers to you, dad. Here's to a night of peace and quiet," Charlie said, a twinkle of defiance in his eyes.

His father stood frozen for a moment before a slow grin spread across his face.

"Well, I'll be damned," he chuckled. "Looks like you've got some of your old man's tricks after all."

Little Charlie ran to the sink and quickly poured alcohol down the drain.

"Did you just pour that out?" his dad said in a rage. "Do you know how much that cost?"

Charlie was now second-guessing what he had just done. His eyes widened, and he knew he was going to pay.

His dad kept a stick next to the fireplace. It was a thick branch that he had found on one of his many hunting trips. He brought it home with him. For weeks, he slowly whittled it down to a smooth texture. He then carved his initials into the creamy white bark. He wrapped the end of the stick in soft brown leather. He said that if anyone ever threatened him or his family, he would use the stick and show them no mercy.

Charlie was fascinated by the pure beauty of the stick, so simple and yet he feared its presence. The stick remained there, leaning against the wall, never moving, only to be looked at as a symbol of power. The stick of power was now in his dad's hand.

Charlie felt a new sense of fear.

"You little punk."

"Sorry, dad. I shouldn't have done that." Charlie darted out of the kitchen, through the family room, up the stairs, into his bedroom, and locked the door. He hid in his closet.

The eerie sound of breaking glass and frantic voices filled the air, creating an atmosphere of dread that enveloped the entire house. Charlie's heart raced as he heard his mother's voice, filled with fear and desperation, followed by a sound so unsettling that it made his blood run cold.

In that moment, time seemed to stand still as Charlie hesitated, unsure of what to do next. The sudden silence that descended upon the house felt suffocating, urging him to take action. With trembling hands, he mustered the courage to follow the sounds.

The dim hallway stretched out before him like a never-ending tunnel, casting eerie shadows on the walls. Ignoring the gnawing fear in his chest, Charlie pressed on, determined to find his mother and unravel the mysterious events that had unfolded.

As he inched his way down the stairs, towards the family room, the sight that greeted him sent a chill down his spine. The room was a chaotic mess, with shattered fragments of glass and crockery scattered across the floor. His mother's motionless figure lay before him, a haunting sight that made his heart lurch in terror.

In that moment, Charlie's instincts kicked in, propelling him forward to his mother's side. He knelt beside her, his hands trembling as he reached out to touch her cold, lifeless hand. The room fell silent, save for the sound of his own ragged breath echoing in the empty space.

His mother's limp body lay on the living room floor, cruelly juxtaposed against the shattered glass that littered the carpet. Her arms and legs bore the cruel remnants of their encounter with sharp edges, a stark reminder of the violence that had taken place.

Little Charlie's eyes darted around the room, finally settling on his father seated at the breakfast table, an eerie calmness in his demeanor. The walking stick, an ominous presence, rested across the table.

As the realization of the situation sank in, Charlie's heart thundered in his chest, a frantic beat that matched the urgency of the moment. He knew he had to act fast, despite the fear and confusion that threatened to overwhelm him.

Still kneeling beside his mother, Charlie hesitated for a moment before steeling himself to face the gruesome task at hand. With trembling hands, he carefully began to extract the glass shards embedded in her skin, each pull accompanied by a pained moan that sent shivers down his spine.

Blood pooled on the floor, a stark and chilling reminder of the severity of her injuries. Desperation gripped Charlie as he darted around the room, his mind racing to find a way to aid his mother.

Grabbing a blanket in a hasty motion, Charlie returned to his mother's side, spreading it gently over the blood-stained body in a meager attempt to offer comfort in the face of chaos, with a resolve that belied his years. With his heightened adrenaline, he lifted his mother, moving slowly step by step.

Charlie and his father's eyes briefly connected as he grabbed the keys with his mouth from the hook on the wall to the car.

It took too long to get his mom into the car. His strength was quickly fading, but fortunately, his mother had enough strength left in her to help him help her.

Charlie gripped the steering wheel tightly, glad that he was already tall enough to see over the steering wheel, as he raced through the quiet streets, his heart pounding in his chest. He had only driven their family's truck once before. Panic and determination fueled his movements as he focused on getting his mother to the hospital as quickly as possible.

"I've got this, I can do this," he muttered to himself, trying to remain calm despite the urgency of the situation. He rehearsed in his head the words he would use to explain to the doctors why they were there, why his mother needed immediate attention.

When the doctors questioned him about that fateful day, Charlie stuck to his story. The weight of his deception pressed down on his shoulders, but he refused to let it crush his spirit. He would do anything to protect his mother, even if it meant bearing the burden of his guilt alone.

She was carrying a glass vase down the stairs. She tripped and fell over some laundry she had left on the stairs.

"You saw this happen?"

"Yes, she rolled down the remaining part of the stairs and smashed her head. She then fell on top of the shattered vase. My father was passed out. I didn't know what else to do."

"You should have called 911."

"I panicked."

"Hmm... that seems hard to believe. Are you sure that is how it happened?"

"Yes, sir."

"You could have killed both you and your mom by driving."

"I understand."

Charlie sat at his mother's bedside, holding her hand and whispering words of love and regret. The scars on her body would fade with time, but the scars on his soul would remain. He should have turned his father in.

As the days turned into weeks and the weeks into months, Charlie's mother healed. And though their home bore no physical traces, with a well-placed area rug, of that tragic day, the shadows of the past lingered in the corners, a silent witness to an untold story.

Charlie told his mother what he had told the doctors.

"Good boy, Charlie. You need to protect yourself." Her voice was a whisper.

That night, as Charlie made his way home, he couldn't shake off the memories of the horrific scene he had witnessed a few hours ago. The image of his mother lying on the floor, blood pooling around her, and the shards of glass embedded in her body kept flashing before his eyes.

As he entered the house through the back door, the same door he had dragged his mother through to his father's truck, a sense of dread washed over him. The kitchen still had a lingering smell of cleaning fluid mixed with something rotting.

His father was still seated at the table, his hand fidgeting with his stick, a telltale sign that he had been drinking. The plastic cup in front of him hid the contents, but Charlie knew it was alcohol. The look in his father's eyes told him all he needed to know - trouble was brewing.

Despite the overwhelming fear gnawing at him, Charlie urged himself to remain calm. In that tense moment, he braced himself for whatever was to come, knowing that he had to navigate through the storm that lay ahead.

Because his father was constantly drunk, he often lost track of time.

"Where the fuck have you been?"

Charlie kept his eyes low and spoke softly. He didn't want to agitate his father in any way. "I was at the hospital with Mom. She's doing better. The doctors said she could probably be released tomorrow."

"Is that right?"

"Mom got a lot of stitches. She was in a lot of pain." Charlie shifted. "They gave her some pain medicine so she could rest."

"So, you're the hero."

"Huh? She could have died. She lost a lot of blood."

"So, little big man saved the day."

Charlie swallowed hard. He could feel the tension rising. "I'm not saying that. But you really hurt mom badly."

"She wouldn't have died, you little prick."

"I don't know, Dad. She was in pretty bad shape."

"So, what did you tell those doctors?"

"I said she fell down the stairs."

"And that your old man did it?"

"No. I never mentioned you."

His dad's voice was getting louder. Charlie shivered. His father terrified him.

"You little liar."

"I told them it was an accident."

"So why the fuck did the police stop by a bit ago?"

"What?"

"Two of them."

"I don't know, dad. I swear."

"Liar!"

His father stood up abruptly and grabbed his stick from the table. The stick accidentally knocked his plastic cup onto the floor. Liquid splattered everywhere.

"Now look what the fuck you made me do?"

His dad came after him. Charlie backed into the counter and realized he was trapped. His father had grabbed him by his shoulders. He was shaking Charlie back and forth.

"I didn't say anything."

"What are you hiding, boy?"

His father kicked Charlie in the knee and pushed him down to the floor. Charlie fell onto his knees. He grunted in pain.

"Please, dad, I didn't tell them anything."

The stick came smashing down on the center of Charlie's back. The pain shot down his legs and he buckled down. It felt as if he was paralyzed, but slowly the pain faded. He tried to stand up, but his father held him down by his leg.

"You're shit, low life filth. You better listen and listen good. I'm the boss around here and you do as I say. You hear me boy? You better keep your mouth shut if you know what's best for you."

The stick once again blasted into his back. Charlie held back tears of pain.

Charlie shivered, thinking about his past. That memory, the one that haunted him like a shadow, felt so vivid, as if it had happened just yesterday. A pang of fear gripped his heart as he saw the resemblance between his actions and those of his father. Emotions, raw and unchecked, seemed to be taking the wheel of his life, just like they did for his old man.

Was he destined to follow in his father's footsteps? Even his uncle Mitch, his father's brother, displayed the same tendencies at times. The realization hit him like a ton of bricks - maybe this was in his blood, an unchangeable part of who he was.

He looked in the rearview mirror of his trusty old truck, feeling like he was staring into the eyes of someone who wasn't him. His eyes were swollen and bloodshot.

Suddenly, a wave of nausea swept over him, catching him off guard. Charlie's clammy hands gripped the steering wheel. He barely had time to react before he swung open the door and leaned out, heaving violently. Yellow liquid splattered on the ground, a physical manifestation of the turmoil churning inside him.

CHAPTER 8

Suspicion

ROBERT SAT SILENTLY in his study, the soft sunlight filtering through the blinds, casting a soft glow over the room. He realized that he had been staring at his screen for nearly twenty minutes, his mind drifting aimlessly. He just couldn't seem to focus.

The past couple of days have been a whirlwind of chaos for Robert. It all started with the mounting problems at work. Each day seemed to bring new challenges and obstacles. Then there was constant bickering with Gwen, Margaret, and Sarah. And finally, there was Charlie...

Ugh, Charlie, a rough-around-the-edges mechanic who had a way of rubbing Robert the wrong way. It took every ounce of Robert's self-control not to throttle the guy last night. Sarah had always had a soft spot for Charlie, but Robert could never quite understand what she saw in him.

For one, the kid needed a serious haircut. His mop of unruly hair always seemed to be in his eyes, giving him an air of mystery that Robert found unsettling. And as a mechanic, Charlie didn't exactly fit the bill of what Robert envisioned for his daughter. Sarah was smart, beautiful, and independent – she could have married any guy she wanted. So why Charlie? Even Gwen seemed to like the pretty boy, Charlie. "If I were a few years younger, I would have my eyes on him too," Gwen once said.

Last night, Charlie made a bold move and blamed his uncle for his own bad behavior. He claimed all his troubles originated from his strained relationship with Mitch, causing him undue stress. Robert, pondering Mitch, couldn't shake off the feeling that something was off about him. Mitch, despite excelling in his business and never disrespecting Robert, carried an air of arrogance around him.

Robert couldn't quite pinpoint what it was, but Mitch's behavior towards women was unsettling. He talked down about them while paradoxically enjoying their company in private. The dynamics between Mitch and Charlie, cohabiting under the same roof and working together, seemed too convenient. A thought crossed Robert's mind - perhaps the two were more similar than he had realized.

Robert sat in his cognac leather chair, his mind a whirlwind of thoughts and emotions. Gwen's betrayal, Margaret's reckless choices, and now the unsettling incident with Charlie Parker and his daughter Sarah weighed heavily on him. As he rubbed his aching back, he couldn't help but wonder how the women in his life could be so entangled in turmoil.

Gwen, once the love of his life, sought solace in the arms of another man despite their seemingly picture-perfect life. Margaret, his oldest daughter, seemed to dance on the edge of disaster with each decision she made. And now, Sarah, his youngest daughter, stood on the precipice of forgiveness for a man who had raised his hand against her.

Robert knew Charlie harbored resentment towards his own father, but he never imagined that anger would manifest itself in violence towards Sarah. The thought made his blood boil, his protective instincts kicking into overdrive. The pressure at the back of his head pulsed in tandem with his racing heart, a physical manifestation of the turmoil within.

Despite the chaos surrounding him, Robert knew he had to find a way to navigate the storm. As he closed his eyes and took a deep breath, a glimmer of resolve flickered within him. He may never understand the complexities of the women in his life, but he knew that he would do whatever it took to protect them, even if it meant facing his own demons along the way.

Robert looked at the clock on the computer. Then he glanced out his window. The day was still young. It was a clear and beautiful day outside.

"I'll drive by the mechanic shop and see if I can get some answers from Mitch without raising any suspicions," Robert thought to himself. "I'll get my car inspected, which I've been putting off."

Robert turned off his computer and straightened his desk a bit. The piles on his desk were getting bigger by the day. The amount of work was overwhelming, but he had gotten nowhere today. He needed to get to the bottom of last night. It would do him some good to put his mind to rest about this.

Hopefully, Mitch would shed some light on Charlie's behavior. He doubted it would lead to anything, but it was worth a try.*

* * *

By the time they finished waxing Margaret's car, an hour and a half had gone by. The sun was high in the crisp blue sky. There wasn't a cloud in sight. There was a subtle wind blowing, and the intense sun highlighted the purple, white and yellow flowers among the vibrant green pastures. Sarah and Margaret were both soaked from head to toe. Margaret's tanned legs glistened in the sun.

Robert walked out to where the girls were leaning against the squeaky-clean car. His dark, grey hair was slicked back, which emphasized his square jaw. He was tall, and his long, lean muscles silhouetted his frame beneath his polo shirt. His stomach protruded slightly from eating too many snacks.

As Robert sauntered over, Sarah nudged Margaret and whispered, "Here comes Mr. Snack-Attack himself."

Margaret stifled a giggle, trying not to make it obvious as Robert approached them with a grin.

"What's so funny?" Her dad said, as if he knew they were laughing.

Sarah looked away from her dad as he walked toward them. She felt embarrassed and angry and tried to hold onto her emotions.

"We're just finishing up," Margaret replied.

"It's the best it's looked in a while," Robert said frankly.

Sarah shot back with a smirk, "We aim to please, especially when the boss is watching."

Margaret nodded. Then a long, awkward silence followed. Robert reached into his pocket and pulled out his keys.

"Hey, I'm going out to run a few errands. I'll be back later on. Let your mom know for me."

"Okay, dad."

"And oh, Sarah, I don't want you talking to or seeing Charlie."

He jumped into his car. The engine turned on. It made a quiet humming noise. He rolled down his windows and looked into his rearview mirror. As he pulled forward, he waved at the girls and drove out of the driveway. The tires crunched over the gravel.

"Did you see that? He won't even look at me."

"That's not true. He looked at you."

"No, he didn't, Margaret."

"How do you know? You didn't even look at him?"

"Well, I didn't want another lecture."

"Yeah... I totally get it."

"Anyway, why doesn't he want you to see him?"

"Because of our fight last night?"

"Oh. Yeah"

Sarah didn't feel like telling Margaret about all the details of the fight. She felt embarrassed. Charlie had hit her, and that's something you just don't talk about, even to your own sister.

"Everyone gets into fights. Relationships suck."

"I was hoping that Charlie and I would get a chance to reconnect."

"If you ask me, you're just wasting your time with him."

"So, you don't like him either?"

"Nah. What you do is your business. Besides, no guy will ever be good enough for Dad's precious daughters."

"Yeah, well, he's definitely got it out for Charlie.

* * *

MARGARET WALKED OVER and sat on the wooden bench on the front porch, looking out at the sprawling garden in front of her. Sarah followed suit and joined her. The wooden porch creaked under their weight. The wooden porch felt warm beneath her damp shorts. As they sat there enjoying the afternoon sun, Margaret turned to Sarah with a thoughtful expression. "What are you going to do now that you're not allowed to see Charlie?"

Sarah sighed, "I don't know." I guess I'll just hang around the house. I could use a good nap. I didn't get a lot of sleep last night."

Margaret smirked, "Ah, the forbidden romance keeps you up at night, huh?"

Sarah rolled her eyes, "Oh please, it's Dad that drives me crazy. He's so uptight."

"I haven't spent this much time with Margaret in a long time," Sarah thought to herself, a mischievous glint in her eye. Margaret, the elusive butterfly, was a creature of whims and fancies, always fluttering off to pursue her own interests without a care in the world.

Margaret had paid Sarah a visit to school once, a fleeting moment of camaraderie amidst the chaos of exams and extracurricular activities. Sarah cherished the memory like a rare jewel, a spark of connection that made her heart flutter with longing.

But Margaret, with her ever-elusive presence, always seemed to slip through Sarah's fingers like fine sand.

"So, why don't the two of us hang out together?" Sarah proposed, a playful twinkle in her eye. "We could go to a movie or go shopping, just like in old times."

Margaret's response was like a cold splash of water on Sarah's enthusiasm. "Sorry, Sarah, I can't. I'm going out later," Margaret replied nonchalantly, her eyes already wandering to the world beyond.

Sarah's heart sank, a wave of hurt crashing over her like a tidal wave. Why did it bother her so much? She pondered this question as she watched Margaret flit away like a rare bird taking flight.

"You'll be home soon enough after you finish up at school. We can spend time together then," Margaret reassured her, a hint of warmth in her voice.

Sarah tried to muster a smile, but the ache in her heart lingered like a stubborn melody. What was it about Margaret that tugged at her soul, that made her yearn for a closeness that always seemed just out of reach?

Sarah knew that when she finally graduated, her life would change. The once inseparable bond she shared with Margaret seemed to be facing an uncertain future.

With a wistful gaze, Sarah turned to Margaret and shared her fears. "I'm afraid things will be different once I start working. We might grow even further apart."

Margaret chuckled softly, a mischievous twinkle in her eyes. "Oh, so you're planning to ditch me for your fancy new job, huh?"

Sarah rolled her eyes, knowing Margaret was just teasing her. "Of course not! But seriously, what if we drift apart like so many do these days?"

Margaret pivoted her weight. "Hey, remember when you said you'd marry Charlie when you graduate?" she said, a playful smirk on her lips.

Sarah's cheeks flushed as she laughed, realizing how much things had changed since then.

Margaret laughed.

"Well, I was serious. I still am. With or without dad's permission? Hopefully with, but without will do."

"You know he'll be hard on you if you marry him against his will. He probably won't give you your trust fund either."

"I know."

If only Margaret knew what really happened last night, Sarah thought to herself.

"Does Charlie know about your trust fund?" Margaret looked at her toes.

"Yeah," Sarah replied hesitantly, her mind racing with uncertainty.

"Maybe Charlie is only dating you because of that," Margaret continued, her words cutting through the air like a sharp knife.

"What?" Sarah exclaimed. A mix of disbelief and doubt clouded her thoughts. "Why would you say that?"

Margaret leaned in, her voice laced with a hint of mischief. "Why would I think that? The guy grew up poor. He's never going to make much money. You're his rich little girlfriend. Maybe Dad has a point."

Sarah's heart sank as she mulled over Margaret's words. A wave of insecurity washed over her. Was she just a trophy girlfriend for Charlie? Was their relationship built on a foundation of wealth and status rather than love and genuine connection?

Maybe Margaret was right. Maybe Charlie was with her for all the wrong reasons. Her thoughts spiraled as she began questioning every shared moment, every exchanged smile between them.

Sarah's mind was consumed by a storm of uncertainty. Was she merely a pawn in Charlie's game, a convenient accessory to fill the void of his own financial struggles?

"Margaret, has Dad seemed different to you lately?" Sarah said, her voice laced with a hint of irony.

"Not really. We never speak to each other. So that hasn't changed," Margaret retorted, her tone as dry as desert sand.

"What about mom?" Sarah asked.

Her mom had always had a way with horses, a bond that seemed unbreakable, especially after arguments with her dad. Sarah couldn't help but chuckle to herself as if the horses were her mom's own personal therapists, whisking her away from the chaos of family life.

"What about her?" Margaret replied, clearly preoccupied.

"Has she been acting differently?"

Margaret paused, her brow furrowed in thought. "No, but she cries a lot more than I remember. Now that I think about it, she seems to be riding more than ever. Some days, that's all she does."

With a smirk, Margaret stood up, announcing her departure for a shower, leaving Sarah to her contemplation.

Deciding to soak up some sun, Sarah settled into a lawn chair, taking in the scene before her. In the distance, her mom rode with such passion and grace, each movement of the horse mirroring her own emotions. Watching her, Sarah couldn't help but wonder if maybe she should take up horseback riding herself – after all, it seemed to be her mother's preferred method of stress relief.

With a sigh, Sarah closed her eyes, letting the warmth of the sun wash over her face. For now, she would just enjoy the peaceful moment, basking in the quirky habits of her family.

CHAPTER 9

The Barn

ASLEEP, her mind slowly drifted into a lifeless slumber, as the moon appeared in the black sky. The blue-white moon's rays began to envelop her body.

Suddenly, she awoke violently from the intense pain she was now experiencing. She sat up, screaming.

"Oh god, please stop the pain!"

Her muscles burned. It felt like her skin was melting. She was so incredibly hot. She pulled on her shirt, trying to peel it off her body. She clawed at her skin that now felt rubbery. The pain rippled through her flesh.

"What is happening to me?"

She had done this many times before, but her mind grew blank with the rising moon. She could never remember these moments of insanity. Then she felt her hands change.

"What is happening?"

In a state of panic, she watched in horror as her hands transformed into something otherworldly. Instead of fingers, she saw long, slender claws protruding from her palms. The burning sensation intensified, making it impossible for her to even touch her own hands. It was like a surreal nightmare unfolding before her very eyes. Her bones felt like they were being crushed in a vise, and she could barely muster the strength to let out a scream.

As the transformation continued, it spread to her feet and legs, contorting her bones in ways that seemed physically impossible. The excruciating pain surged through her body, causing her to let out a piercing scream that echoed through the forest. She felt a fierce struggle brewing within her, a battle between her humanity and an unknown force trying to overtake her.

But the most harrowing part of the transformation was yet to come. She felt a searing pain in her head as it began to crack and shift in shape, extending beyond the confines of anything remotely human. Her jaw cracked open, revealing large, menacing fangs that filled her with dread and revulsion. The agony was so unbearable that she felt as though her very sanity was slipping away.

Just when she thought she couldn't bear the torment any longer, the intensity of the pain overwhelmed her, and she collapsed to the ground, her body spent and her mind reeling from the sheer absurdity of what had just transpired.

As she lay there, unconscious and battered, a lone shadow flickered across the moonlit forest, leaving behind an eerie sense of foreboding. What fate awaited her now that she had been touched by something unknown and otherworldly? The once demure Sarah Paige had morphed into something wild and untamed. She was a ravenous beast on a mission.

Her eyes glowed with mystical light, cutting through the darkness like two fiery orbs. A mass of hairy fur covered her body, adding to her ferocious appearance. As her voice echoed through the night, even the crickets fell silent in awe of her presence.

With a swish of her monstrous tail, Sarah - or rather, the beast - set off into the woods, her senses sharp and her determination unwavering. Her destination was a mysterious clearing where other creatures like her gathered, each with a mission calling them.

As she trudged through the undergrowth, Sarah couldn't help but feel a twinge of excitement at the prospect of what lay ahead. After all, who wouldn't relish the chance to unleash their inner beast and join forces with a pack of like-minded creatures on a quest for dominance? She was alive!

Sarah sat up in the lawn chair, frightened. Her heart was pounding in her chest. "What the hell was that?" The sun was beating down on her face, casting a warm glow around her. She squinted to see her mother riding in the distance, the wind tousling her hair like golden ribbons. "God, what kind of nightmare was that?" Sarah muttered, rubbing her eyes in disbelief. She had fallen asleep under their old oak tree. The horrible dream that felt too real was hard to shake off.

Then it hit her—it was the moon. The looming full moon that would rise in two days. She had always heard about the strange way people's behavior changed with the lunar cycle, but she had never paid much attention to such superstitions. Until now. "Everyone has been acting so weird since I got home," she mused, running a hand through her tangled hair. "No wonder I'm having nightmares," she thought, piecing things together in her mind.

As she brushed off the fallen leaves from her clothes, Sarah felt a prickling sensation on her skin. She chuckled to herself, nervous laughter bubbling up. "Werewolves, what the hell! Next thing you know, I'll be howling at the moon," she joked, trying to lighten the eerie atmosphere around her. The thought of turning into a creature of the night seemed both ridiculous and intriguing at the same time.

* * *

SARAH WATCHED, puzzled, as her mom disappeared into the barn. Her skin felt like it was trying to bond with the chair as she peeled herself from its sticky embrace. Sweat cascaded down her legs, around her ankles. The day was getting hotter by the minute. Summer is here.

As she made her way towards the barn, the wispy grass gently tickled her ankles, offering a welcome distraction from the unforgiving sun above. The barn sprawled out before her, its long and narrow structure dominating the landscape. With double doors on each side, the building seemed to hold secrets waiting to be discovered.

Sunlight filtered through the cracks in the wood, casting golden ribbons onto the dusty ground. The path in the middle of the barn stretched like a lifeline, dividing the two sides, that housed the horse stalls. Sarah counted the stalls absentmindedly, noting that only six out of ten were occupied. Her mom's dedication to these majestic creatures was something beyond her comprehension.

The pungent smell of hay and manure assaulted her senses, making her wrinkle her nose in distaste. Sarah had never understood the allure of horseback riding; the thought of getting on a horse's back was enough to send shivers down her spine. She had always been more inclined towards books and quiet afternoons.

As she stood at the barn's entrance, Sarah couldn't help but wonder what drew her mom to this place day after day. Maybe there was more to these animals than meets the eye, hidden beneath their graceful exterior. Or maybe her mom found solace in their silent companionship, a bond forged in quiet understanding.

A light breeze was blowing through the corridor of the barn, which drifted the different smells of horse and hay. Her mom was removing a saddle from one of the horses. Her long blonde hair was braided, and her braid fell forward as she leaned over to unbuckle the dark leather saddle. Her mom was wearing faded jeans and a black tank top. Her shoulders were pink from riding in the sun. The horse's hair was wet beneath where the saddle had been, and its black hair looked glossy. Gwen looked up when she heard the crunching of hay.

"Oh, Sarah, I didn't see you there."

"Hey, I saw you riding out there."

Her mom smiled. Her blue eyes sparkled. "Yeah, I rode him hard today," Gwen patted the black horse on his back.

"I saw that. It looks like hard work."

"Not at all. It relaxes me."

Sarah thought about swimming. That always seemed to relax her, she thought. Her mom rubbed her forehead.

"What's wrong, mom?"

"Oh, it's nothing. I have this headache that won't go away. I thought riding would help."

Sarah could tell her mom was feeling worse than she admitted.

The horse snorted. "Hey there, pretty boy." Sarah rubbed the stallion's side.

"He's had a bad leg for a while. He is just now getting better."

"He looks good out there."

"You should have seen him two months ago. Poor baby. Today was his first hard ride in a while. Isn't that right, Rudy?" Her mom stroked the horse's black face. She leaned over and picked up the brush and started brushing his coat.

"Can I help?"

"Sure. Grab a brush."

Sarah grabbed a brush from the shelf.

"So, are you feeling any better after last night?" her mom asked with sad eyes.

"I didn't get much sleep. I feel kind of weird. I had this really strange dream."

"What was the dream about?"

"I don't really want to talk about it."

"Do you want to talk about Charlie?"

"Nah..."

"Your dad is pretty mad."

"He is always mad. Nothing is ever good enough."

"Yes, your father is a stubborn man."

Sarah paused. "How did you know dad was the one for you?"

Gwen smiled. Her eyes lit up as she thought about Sarah's question.

"That was so long ago. I was so young. Just a girl like you."

"Mom, I'm not a little girl anymore."

"You're still my little girl."

Sarah laughed.

"Your father caught me by surprise. I wasn't expecting to meet anyone."

"You two met in Austria."

"Yes, in Klagenfurt. I was on a ski trip with a friend of mine. She trained me to ride. We had been competing for about six months. We both needed a break. One of my father's friends told me about Klagenfurt."

"Oh... I bet it's pretty there."

"It's absolutely beautiful. The Carnic Alps are breathtaking. It is one of your father's favorite places."

"So, you know how to ski?"

"I used to ski a lot with my father."

"In Montana?"

"Mostly in Colorado."

"My father loved to ski, and he would volunteer frequently to go skiing with us kids in high school."

"Yeah, I remember grandpa being strong. I remember him showing us how he could walk on his hands."

"He was funny that way. He was always in such good shape."

"From working in the mines?"

He drilled for natural gas, right?"

"Yes."

"Wow, that sounds dangerous."

"It was, but he never gave it much thought. Mining has been in our family for years. He learned it from his father."

"Did he want you to work in the mines too?"

"When he found out that my mom was having a girl, I don't think my father knew what to do with me. He didn't grow up with any sisters either."

Sarah laughed. "That must have been different for him."

"I think he had to figure out what to do with me."

"Like riding horses?"

"Yeah."

"Did you always know you wanted to ride?"

"I guess so, but not until I was eight or nine. One day I told my father I wanted to be an equestrian, like in the books. My family's friend let me hang around his horses all the time."

"Like how I told you I wanted to be a princess?"

Gwen laughed. "Yes, exactly like that."

"But I'm not a princess."

"You are to me."

"So, your dad let you follow your dreams?"

"At first, I think he tried to talk me out of it. I was such a timid little girl. He was worried that it would be too much pressure for me. But he came around, and he supported me. My father was great. He supported me all the way."

"You were really good, weren't you?"

"I was good, but it was more than that. I loved the freedom of riding."

"So why did you give it up?"

"Oh, sweetie. I have so many reasons."

"Was it because of dad?"

"Um... That was one reason. When I met your father that day at the lodge, I was exhausted from all the training. I had never dated anyone before, because my main focus was on training. He was so charming, and I played hard to get. It was such a fun time."

"But how did you know he was the right person for you?"

"I didn't know. He made me feel good. He kept trying."

Sarah brushed Rudy's long black tail absentmindedly, lost in her own thoughts. Charlie's image lingered in Sarah's mind once again. He was the first guy who really made her feel appreciated, unlike all the others who seemed more interested in her sister. Margaret was always quick to point out Sarah's flaws with Charlie, but Sarah couldn't care less. Their bond was strong despite Margaret's tease.

As she thought about how Charlie made her feel special, a mischievous smile crept across Sarah's face. The idea of annoying Margaret with their enduring love brought her a sense of satisfaction. It was a petty yet fulfilling feeling.

Sarah knew that Margaret's taunts were just a reflection of her own insecurities, but that didn't stop her from relishing in the small victory of proving her wrong. With a playful glint in her eye, Sarah continued to brush Rudy's tail.

Her mom handed Sarah the large, oversized brush she had just used to brush Rudy.

"Would you be a dear and put these back on the shelf?"

Her mom walked the horse into its stall. Rudy's tail flickered back and forth. "He had a good workout. He's tired," Rudy nickered.

"Mom, how has Margaret been?"

"What do you mean?"

"She seems distant from her dad. I don't know. The two of them pretending that the other one is not around. Isn't that weird?" Sarah paused. "I guess I'm not doing much better."

"No one is these days." Her mom stated. "Those two just don't get along. He was so hard on her. I wish I could help Margaret, but she won't let me in."

Sarah could hear the strain in her mom's voice. Her mom rubbed her eyes.

"I don't know what to do," her mom said as she closed the gate to the stall. Rudy seemed content.

"You are so good with horses," she said.

"Thanks, sweetie," her mom replied.

"Do you regret that you didn't continue to compete?"

"All these questions. You've heard all this before. Why the sudden interest?"

"Can't I be interested?" she asked, in a casual tone.

Her mom smiled. "Of course. Sometimes I do, but I wouldn't trade my two amazing daughters for the world."

Sarah once again heard the strain in her mother's voice. She looked at her mom, whose eyes were teary, lost a million miles away. "What's up, Mom? You look like you just finished watching 'The Notebook' for the tenth time," Sarah teased.

"Oh no, I'm fine. Just tired, and this nagging headache is killing me."

Gwen had been deep in thought about her husband. "Why was he being so hard on Margaret? Why had their marriage fallen apart?" Gwen pondered, her mind swirling with questions. She had been holding onto her anger towards Robert for what felt like ages. She wondered why Sarah was asking her so many questions. Could it be possible that her daughter had figured out the secret chaos unfolding in the household?

"Mom, are you okay? Really?"

"Yes, I promise. I think I'm going to go upstairs and take a nap."

CHAPTER 10

Mitch

MITCH CONNORS' shop stood out like a newly polished hubcap on a vintage car. The one-story building, freshly painted in pristine white, stood in contrast to the other wood and brick buildings along the street. It exuded a sense of orderliness amidst the chaos of grease and tools on the inside. As customers walked in, they were greeted by a small lobby that was bare, save for a few chairs, a T.V., a couple of struggling plants that desperately clung to life and two vending machines.

Beyond the lobby lay a narrow hallway, reminiscent of a racetrack, leading to various sections of the shop. There was a back office, with a bed, a closet and a small bathroom with a shower, where Mitch Connors could be found buried under a mountain of paperwork. On the other side of the hallway was an eating area for employees, where grease-stained burgers were hastily devoured, and two guest bathrooms. Attached to the lobby were five bustling garage bays, each filled with the hustle and bustle of mechanics hard at work. The air was thick with the smell of oil, and the noise of clanking tools reverberated off the cold concrete walls.

Amidst the organized chaos, four burly men toiled away on engines and exhaust pipes, their grease-stained overalls telling tales of hard work and dedication. Meanwhile, Mitch, the shop owner, leaned against the hood of a car, overseeing operations with a keen eye. However, there was one crucial member missing from the lineup – Charlie, the elusive mechanic whose absence made Mitch want to punch the wall.

As the mechanics went about their business with the precision of a pit crew during a high-speed pit stop, a young, pretty girl sat at the reception desk, her nails perfectly manicured, filing away the monotony of the day. The rhythmic sounds of machines and equipment hummed in the background, creating a mechanical symphony that resonated through the shop like a well-tuned engine.

"May I help you?" the receptionist asked.

"No, actually, I just stopped by to see Mitch."

"He's in the..."

The young girl pointed in the direction of the garage.

"I see him, thanks."

"I can get him for you." She said politely.

"No, he knows me."

Mitch was discussing some car troubles with one of the mechanics when he caught sight of Robert in the distance. Without missing a beat, Mitch excitedly raised his hand and waved at Robert, who reluctantly waved back with a small smile.

As Robert made his way over, Mitch's face lit up with delight, as if they were the best of buddies. Robert, on the other hand, remained reserved, not particularly eager to engage with him. But he put on a friendly smile as he approached Mitch.

"Hey, Robert, how's it going?" Mitch asked cheerfully.

"Good, thanks," Robert replied with a polite nod.

Undeterred by Robert's reserved demeanor, Mitch reached out and shook Robert's hand, fully embracing their interaction with a casual tone that belied the underlying tension between their differing levels of friendship.

"What can I do for you, Robert?"

"I was wondering if one of your guys could do an inspection for me. I've been putting it off for weeks and I'm overdue."

A small radio was playing music in the background.

"I got a warning the other day, and I need to get this updated before I get pulled over again."

"No problem. Hey, Chris, could you come over here for a minute?" Chris looked up. He was tightening a bolt.

"Just a second, I'm just finishing up."

"How's the family?"

Robert crossed his arms. "Good. Sarah's back in town for a couple of days."

"That's right... End of school. Come to think of it, have you seen Charlie today?"

"Isn't he here?" Robert looked around. Charlie seemed MIA.

Robert could tell Mitch was holding back his anger. He got more jittery by the minute, and his face was turning into a sunburned reddish color.

"So, how's business?"

"Whew, we've been swamped. That kid has no sense of responsibility. He knows how busy we are. Thank god today has been a bit slower."

"So, he didn't call in?"

"Not a word. We can't keep up with things around here. I'm downright exhausted these days. I'm not complaining or anything. The money has been great. I could use a little more, but... when business is good, you can't complain."

"I guess not. Seems irresponsible of Charlie."

Mitch nodded his head in frustration. "Charlie has been pulling a lot of crap lately."

"How so?"

"We had a run-in the other day. Not proud of it."

This didn't surprise Robert at all after last night's scene.

"I had a long, nice talk with him. He's been slacking way too much. He better get his act together because I'm not going to keep putting up with this shit."

"Sounds like Charlie is taking his job for granted."

"Pretty much. That's the thanks I get for letting him come live with me and giving him a job. He would be on the streets right now if it weren't for me."

Charlie had an attitude, all right, just like Mitch, he thought. Robert listened as Mitch went on.

"Goddamn Patty, always comes to his rescue."

Mitch seemed extremely irritated when he mentioned her name.

"But the first chance I get, I'm going to knock some sense into that boy, if you know what I mean."

"Are you and Patty having some problems?"

"Uh...no. Why do you ask?"

Robert could see that the question made him nervous.

"No reason."

"You know women? They don't know when to mind their own business."

"Is she okay with you staying late at the office?"

Mitch darted his eyes. He rubbed his hand along the side of his jeans.

"She nags all the time, but she knows I have a lot going on. I'm sure you know what that's like."

"Yeah."

It sounded like Robert's current situation. He wondered if he was anything like Mitch. Robert was always busy with his job, and his family had been sacrificed at times.

"As a matter of fact, I can't remember the last time I saw her," Robert said.

"Yeah, Patty's a homebody. Doesn't like getting out much," Mitch replied.

Robert had always considered Patty a spunky girl. She was ten years younger than Mitch, and he couldn't imagine her enjoying staying home alone. Patty was always the type to go out and do things, which reminded Robert of his own relationship with Gwen. There was a thirteen-year age gap between them, and Gwen despised being by herself. As he pondered this, a twinge of anxiety crept into his stomach, leaving a gaping hole of uncertainty. Was that perhaps the reason she...? Robert shook his head, trying to dispel the troubling thoughts swirling in his mind.

"Robert?"

Robert pulled himself back into reality.

"Sounds like things have been kind of crazy for you," he replied.

"You could say that. Ah, Patty is the least of my problems. I can handle her. Gotta keep up with business. If you see Charlie, you might advise him to stay clear of me for a while. I'm not feeling too calm these days," he laughed. "Hey, Chris, you done over there?"

"Yeah, I'm coming."

"Good talking with you. Be sure to say hi to Gwen for me."

Robert nodded. "I will."

* * *

MITCH DECIDED to leave work early, even though he had a lot more work to do.

"Hey Fred, I'm taking off. There's something I have to take care of."

"Yeah, sure."

"Call me on my cell phone if you see Charlie."

After talking to Robert, Mitch realized that instead of avoiding Charlie, he could wait for him to show up at his place. He needed to deal with Charlie. He wasn't going to tolerate Charlie blowing off work whenever he pleased. He wasn't going to put up with this behavior any longer. He would have to take control of the situation and teach Charlie a lesson.

Mitch thought about his night with Charlie yesterday evening, when the two of them were closing the shop.

"What were the two of you talking about the other night when I came home?" Mitch asked obnoxiously.

"What?" Charlie turned off the radio.

"You and Patty."

"You spying on us?" Charlie looked at Mitch. He could see the angry stare that was directed at him.

"What were you talking about?"

"When?"

"The other night." Mitch retorted.

"Shit. I don't know."

"It looked like the two of you were having fun."

"What are you talking about Mitch? I don't have time for this."

"I told you to leave Patty alone." Mitch's tone was stern.

"I wasn't doing anything, Mitch. Why would you care about what she does?" Charlie could see Mitch's face turning red.

"I told you to leave Patty alone."

"What the fuck is your problem, Mitch?"

"I don't want you talking to her. Is that clear?"

"I live in the same house as her. What do you want me to do? Ignore her?"

"Yeah, I want you to ignore her."

"Fuck you ,Mitch. You don't own me."

Charlie started to turn towards the garage door, and out of nowhere, the backside of Mitch's hand landed across Charlie's face. His ring cut into Charlie's cheek, and blood slowly trickled out of the fresh wound. He stumbled into the wall next to a pile of parts and tools. Charlie, out of extreme anger and fear, picked up a pipe.

"What are you going to do? Hit me with that?" Mitch said sarcastically. Mitch's voice echoed as he laughed out loud.

Charlie stood firmly. The pipe was high in the air. "You're a fucking asshole, Mitch. I swear..."

"You swear what?"

Charlie dropped the pipe onto the hard concrete floor. The sound reverberated throughout the space.

"Don't ever touch me again." Charlie walked out of the shop.

Mitch watched Charlie walk quickly towards his truck. He knew Charlie wouldn't hit him back. He knew Charlie was too scared to cross that line.

* * *

Mitch felt more agitated after speaking to Robert. He got into his truck. I'm exhausted, Mitch thought to himself as he pulled into his driveway. Mitch walked through the side door into the kitchen. Patty was cooking something on the stove. He went straight past her to the refrigerator and grabbed a beer. He needed to drink a couple of beers so he could relax.

"Well, hello to you too," Patty said without looking at Mitch. "I didn't expect you."

"It's none of your business what I do."

"I thought you had a lot of work to do."

"I didn't come home to see you."

"You're such a dick."

"If you have to know, I plan on having a nice long talk with Charlie." He opened the beer and flicked the lid onto the counter.

"What's going on?"

"Nothing you need to worry about."

"What are you planning to do?" Patty's voice sounded concerned. Patty knew that Mitch was in one of his moods.

"Think I might hurt him? Nah, just want to talk," Mitch said, trying to decide what he was going to do.

He took a long swig of his beer. Patty knew that if Mitch got any angry, it could go a lot further than just talking. She knew he had it out for Charlie for a while, and things were building up between the two of them.

"Besides, he needs a good ass-kicking. Maybe that's what I'll do." Mitch stated.

"Why don't you leave him alone?" Go out with your buddies. What do you have to prove, anyway?"

"You gonna protect him?"

Mitch looked at his wife. He looked at her up and down. "You disgust me," he thought. He took another drink of his beer. The cold fizz felt good going down his throat. He was lost in thought for a while. What had he seen in her? It wasn't like him to make such a mistake. Patty used to be the envy of the town. She was a knockout, but now she looked like every other housewife. She was no longer the long-legged redhead that he first married.

He remembered when the two of them used to have great sex. They looked good together. It made Mitch feel more like a man. Mitch took pride in showing her off to all his buddies. Now he never went out in public with her. She was an embarrassment.

"God, you can be so mean," Patty said fearing what Mitch might do to Charlie, her eyes filling up with tears.

"Then stay out of my face, and you won't have to deal with me."

Patty lunged out and tried to slap his face. She regretted it immediately. He grabbed Patty by her hair and flung her down to the ground. She flopped down heavily on her knees. Her knees burned, and it felt like her hair was going to rip out of her head at any moment.

"You like this?"

"You're hurting me," she said as the pain increased.

He grabbed the skin on the side of her waist and firmly pinched his fingers together. Tears filled her eyes.

"Good thing you have all this extra skin on ya."

"Mitch, please?"

"Now listen carefully. I don't have time to deal with you right now. Go to your room and take a nice long shower.

Don't come back in here, because if you do, well, you're not going to like it. Do you understand me?"

Tears rolled down her face.

"Yes."

"Yes, what?"

"Yes, I will stay in my room."

"Very good."

She pulled her knees into her chest and sobbed.

"Go now!"

CHAPTER 11

The Clearing

ROBERT DROVE AROUND FOR A WHILE, the familiar streets passing by in a blur of colors and sounds. The radio played softly in the background, but his mind was elsewhere. Lost in a sea of thoughts, he finally pulled his car off the road, to a secluded spot with a view of the city's skyline in the distance.

Their marriage, once filled with love and laughter, had crumbled before his very eyes. Gwen's bitterness and anger had become a formidable barrier between them, a wall that he couldn't breach no matter how hard he tried. The woman he had always loved now seemed like a stranger, a distant figure lost in a sea of resentment.

What had happened to Margaret? He no longer had a true relationship with her. They had grown distant, barely talking or looking at each other as they pretended the other one didn't exist. It was like they were living in parallel worlds, their once-strong connection fading away into nothingness.

And then there was Sarah, his precious baby girl, now a young woman navigating the turbulent waters of love. But Robert couldn't shake off the fear that Charlie, the man she had fallen for, was not the right choice. To add fuel to the fire, what was going on between Charlie and Mitch? The shadows of Charlie's past haunted him, the echoes of his own mistakes whispering warnings of a dark future.

As if these personal struggles weren't enough, Robert also faced the looming threat of the collapse of his company, the one thing he had poured his heart and soul into for years. The challenges ahead seemed unsurmountable, the burdens too heavy to bear.

Feeling defeated, Robert slumped forward, resting his head on the steering wheel. Tears welled up in his eyes, a mix of anguish and frustration threatening to over-flow. In that moment of vulnerability, he realized that he was at a crossroads, a moment where he had to decide whether to succumb to darkness or fight back with all his might.

With a heavy heart, he closed his eyes and allowed the gentle breeze to envelop him, offering a moment of solace, amid his turmoil. In that fleeting moment of stillness, he found a glimmer of hope amidst the chaos, a reminder that even in the darkest of times, there was always a flicker of light waiting to guide the way. Taking a deep breath, Robert wiped away his tears and straightened up in his seat. He may have been battered and bruised by life's cruel twists, but he refused to be broken.

* * *

IT WAS 5:30 PM when Charlie walked into Mitch's house, with the weight of sleep deprivation pulling at his eyelids. He let out a heavy sigh, feeling the fatigue in his bones after spending the night in his car and restless hours driving around. All he wanted was to collapse into a cozy bed for a brief respite.

As Charlie entered the living room, the sharp tone of Mitch's voice startled him from his daze. "Where the fuck were you today?" Mitch's words pierced the air, echoing with a mix of frustration and concern. Perched in his leather recliner, a beer in hand, Mitch exuded an aura of anxiety, his gaze flitting around the room.

Charlie mustered a calm response, trying to diffuse the tension. "Hey, Mitch," he greeted softly, sensing the underlying tension brewing beneath the surface.

"I asked you a question," Mitch's voice persisted with a casual yet firm tone, his fingers tapping a restless rhythm on the arm of his chair.

Taking a moment to collect his thoughts, Charlie braced himself for the inevitable conversation ahead, knowing that Mitch's anger stemmed from the pressures of work and their heated fight. The room seemed to hang heavy with unspoken words, awaiting the unraveling of a story that had been brewing between them for far too long.

"Did you hear me?"

"Yeah, I heard you."

"So?"

"Look, Mitch, I'm really sorry about that. I had a shitty night. I know I should have called you, but I wasn't thinking straight."

"You had a bad night? So, is that your excuse?"

"Yeah, that's right."

"That's not good enough. I told you there are no free rides around here. I took you in, and this is how you repay me? I should have known you were a shitty asshole just like your good-for-nothing father. You remind me more of him every day."

"Don't you think you're overreacting?"

"There is no way someone like you is going to get a free ride. Not in my house, and you aren't going to come and go as you please at work. It's my business, and I call the shots."

"I don't see what the big deal is." Even though Charlie knew he should have let Mitch know, Charlie felt his tension start to rise. His face was beet red, as he was breathing hard.

"Look at you. You can't even handle a hard day." Mitch had a big smile on his face.

"I don't need to explain this to you."

"You're not going to ruin my business."

"It was just one day."

"I've worked hard and no little shit is going to push me around."

Mitch stood up from his leather recliner. He moved back and forth in the family room. "I have made something of my life and it's good."

"You call your life good? You can't even have a relationship with your wife. You're out fucking every other woman you can pick up at the bar."

"I told you to stay out of my business and I meant it. You

better watch your step or you're gonna pay the consequences."

"Is that a threat Mitch, 'cause I'm real scared?"

"I think it's the other way around. I've got friends in high places. So you better just keep your distance if you know what's best for you."

Mitch was trying to control his anger. "People in high places? Who? Sarah's dad?"

"He'll back me up," Charlie exaggerated.

Mitch laughed. "Well, I don't think that Robert will be sticking up for you. I told him all about your lazy ass."

"What are you talking about?"

"Robert paid me a visit. Like I said, you better watch your step."

"You're a goddamn liar."

Mitch's fists were clenched.

"Go on. Hit me." Charlie bated him on.

"You think you're onto something, dating that pretty little, rich girl. You think you can charm your way into their lives without them smelling your stinking ass? They'll catch on."

"No, Mitch, they won't, and that fucking drives you crazy, doesn't it? To know that I'm going to make something of myself. I'm going to leave all this shit behind, and there is not a fucking thing you can do about it."

Charlie turned his back on Mitch and headed toward the staircase. Then suddenly, Charlie saw blackness.

* * *

AFTER SARAH GOT off the phone with Lou, she realized how long they had talked. It was already 8:30 PM. Where was everyone? Margaret and her father hadn't returned since they had left earlier that day. Her mom was still in her room, closed off from the rest of the world. The house felt empty, too still, too quiet.

Sarah's stomach churned as she stood in front of the half-empty refrigerator. The flickering light illuminated the sparse items within. "Doesn't anyone eat around here?" She muttered quietly. Her frustration was evident in her voice.

The sight of a carton of milk, a bottle of ketchup, mustard, mayonnaise, butter, cream cheese, jelly, a few yogurt cups, five lonely eggs, one red pepper, a carton of mushrooms, a dwindling chunk of cheese, two hotdogs in a zip locked bag, a carton of raspberries, 3 bagels, a six-pack of seltzer water, and a near-empty container of lunch meat did little to assuage her hunger.

She sighed, her mind racing on what to make with such limited ingredients. "I can make an omelet with this, I suppose," she mumbled. As she cracked the eggs into a bowl, added milk, chopped the red pepper, mushrooms and the last bit of cheese. Sarah couldn't shake the feeling of unease in the house. The silence was oppressive, and the darkness beyond the kitchen seemed to creep closer, enveloping her in its suffocating embrace.

Sarah jumped as her phone buzzed. "Crap!"

Sarah's heart raced as she heard Charlie's voice on the other end of the line. Her hand trembled slightly as she gripped the phone tightly.

"I had to call you, Sarah. I couldn't go another minute without hearing your voice," Charlie said urgently, his tone filled with emotion.

Sarah's mind raced with conflicting thoughts and emotions. She knew she shouldn't be talking to Charlie, but her heart ached for him. Memories of their time together flooded her mind, causing a deep longing within her.

"I miss you, Charlie," Sarah whispered, her voice filled with longing and regret.

"I miss you too, Sarah. I can't stop thinking about you," Charlie admitted, his voice raw with emotion.

Tears welled up in Sarah's eyes as she struggled with her feelings. She knew that talking with Charlie was risky, but she couldn't deny the love she felt for him.

"I have to go, Charlie. My dad will be home soon," Sarah said, her voice filled with sadness.

"Wait, Sarah. Meet me at our spot by the lake tonight. I'll pick you up from there. Please, I need to see you," Charlie pleaded, his desperation evident.

Sarah hesitated, her mind and heart warring within her. Finally, she made a decision.

"Okay, Charlie. I'll meet you there," Sarah said softly, a sense of determination in her voice.

As she hung up the phone, Sarah felt a mix of excitement and fear. She knew that seeing Charlie would bring consequences, but she couldn't resist the pull of their love.

Thoughts raced through her mind, each one more unsettling than the last. What was that about? He had such urgency in his voice.

As she stared at her half-eaten omelet, the sight of it no longer held any appeal for her. Sarah dumped the food into the trash with a huff. "What am I doing?" she thought, feeling a mix of anger, confusion, and worry swirling in her mind. Glancing at the time on her phone, the numbers mocked her — 8:50 PM and still no sign of anyone around.

Panicking, Sarah dashed up to her room, the thud of her heart loud in her ears. She changed her shirt and shorts in a frenzy, clumsily putting on some earrings and running a brush through her hair with trembling hands. Her stomach churned, but it wasn't from hunger anymore; it was from fear and the creeping sense of dread that gripped her tightly.

If her father found out about this, it would be a disaster. The weight of potential consequences hung heavy in the air, suffocating her. Sarah knew she had to meet Charlie, the mystery consumed her, driving her forward into the unknown with a fierce resolve.

Sarah waited by the lake, nerves buzzing beneath her skin like a live wire. The mild night air seemed to hum with a sense of foreboding, a feeling that matched the churning unease in her gut. A light wind whispered through the tops of the trees, a haunting melody that seemed to echo her own sense of trepidation.

She couldn't shake the memory of a few minutes ago, the way Charlie had sounded so desperate on the phone. His words had been a tangled web of fear and urgency, pulling her into a vortex of confusion and doubt. And now here she was, on the edge of a dangerous precipice, teetering between what was right and what was necessary.

The moon began its ascent above the shadowed canopy of trees, casting a silvery glow over the lake. Sarah sat on the bench next to the lake. Was this a mistake? Was she walking willingly into the jaws of danger, fueled by curiosity and a thirst for answers?

Suddenly, a memory of her vivid dream flashed through her mind, a surreal image of Charlie transforming into a werewolf before her eyes. No that was her. The absurdity of the thought made her laugh out loud, a nervous sound that rang hollow in the stillness of the night.

And then, as if on cue, he arrived. Ten minutes late, but there he was, his presence filling the space around her with a palpable intensity. The way he said those two words, "Get in," sent a shiver down her spine, a warning that she couldn't ignore.

As the truck sped down the deserted road, Charlie's grip on the steering wheel tightened, and his eyes were fixed on the ahead with determination. Sarah, sitting beside him, could feel the tension in the air, almost suffocating her.

"Charlie, please, just slow down!" she pleaded. Her voice was edged with fear.

But Charlie paid no attention, his focus solely on the road ahead. The tires screeched against the pavement, leaving a trail of black marks as they tore through the night. The smell of burning rubber filled the truck, mixing with the heavy beats of 'The Doors' blaring from the speakers.

"Are you trying to get us killed?" Sarah's voice rose with panic, her heart beating rapidly in her chest.

Charlie's jaw clenched, his knuckles turning white as he gripped the wheel tighter. "Don't worry about my driving, Sarah," he growled, his tone laced with urgency.

Sarah could sense his anxiety, his desperation noticeable in the air. She knew something was wrong but couldn't quite put her finger on it. Leaning over, she tried to reason with him, her hand reaching for the volume knob to reduce the music.

But Charlie's eyes flashed with a mix of determination and defiance as he cranked the music volume up even louder. The haunting lyrics filled the cabin, drowning out any attempts at conversation.

"Turn it down, Charlie," Sarah insisted, her voice barely audible over the music.

"We'll talk when we get there," he replied, his voice cutting through the loud music.

As the truck continued along the rough dirt road, Sarah's anxiety grew with each passing mile. She couldn't shake the feeling that something was off, that they were heading towards an unknown destination that held secrets waiting to be uncovered.

The trees seemed to loom closer, blocking out the moonlight and casting eerie shadows on the path ahead. The air grew thick with tension, suffocating her as she tried to make sense of Charlie's sudden detour.

Her heart pounded in her chest, the rhythmic beat echoing in her ears like a warning. She stole glances at Charlie, searching for any sign of reassurance in his demeanor, but finding none. His gaze remained fixed on the road ahead, his expression unreadable.

As they rounded a bend, the truck came to a sudden halt, kicking up a cloud of dust that obscured their surroundings. Sarah's breath caught in her throat as she peered through the haze, her eyes widening in disbelief at what lay before them.

A hidden clearing emerged from the shadows, bathed in a surreal light that seemed to beckon them closer. It reminded her of the meadow in her dream where all the beasts came together. Charlie turned to look at Sarah. His eyes gleaming with a newfound intensity that sent shivers down her spine. Without a word, he reached out his hand towards her, his touch cold against her skin.

"Trust me," he said softly, his voice barely above a whisper.

Sarah hesitated, her instincts screaming at her to flee, but a strange sense of curiosity tugged at her, compelling her to take his hand and step out of the truck.

"Where are we?"

"I found this place a while ago. I sometimes come here to get away."

"You do? You never mentioned it before."

"Come on."

Charlie jumped out of his truck and slammed the door shut, the sound echoing through the empty field. The night was dark, and the air was filled with an eerie stillness. He walked over to the bed of his truck, the gravel crunching beneath his boots, and rummaged through his tools until he found a flashlight. With a determined look on his face, he then reached into the crevice and pulled out two thick wool blankets, old and worn with several holes in them. The blankets had been with him for years, trusty companions on many cold nights.

Meanwhile, Sarah stood silently, her heart racing as a strange sense of déjà vu washed over her. The scene seemed oddly familiar, as if she had been there before. But that couldn't be possible, could it? It was just a dream, she reminded herself. She couldn't have dreamed of a place she had never seen before.

The moon cast a ghostly light over the field, casting long shadows that danced in the darkness.

"Follow me," Charlie whispered in the still night air, sending shivers down Sarah's spine.

As she tentatively took a step forward, the ground beneath her feet felt strangely solid, as if it were leading her somewhere. She followed the invisible path, the sound of her own footsteps echoing in the silence. The air grew colder, the wind rustling through the trees as if whispering secrets that only the night could hear.

And then, as if drawn by an unseen force, Sarah found herself face to face with Charlie, his dark eyes gleaming in the moonlight. The beam of his flashlight cut through the darkness, illuminating the worn blankets in his hands. Without a word, he held out one for her, a silent offering of protection and warmth on a chilly night. With a sense of recognition that defied explanation, Sarah reached out and took the blanket, feeling its rough texture against her skin. As she wrapped it around her shoulders, a wave of comfort washed over her, as if she had finally found a piece of herself that had been missing.

"Charlie, this is weird."

"I thought you would like it here."

"I don't. Let's leave."

"Come on, it's not so bad."

He laid out the second blanket on the ground in the center of the meadow. This all seemed so weird. Last night, he had hit her, and now he was taking her to a secluded area. Sarah didn't feel like sitting.

"What's wrong? I don't believe you. You called me. You said you needed to talk, and you sounded so... Was all that a lie to get me out here?"

"What are you talking about, Sarah?"

Sarah realized that her heart was racing. She felt like she couldn't breathe. "I don't know."

"Sit down."

He patted the blanket next to him.

"This better be good."

* * *

THE TWO OF them sat in the middle of the clearing. The moon was high in the night sky. They sat cross-legged on the blanket. "So, what's going on, Charlie?"

Abuse had been a constant companion in Charlie's life, haunting his every step, weaving its way through his relationships like a venomous thread. The air was heavy with unspoken words, the tension palpable as Charlie's hands fidgeted nervously.

"I had another fight with Mitch." Charlie's voice was low, filled with a mixture of anger and hurt. Sarah's eyes widened slightly, a flicker of concern dancing in their depths as she leaned in, urging him to continue.

"Things have spiraled out of control with Mitch. He's just like my old man. Always drunk, always angry, always looking for a reason to unleash his fury on me," Charlie's words tumbled out in a rush, each syllable tinged with raw emotion.

Sarah's brow furrowed in confusion, her mind racing to make sense of the tangled web of emotions that Charlie was unraveling before her. "What do you mean, Charlie?" She prodded gently, her voice a soothing balm against the storm raging within him.

"He's paranoid about Patty," Charlie's voice cracked, memories of past confrontations resurfacing like a tidal wave threatening to drown him. "He thinks I'm talking to her, even though he couldn't care less about her. He hit me, Sarah. Just like my father used to. The same rage, the same brutality."

Sarah's eyes were wide with a mix of shock and worry as Charlie recounted the events of the night.

"He hit you?"

"I almost used a pipe on him," Charlie's admission hung heavy in the air, suffocating the space around them with its weight. Sarah's breath caught in her throat, her mind reeling from the darkness that threatened to engulf him.

Charlie winced as he recalled the moment. "Yeah, he did. It happened so fast. I never saw it coming. He hit me again tonight. I didn't go to work. He was pissed. I blacked out."

"What?" Tears welled up in Sarah's eyes as she wrapped her arms around Charlie, pulling him close. "Charlie, we have to do something about this. We can't let him get away with hurting you," she said, her voice filled with determination. Charlie sank into her body.

"God, it must have been so painful. You might need stitches for that head wound," Sarah said. Her brow furrowed in worry.

Charlie shrugged off the suggestion. "Nah, I'll be fine. It's my arm that hurts more from when I fell."

Grabbing a flashlight, Sarah examined Charlie's arm, which was red and swollen. She gasped at the sight.

"Oh my gosh, Charlie. This looks bad. You have to tell someone about this," Sarah urged, her voice pleading.

Charlie let out a bitter laugh. "When I woke up, my head was pounding. My arm hurt like a mother fucker. Patty was there, trying to help me."

"Patty helped you? But where was Mitch?" Sarah asked, her tone dripping with disdain.

"Patty said Mitch had left the house," Charlie replied, his voice heavy with disappointment.

"That coward! He left you like that," Sarah spat out, her fists clenched in anger.

"I saw the broken beer bottle on the floor. It all started to make sense," Charlie continued his eyes narrowing in determination.

"You need to tell the police about this. Mitch can't get away with this," Sarah insisted, her voice growing more intense.

Charlie hesitated for a moment before finally responding, "I'm not telling the police, Sarah. I can handle this on my own."

"Charlie, he could have killed you. You can't let him get away with it," Sarah pleaded, her voice filled with worry for him.

Charlie shook his head, a sense of defeat washing over him. "I don't know what to do, Sarah. Mitch is unpredictable, and I'm afraid of what he might do if I try to stand up to him," he confessed, his voice trembling with fear."

"Charlie, he's dangerous. You need to move out of there, Charlie," she said softly, her voice tinged with anxiety.

Charlie's eyes flickered with an emotion Sarah couldn't quite place as he responded, "No, I can't."

Perplexed, Sarah asked, "What do you mean you can't?"

Charlie hesitated before replying, his tone defensive. "I mean... I just can't."

Sarah knew there was more to Charlie's words than meets the eye. She pressed on, her voice growing more intense. "Charlie, you need to get out of there before he really gets mad at you. Patty is an adult. She can take care of herself."

Charlie's voice turned abrasive as he retorted, "Sarah, I'm not going to abandon her. She needs my help."

"Why is she so important?"

Charlie's gaze bore into Sarah's, his eyes revealing a past she could only imagine. With a sense of urgency, she probed, seeking answers buried deep within his troubled heart.

"I know how she feels. I was there too. "Mitch is just like my father," Charlie confessed, his voice imbued with a pain that mirrored hidden scars.

As Sarah's mind raced, a torrent of emotions flooded her senses. Was it love that stirred Charlie's guarded heart? Or was it a bond forged by shared experiences and unspoken truths?

Doubt clouded Sarah's thoughts, uncertainty gnawing at her heart. Could she trust the flicker of hope that burned in

Charlie's eyes, or was it merely a facade veiling her darker intentions?

With a trembling voice, Sarah spoke, her words heavy with unspoken truths and unshed tears. "You're right, Charlie. I'm sorry."

Sarah paused. He can't leave Patty by herself with a madman.

"I can't just sit around and wait for this to happen again," Sarah insisted, her voice filled with determination. "I can't let you go through this alone. My father can help. I know he can."

Charlie shook his head, the weight of the situation bearing down on his shoulders. "I appreciate your offer, Sarah, but your father...he's not exactly thrilled with me right now. After what he witnessed last night, I doubt he'd be willing to lend a helping hand."

Sarah clenched her fists, frustration bubbling to the surface. "Then what, Charlie? Do you expect me to just stand by and watch as things spiral out of control? This is not just your problem, it's mine too. I can't let you face this alone."

Charlie looked up at her, the intensity in her eyes reflecting his own inner turmoil. "I hate myself for what happened last night, Sarah. I can't bear to see you hurt because of me. I won't let myself become like my father."

Sarah bit her lip, trying to control the flood of emotions welling up inside her as she sat face-to-face with Charlie. His words cut through her heart like a knife, yet she refused to show any weakness.

"What can I do to help you?" Sarah's voice quivered with a mixture of concern and frustration. She had been trying so hard to reach out to him, to break through the walls he had built around himself.

"Nothing, Sarah... just stay out of it." Charlie's tone was cold and distant, his eyes avoiding hers as if unable to bear the weight of her gaze.

"What about us? Things haven't seemed right between us lately," Sarah pressed on, her voice tinged with desperation. She needed him to understand, to see the turmoil within her.

"I know," Charlie finally met her eyes, his gaze heavy with unspoken words and emotions.

"You should have told me about this sooner," Sarah's voice softened. A glimmer of hope shone through the darkness that threatened to engulf them.

"I didn't want to get you worried. I know you have so much going on at school." Charlie's voice was barely above a whisper, filled with regret and longing.

"Charlie, you are more important to me than school," Sarah's words hung in the air, the gravity of her confession settling between them like a heavy fog.

Charlie looked up at the sky, his eyes searching for answers in the vast expanse above. Then he closed his eyes, as if trying to shut out the world and its complexities.

"Have you even missed me, Charlie?" Sarah's voice trembled with unspoken fears. Her heart lay bare before him.

The silence that followed was deafening. The unspoken words echoed in the space between them like a haunting melody. Sarah's heart raced with anticipation, waiting for

Charlie's response, for a glimmer of hope to break through the darkness that threatened to consume them both.

As the moon rose higher in the night sky, casting a silver glow over the meadow, he gazed deeply into Sarah's eyes. An intensity burned within him, a desire that could not be denied. He felt drawn to her in a way he hadn't felt in a while.

Without hesitation, he closed the distance between them, his lips meeting hers in a passionate kiss. Sarah's response was immediate, her body responding to his touch with an urgency that matched his own. In that moment, they ignited a fire that had smoldered between them for far too long.

Under the blanket of stars that stretched endlessly above them, they became entwined in a dance of desire and longing. Their bodies moved as one, fueled by a primal need that consumed them both. The sound of the swaying trees served as a backdrop to their union, a symphony of love and lust that filled the night air.

Afterward, they lay together in a tangle of limbs, their breath coming in ragged gasps as they tried to catch their bearings. Sarah's skin glowed in the moonlight, a vision of beauty that took his breath away. He caressed her hair, his touch gentle yet bathed with a quiet intensity.

"Charlie, do you believe in werewolves?" Sarah whispered, her eyes scanning the vast horizon with a mix of curiosity and fear. "It's going to be a full moon tomorrow night," she added, her voice barely above a whisper.

Charlie turned to face her, a mischievous smirk playing on his lips. "Oh, most definitely."

Sarah studied Charlie's expression, trying to decipher the hidden depths behind his playful demeanor.

"Why, 'cause it's almost a full moon? All the werewolves coming out?" Charlie raised an eyebrow, his eyes twinkling with amusement.

"Yeah, that, and I was just wondering." Sarah's voice trembled slightly as she spoke, the words hanging heavy in the cool evening air.

"Sometimes I think I could believe anything," Charlie mused, his smile fading as he gazed into the distance.

Charlie suddenly sat up straight. His eyes were wide. "There is something else I need to tell you." His voice was penetrated with a mixture of guilt and apprehension.

"What is it, Charlie?" Sarah's voice was barely above a whisper. "It's your mom," Charlie stammered the words.

"My mom?" Sarah's voice was barely audible as she struggled to comprehend the gravity of Charlie's words.

"Yeah, she's been sleeping with Mitch."

CHAPTER 12
Momma

MITCH SAT in the dimly lit bar, lost in his own thoughts as the world around him buzzed with life and energy. The music blared, the chatter of the crowd melded into a deafening roar, but Mitch seemed untouched by it all. His eyes were fixed on the bottle of beer in front of him, the amber liquid inside swirling in lazy patterns. Outwardly, he appeared unfazed, but inside, turmoil raged like a stormy sea.

The bar had filled up since Mitch arrived. The once sparse space was now teeming with people. Amidst the throng, a brunette woman caught his eye. Her gaze was intense, filled with desire and longing. She held his gaze with a silent invitation. Her body language spoke volumes. Others might have seen an opportunity, a chance for excitement and pleasure, but Mitch saw only a painful reminder.

The woman's features, her curves, her very presence, all echoing someone else's image in Mitch's mind. Patty. The name brought a surge of conflicting emotions, a jumble of love, disapproval, and regret. It was as if a curtain had been pulled back on his feelings, revealing truths he had long kept buried.

Patty, once the fun, hot girl of his life, is now a shadow of her former self. The weight gain, the loss of firmness and grace, it all struck a nerve deep within Mitch. He remembered the days when they were young, carefree, and in love. But now, staring at his wife, he saw only a painful reminder of his mother, her "fifteen-pound" weight gain, her struggles, her presence like a heavy cloud over their marriage. It all seemed to go down-hill, ever since Charlie arrived

Growing up, Mitch and his brother were tormented by the cruel laughter of their peers. Their mocking words etched scars on their fragile hearts. They sneered at Mitch and his brother, their taunts piercing deeper with each passing day. But it was the weight of his mother's disappointment that crushed Mitch the most.

His mother, a woman once vibrant and full of life, had become trapped within the confines of her own flesh, imprisoned by layers of fat that shielded her from the world outside. Her voice, once gentle and soothing, had become a sharp blade that sliced through the fragile peace of their home.

Their father, a ghost of a man, drifted through the shadows of his own making, bearing the brunt of his wife's wrath with a silence that screamed louder than any words could. He tended to her every need, a servant to her whims, a prisoner of his own making.

Mitch and his brother became the caretakers of their crumbling home, their childhood stolen by the weight of their responsibilities. They cooked, they cleaned, they toiled away in silence, their laughter a distant memory.

But beneath the layers of shame and despair, a flicker of defiance burned in Mitch's eyes. A flame that refused to be extinguished, a spirit that longed to break free from the chains that bound him.

And so, as the echoes of laughter faded into the night, Mitch vowed to rise above the darkness that threatened to consume him. He would forge his own path, carve out a future free from the shadows of his past.

Mitch lifted his bottle. "Hey Bill, another beer?"

He remembered the awful smell of her breath. It smelled rotten from never brushing her teeth or going to the dentist. She consumed food like a garbage disposal. She didn't chew, she just swallowed. Mitch was hoping for God that she would just choke to death. He fantasized about watching her as she gasped for air. Her fat body would buckle as she tried to pull air into her lungs. Her large hands would reach for her obese neck. Little coughing and yelping sounds would leave her disgusting mouth. "Please help me," not said but seen through the desperation in her eyes. Her eyes would bulge, and her body would thrash like a beached whale. Very slowly, the uncontrollable spasms would cease, and her fleshy body would no longer move. As much as Mitch fantasized about it, it just never happened.

If Mitch and his brother failed to do exactly as they were told, their mother's wrath would come crashing down upon them like thunder. Her big hands would strike them hard, leaving behind bruises as dark as midnight. The boys quickly learned to obey her every command, for the consequences of disobedience were too painful to bear.

Mitch and his brother, James, always felt suffocated by their overbearing mother's constant need for affection. If she wasn't shouting at them, demanding declarations of eternal loyalty, she was smothering them with her heavy, odorous embrace. The boys felt trapped in a cycle of guilt and revulsion, counting the moments until they could break free.

"Momma's never going to let you go. I don't care how big you get, you're always going to stay with me. Now say it. "Tell Momma you're never going to leave her, not ever," she would insist, her arms enveloping them in a stifling grip.

One day, Mitch couldn't bear it any longer. The weight of his mother's expectations and the burden of her suffocating love became too much to bear. He made a decision that would change his life forever.

"I can't take this anymore," Mitch finally admitted to his father. His voice permeated with a mix of anxiety and determination.

Mitch had made the mistake of speaking his mind a little too loudly within earshot of his mom. Little did he know that those few words would set off a chain of events that would test his courage to its limits.

As his mom stomped her way towards him, her anger visible in the air, Mitch felt a shiver run down his spine. But this time, he refused to cower in fear.

"Come here, Mitchy," his mom's voice boomed through the room, demanding his immediate attention.

Mitch stood his ground, a steely resolve forming within him. He wasn't going to back down this time.

"I said, come here," his mom repeated, her voice growing more menacing with each word.

With a deep breath, Mitch finally turned to face his mom, his eyes meeting hers with a newfound determination.

"I'm done obeying blindly," Mitch spoke, his voice steady despite fear gnawing at him. "I deserve to be heard too."

His mom's expression softened, a hint of surprise flickering in her eyes. For the first time, she truly saw the strength within her son, a strength that had been silently growing beneath the surface all along.

"So boy, you're not gonna listen to your momma?" Her voice boomed. "So, you think you're gonna win this one, do ya? Let's see, what's you gonna do?"

Her fat face loomed closer to Mitch's, a sneer playing on her lips. "You go first, make the first move."

Mitch stood his ground, unmoving despite the pressure. His mother's words echoed in his mind, but he refused to back down. He knew that this was his moment to stand up for himself, no matter how daunting the opponent.

"Are you deaf, boy?" She taunted, poking him in the ear. The sharp pain jolted through Mitch's head, but still, he didn't flinch.

"I think he's deaf, Father," Momma called out, looking over at her weak husband who stood by, watching the scene unfold.

Father just shook his head in approval, a hint of amusement in his eyes. "Maybe we need to pour some water into your ears..."

Mitch knew he had to stay cool before things escalated further. "Hey Mitchy, wanna play?" she said with a mischievous grin.

Mitch looked up at her, uncertain of what was coming. He knew that when his mom had that look on her face, trouble wasn't far behind.

She swung her hand and smacked him across the head. Mitch flinched, more out of surprise than pain.

"Did that hurt Mitchy? Poor baby. "Father, he's hurt," Momma teased, glancing over at Mitch's father with a sly smile.

Mitch's father chuckled, shaking his head.

Momma turned back to Mitch, her smile widening to reveal a mouth full of crooked, yellowed teeth. "So, I heard you tell Father that you were sick of the shit around here. That's good, Mitchy. We're communicating like family now. But the problem is, I think you were talking about me. Instead of coming to me, you went straight to Father and got him all worried."

Mitch felt a knot in his stomach. He knew his momma could be unpredictable.

"I knew this day was a-comin'," she began. Her voice was tinged with a hint of sadness. "Momma knows these kinda things. It's good you're a tough boy, Mitchy. But you're stuck thinkin' there's something better out there. That's the problem. It ain't better. This is it. Do ya understand me?"

Mitch felt his stomach churn, unsure of what his mother was trying to tell him. But her gaze was steady, her words filled with a quiet strength that brooked no argument, she continued, her tone casual yet steeped in gravity.

"Your momma and father are going to be needing you now, especially because we're getting on in age. So I'm going to have to teach you an important lesson about not leaving family and all," she said, her eyes searching his face for understanding.

She grabbed his hair and yanked it hard, causing a sharp pain to shoot through his head. Mitch stumbled back, crashing into the nearby table, which skidded across the floor, creating a cacophony of screeching sounds. He winced as he felt a dull throbbing in his side from the impact and fell to the floor.

As Mitch lay sprawled on the ground, his mother loomed over him. Her face was flushed with anger and sweat glistening on her brow. Her breath was hot and pungent as she leaned in close, her intense gaze fixed on him.

"So, how ya feelin?" she asked, her voice deceptively casual despite the tense situation.

Mitch stared up at her, a mix of fear and confusion clouding his expression.

He couldn't believe what was happening. To his horror, his mother slowly spread her legs open, revealing her oversized, stained underwear. With a sudden movement, she straddled him, her weight pressing down on his chest.

Gasping for air and feeling a sharp pain in his left rib, Mitch struggled to move, his arms and feet being the only parts of him able to squirm. In a desperate attempt to reason with his mother, Mitch mustered all the strength he had left to nudge her with his arm.

"Momma, please," Mitch managed to croak out, his voice barely above a whisper as her weight bore down on him. "Let me go."

His mother looked down at him, her eyes filled with an unsettling mix of determination and something else that Mitch couldn't quite place.

"So Mitchy, what's it gonna be, me or nothin'?" she asked, her tone demanding.

Struggling to breathe under her immense weight, Mitch felt a sense of fear wash over him. He knew he had to make a choice, and it wasn't going to be an easy one.

In a moment of desperation, Mitch's response escaped his lips in a hoarse whisper: "Yes, Momma, I wanna stay with you."

A flicker of satisfaction danced across his mother's face as she patted him on the head with surprising gentleness.

"That's my good boy," she whispered before finally lifting her weight off him.

"Father, help me here," Momma stammered.

"Help me to the couch, Father, my legs are killing me." She didn't look back.

"Mitchy, get your Momma a piece of cake. A large piece. I've worked up an appetite."

Mitch just lay on his side.

"Oh God, please."

A year later, without a second thought, Mitch left everything behind, including his younger brother three years his junior, and drove off into the unknown night. The truck roared down the empty highway, swallowing the distance between him and his past.

As the wind whipped through his hair, Mitch felt a mix of exhilaration and fear. It was both liberating and terrifying to leave everything he knew behind. He couldn't bear the weight of his old life any longer, so he chose to shed it like a snake sheds its skin.

Leaving his family, his belongings, and even his identity as Mitch Parker, he embraced a new beginning as Connors. It was like a rebirth, a chance to rewrite the story of his life on a blank page. The road stretched out before him, full of twists and turns, mysteries waiting to be unraveled.

Mitch finished his sixth beer as he sat in the bar, surrounded by half-drunken people. Tonight, after hitting Charlie over the head he had made the decision to spend the night at the shop, away from the drama unfolding in his own home. He didn't feel like dealing with Patty's shenanigans, especially now that he sensed something fishy going on between her and Charlie.

Lately, Mitch had noticed Patty and Charlie spending more time together, whispering and exchanging secretive glances. He was certain they were communicating a lot behind his back, probably even texting each other. The fact that Patty wasn't as intimidated by him as she used to be set off alarm bells in Mitch's mind. A wave of frustration washed over him as he realized that Patty was likely going to let Charlie stay in the house, despite his explicit instructions for her not to.

"Fucking kid knows too much," Mitch muttered to himself, running a hand through his unkempt hair. Charlie seemed to have a knack for picking up on Mitch's fights with Patty and his extramarital affairs. This precarious situation put Mitch in a tight spot, and he knew he had to tread carefully.

He had warned Charlie multiple times to stay out of his business, emphasizing the consequences if he didn't comply. But it seemed like Charlie had his own agenda, and he wasn't backing down anytime soon. Mitch took a swig of his beer, contemplating his next move as he pondered the tangled web of relationships and trust that was slowly unraveling before his eyes.

"How much do I owe you, Bill?"

"Thirty bucks."

"Geez."

Mitch took out three tens and a five-dollar bill from his money clip and laid it on the counter.

"Keep the change."

CHAPTER 13

Secrets

SARAH STARED AT CHARLIE, which felt like hours. Charlie finally mustered the courage to reveal a truth he had kept hidden for so long.

"What are you saying?" Sarah asked, a hint of confusion in her voice.

"I wasn't sure how to tell you," Charlie hesitated, his heart racing with apprehension.

Sarah's reaction was not what he expected. She jumped up from the blanket, her eyes watery, and stood over him with a mix of shock and disappointment.

"It's not true. My mom isn't sleeping with Mitch." Sarah yelled nervously, the sound echoing through the silent night. But as she felt adrenaline pumping through her veins, she could almost believe his words to be true. Her senses seemed heightened, every rustle of leaves and hoot of an owl sending a shiver down her spine.

Her heart raced as she imagined the moon turning her into a creature of the night, her blood running hot with newfound power. The hairs on her arms stood on end, as if reaching out to touch the moonlight bathing the forest in its silvery glow.

Her imagination continued. In that moment, after transforming, she felt alive in a way she had never experienced before. The thrill of the unknown, the rush of danger lingering in the air - it all filled her with a sense of exhilaration she could not deny. The human side of her was gone.

"Are you lying to me about this?" she demanded, her voice trembling with emotion.

Charlie shook his head in denial, trying to make sense of the sudden tension that filled the air. As he reached for the flashlight to shed some light on the situation, Sarah's piercing gaze bore into him.

"How long have you known?" she asked. Her tone was a mix of hurt and frustration.

"I don't know... for a while, I guess," Charlie admitted, feeling the weight of his secret crushing down on him.

"And you're just now telling me?" Sarah's voice rose with a mix of anger and betrayal, making Charlie realize the gravity of the situation.

"Why are you overreacting?" Charlie tried to defend himself, but Sarah's fiery glare silenced him.

"Overreacting?" Sarah's words cut through the darkness, echoing in the still night air.

As Charlie reached down and grabbed the blanket, Sarah stood there, her patience wearing thin. She watched as he nonchalantly rolled up the blanket with the flashlight tucked under his arm. In that moment, she felt a surge of energy, almost like a werewolf with her blood running hot and her hair standing on end.

"Forget about the blanket! What were you waiting for? You should have told me!" Sarah's frustration was evident in her voice.

"Calm down," Charlie replied, his tone steady and composed.

"Why should I calm down?" My mom is sleeping with that raving idiot. What is she thinking? "What's wrong with everyone?" Sarah's words spilled out in a rush, her emotions raw and unfiltered.

Without another word, Sarah stormed ahead and climbed into Charlie's truck, the anger simmering beneath the surface. She watched as Charlie approached the truck leisurely, seemingly unperturbed by the chaos around them. As he placed the blanket and flashlight in the truck bed, Sarah couldn't help but wonder how he remained so calm in the midst of it all.

Finally, Charlie climbed into the driver's seat and started the engine. The roar of the engine shattered the stillness of the woods, the sound echoing through the trees. Sarah's confusion grew as she wondered why he hadn't told her sooner. The truck jolted into motion, tires squealing against the gravel as they navigated the dark, narrow lane.

The silence was deafening, only broken by the hum of the engine. Charlie didn't turn on the radio. The only sound was the rhythmic thud of Sarah's heart. Minutes passed in tense silence until Sarah couldn't take it any longer.

"I can't believe you didn't tell me," she blurted out. Her voice was tinged with frustration.

Charlie glanced at her, his eyes unreadable. "Look, don't be mad at me about this. It's your mom you should be mad at," he replied, his tone calm.

Charlie sat nervously while driving his truck, his mind racing with the snippets of conversation he had unintentionally overheard.

"How do you know for sure?" Sarah's words echoed in her mind, making her question everything she thought she knew about her mom.

"I heard him talking on the phone, in his office, after everyone in the shop had gone home. He didn't know I was still there. He said her name several times. He even said your dad's name," Charlie recounted the details to Sarah.

"But it could be someone else?" Sarah suggested, trying to offer a glimmer of doubt to Charlie's burgeoning suspicions.

"It could be, but I doubt it," Charlie replied, his certainty unwavering.

"I think you're wrong," Sarah said.

"Maybe they were just talking business," Charlie attempted to rationalize why Sarah wanted to hear something different, although deep down, he knew that wasn't the case.

"No, Sarah, they weren't talking about business," Charlie remarked firmly, his hands clenching the steering wheel.

Sarah looked at Charlie, her expression pleading for understanding, for guidance.

"What were they talking about?" she inquired, desperation lacing her voice. Sarah hesitated, knowing the weight of her next words. "I need to tell my father about this," Sarah declared, the decision solidifying in her mind.

"God, Sarah, I don't think that's a good idea," Charlie cautioned, concern etched into his expression.

"He has a right to know," Sarah countered, her resolve unwavering.

"Maybe, but you shouldn't be the one to do it," Charlie urged, trying to protect Sarah from what could potentially unravel if she decided to confront her father.

Sarah sat in Charlie's truck, her hands nervously fidgeting with the hem of her top. "What am I going to do?" she muttered under her breath, her thoughts swirling around like a whirlwind in her mind. The silence between her and Charlie was heavy, the tension palpable.

As they drove closer to her house, Sarah's anxiety grew stronger. Charlie's words about Mitch had planted a seed of fear in her heart. Could he really be capable of hurting her mom? The mere thought made her stomach lurch with dread. She couldn't shake off the worry that gnawed at her insides.

Margaret's words echoed in her mind - how she had noticed their mom's tears, her sadness hidden behind a facade of strength. Sarah felt a pang of guilt, knowing she shouldn't be the one to tell her father. What if something happened to her mom because of her silence? Maybe it would have to be her duty? The weight of responsibility bore down on her, making her chest tight with worry.

Charlie turned off the car's lights as they approached Sarah's house, casting a shadow of darkness over the familiar surroundings. The stillness of the night added to the eerie atmosphere, heightening Sarah's apprehension. She took a deep breath, steeling herself for what lay ahead.

"I wonder if my father has been looking for me. I hope he doesn't catch us."

"He won't."

Charlie drove a little past her house. "He can't see us from here. Walk around the driveway."

"Yeah."

"What are you going to do about your mom?"

Sarah sighed. "I don't know yet."

"I don't think you should say anything. It's just going to cause more problems."

"Yeah, well, Mitch is dangerous."

"I will deal with Mitch." Charlie retorted.

"How are you going to do that?"

Charlie didn't respond.

"How long do you suppose they've been seeing each other?"

"You're asking me? I don't really know. A while I guess."

"Well... you knew something about it and kept me in the dark."

"I was planning on telling you."

"When? You never include me in anything anymore."

"Sarah, I..."

"Never mind, Charlie. I need to go."

Sarah opened her door. Charlie yelled out the window, "Hey, I'll be at John's if you need me."

Sarah quietly ran up and around the driveway to the back of the house. The moonlight's rays peeked beneath the wispy clouds, and then Charlie watched Sarah disappear into darkness.

* * *

SARAH CAME in quietly through the back door, her heart pounding in her chest. She did not want her father to know that she had been out late. As she stood in the kitchen, trying to calm her racing thoughts, a shiver ran down her spine. Everything seemed normal in the house at first glance, but nothing felt normal anymore.

Charlie and Mitch, their horrible night, both their violent sides being exposed. Margaret had been acting strangely, disappearing for hours at a time and returning with a distant look in her eyes. Her mom. Mitch, her lover? What world was she living in?

"It must be getting late," Sarah whispered to herself, glancing at her phone. She kicked off her sneakers and placed them by the back door, ensuring she made no noise as she crept through the darkened house. The soft glow of light spilled from her father's study, drawing her in like a moth to a flame.

As she approached the study, Sarah heard muffled voices coming from within. Her father was on a speakerphone call, his voice calm and authoritative. Sarah hesitated for a moment, debating whether to eavesdrop or retreat to her room.

Curiosity got the better of her, and she pressed closer to the door, straining to catch snippets of the conversation. Her father was discussing Charlie's parents. Sarah's breath caught in her throat as she realized the seriousness of the situation.

"Hey, Harry, it's Robert. Sorry to be calling you so late, but I need you to do me a favor."

Sure, Robert, what is it?

"Could you do some checking on James and Doris Parker and their son Charles?"

"Slow down."

"And Mitch Connors."

"I'm writing this down... James and Doris Parker? Charlie Parker and Mitch Connors?"

"Yeah, that's right. James and Doris were killed in a car accident almost 5 years ago. Their son Charles went to live with Mitch Connors, James' older brother. I believe they lived in a town called Riddle. It's a small town outside of Boise, Idaho."

"What's this all about?"

"Just doing a little research. Can you get me some background on what kind of people they were? Can you do that for me?"

"Sure, Robert, no problem. It might take me a day or two."

"Hurry it up, will you, Harry?"

Sarah could not believe what she was hearing. Her father had always been a pillar of strength and wisdom in her life. So, what was he up to now? Sarah felt her legs turn to jelly as she leaned against the wall outside his office. The words she had just overheard echoed in her mind, making her head spin.

"Oh my God. What is going on around here?" she whispered to herself, unsure of what to make of the situation. As tears threatened to fall, she slumped to the floor, overwhelmed by a wave of disbelief and confusion.

Inside the office, her father was engrossed in his computer, seemingly oblivious to the turmoil brewing just outside his door. Sarah couldn't understand what was happening and what was about to unfold. Was there more to this story than she had been led to believe? She questioned everything she thought she knew.

* * *

SARAH DIALED CHARLIE'S NUMBER, her heart racing with anticipation. Two rings, then a voicemail. She sighed in frustration and redialed, hoping for a different outcome. Again, no answer. Sarah paced the room, her thoughts swirling like a storm in her mind.

Minutes ticked by as she mindlessly scrolled through Facebook, a habit she despised but found oddly soothing in moments of distress. Images and updates flashed before her eyes, but none of them held her attention. "Why am I wasting my time on this?" she muttered to herself, throwing her phone onto the bed.

An idea suddenly struck her, and she dialed John's number. The familiar ring brought a sense of relief. "Hey John, it's Sarah," she said when he answered.

"Hey Sarah, how are you doing?" John's voice was warm and friendly, easing some of the tension in Sarah's chest.

"I'm good," she replied, grateful for his easy-going demeanor. "How's everything going?"

"Not bad, nothing too exciting," John replied, his tone comforting.

"Charlie mentioned something about going back to summer school," John said, curiosity lacing his words.

Sarah chuckled at the other end of the line. "Ah, yeah. Nothing to worry about. I just have a few classes to catch up on. Sarah paused. John, I'm sorry to cut you off, but I really need to talk to Charlie. Is he there?"

"Yeah, hold on for a minute," came the muffled response from the other end of the line. She fidgeted nervously.

"Sarah?" A voice brought her back to the present. "Hello? Sarah?"

Sarah let out a sigh of relief. "Hi, Charlie," she replied, trying to keep her tone casual despite the turmoil within her.

"Is everything okay?" Charlie asked, concern evident in his voice.

Sarah hesitated, taking a deep breath before plunging into the depths of her fears. "Why aren't you answering your phone?" she asked, her voice breaking slightly.

"I didn't get a chance to charge it today...well since sleeping in the truck last night and all." Charlie responded matter-of-factly, but Sarah could sense the underlying tension in his words.

"What's wrong?" Charlie pressed, his voice soft and reassuring.

Sarah closed her eyes, steadying herself to reveal the truth. "My father," she whispered. The weight of the words was heavy on her tongue.

Charlie cut her off. "You told him about your mom?" Charlie's question hung in the air.

Sarah sighed. "No, I didn't talk to him. I overheard him talking on the phone to his lawyer."

"Yeah, and...?"

"He asked him to do some checking around on you and your parents," Sarah revealed with a tense voice.

"What?" Charlie exclaimed. His disbelief expressed in his voice.

"He's also doing some checking on Mitch," Sarah added. Her voice was tinged with concern.

"Why would he do that?" Charlie sounded mad.

"For one thing, you hit me. Did you forget about that?" Sarah reminded him, her tone hinting at a lingering hurt.

"No, I didn't forget about that," Charlie answered quietly, a sense of regret evident in his voice.

"Maybe he thinks you're crazy, and he probably thinks Mitch is crazy too," Sarah suggested.

"How would he know anything about Mitch?" Charlie inquired, his confusion detectable.

"Last night you mentioned to my father that Mitch was giving you trouble. He saw the cut on your face. Maybe he suspects something?"

"Yeah, maybe."

"Maybe he also knows that my mom is sleeping with him," Sarah confessed, her voice lowering.

"You think?" Charlie uttered in disbelief, processing the news.

"Well, something is up," Sarah pointed out. A sense of unease settled between them.

"Charlie, is there something you're not telling me?" Sarah asked, her concern growing with each passing moment.

But Charlie wasn't listening. His mind was racing with a whirlwind of thoughts and emotions, trying to make sense of the tangled web of secrets and suspicions that threatened to unravel their relationship.

"Charlie, what's this all about?"

"I have no idea."

"Are you sure?"

"What, you don't believe me?" Charlie retorted in quiet anger.

"Charlie. I believe you. It's just that things seem to be really strange lately."

Charlie went silent.

"Charlie, are you listening to me?" Sarah's voice echoed through the phone.

After several seconds, he answered. "Yeah," Charlie muttered.

"You messed up badly. Unlike you. I think our relationship is important." Sarah's frustration was evident.

"Who says our relationship isn't important to me?" Charlie iterates.

"My father obviously thinks something is up with you."

"Shit, Sarah, I can't take back what happened. If I could, I would," Charlie's tone softened.

"You need to get your shit together. You need to stop keeping secrets from me," Sarah insisted.

"Whatever Sarah," Charlie's voice was overlayed with resignation.

"I thought you cared about me," Sarah's voice wavered.

"I'm just tired of all this bullshit," Charlie admitted, his voice heavy with emotion.

And then, the phone went silent.

CHAPTER 14

Control

CHARLIE COULDN'T SHAKE off the weight of regret that had settled in his chest. The memory of the argument with Sarah replayed in his mind like a broken record. He wished he could turn back time and erase his moment of rage that had led to a physical outburst.

Sinking into the couch, Charlie tried to focus on the basketball game blaring on TV. John's enthusiastic commentary on the Mariners' lead barely registered in his mind. His thoughts were consumed by guilt and self-reproach.

With a heavy sigh, Charlie finally turned to face John. "I messed up, man. I messed up big time," he admitted, his voice filled with a mix of regret and self-loathing.

John glanced at Charlie, momentarily torn between the excitement of the game and the serious tone of Charlie's voice. "What happened, Charlie?" he asked, concern etched on his face.

Charlie hesitated, unsure of how to explain his actions. "I

let my anger get the best of me. I hit Sarah," he confessed, his voice barely above a whisper.

John's expression darkened as he processed Charlie's words. "Shit, dude. That's rough," he replied, his tone understanding but firm. "You need to talk to Sarah, apologize, and make things right."

John got up from the couch and stretched his tired muscles. "Hey, do you want another beer?" he asked Charlie, who was lounging on the adjacent couch.

Charlie nodded and replied, "Sure, bring me one."

John made his way to the small kitchen, muttering under his breath about the temperamental fridge. He opened the door, and with a sigh, he realized there were only three beers left.

"Piece of crap fridge," he muttered to himself. John called out from the kitchen, "Wow, man, there are only three beers left?"

John peered into the nearly empty refrigerator, finding only condiments and a few food items. He shook his head in disappointment. "So, why don't you go and talk to her old man? Try and make amends," John suggested.

John grabbed a bag of pretzels from the kitchen table before returning to the living room with a beer for Charlie.

"Thanks," Charlie said as he accepted the drink.

John sank back onto the couch, munching on pretzels as he contemplated Charlie's words. "You know, I can see why her old man is so protective. That family is worth a lot of money," John remarked casually.

John and Charlie sat on the worn-out sofas in John's tiny apartment, bottles of beer in hand, watching the basketball commentators on TV. The sound of their half-empty bottles clinking against the coffee table filled the small living room.

As the commentators continued, John took a long swig of his beer, the amber liquid gliding down his throat, easing his stress momentarily. "Man, I wanted to see the ending," he lamented, disappointment evident in his voice.

"You knew they were going to win," Charlie remarked, his eyes fixed on the screen. He could feel the tension in the room dissipating as the final moments of the game played out in a loop on rewind.

"Shit, Sarah and Margaret are going to be loaded," John muttered. The thought of their lavish lifestyle made him yearn for a taste of that wealth.

"Yeah. I could use some money. I'm behind on my truck payment. I need to find a place of my own. "Freakin' Mitch doesn't pay me shit," Charlie vented, frustration evident in his tone.

John nodded in agreement, empathizing with his friend's financial struggles. "Yeah, look at my crappy apartment. Mitch hasn't given me a raise in years."

"He's a cheapskate. I could be rich with Sarah."

"That's for sure. Being rich... that's the life. Who wouldn't want to be rich like that? "Man, I would quit the job and sit around and play video games all day," he mused, a hint of longing in his voice. John shoved pretzels into his mouth. Suddenly John began to choke.

Charlie glanced at John with a mix of concern and amusement. "Dude, are you okay?" he asked.

John seemed to stop breathing. Between coughs and gasps for air, John managed to nod, his face now a deep shade of red. Charlie rushed to grab a glass of water for his choking friend.

After a few sips of water, John finally caught his breath and wiped his watery eyes. He sheepishly grinned at Charlie and said, "Note to self: don't talk with my mouth full."

Charlie chuckled. "You're just drunk." Charlie patted John on the back. "You're okay buddy."

* * *

MITCH DIALED THE NUMBER AGAIN. No answer.

Deciding to stay put in the shop for the night, Mitch begrudgingly accepted that rest would not come easy. His mind replayed the events of the day, anger bubbling up once more at the memory of hitting Charlie over the head. That kid was always pushing his buttons, testing his limits.

Mitch has always been a hard worker, putting in long hours to keep the bills paid and the lights on. But what did he have to show for it? A wife who seemed to grow plumper by the day, and a nephew who had all the attitude of a rebellious teenager.

Charlie, Mitch's brother's son, strutted through life like he owned the place. He didn't bother to offer a helping hand, instead choosing to focus on his own selfish desires. Mitch couldn't stand the way Charlie disrespected everything he had worked so hard to build.

As the days passed, Mitch's frustration bubbled beneath the surface, ready to boil over at any moment. He was sick and tired of being taken advantage of, of constantly sacrificing his own happiness for the sake of others.

Mitch made a tough decision to leave home, feeling like he was leaving his brother, James, vulnerable and unprotected. The guilt weighed heavily on him as he knew his absence meant his brother would have to face the abuse alone. Mitch couldn't shake the feeling of remorse for not taking his brother with him when he left. He couldn't forgive himself for leaving him to face such troubles on his own. Every now and then, when guilt became unbearable, Mitch would dial his brother's number just to make sure he was okay. But the last time he tried calling, there was no answer.

Mitch eventually made a silent pact with himself to forget about his brother. He buried memories deep within his mind, pushing aside the pains of the past. Days turned into weeks, weeks into months, and soon, Mitch found himself hardly thinking about his brother at all.

But life had a funny way of bringing back the ghosts he tried so hard to forget. One day, out of the blue, Mitch received a call from the authorities. His brother and sister-in-law had tragically perished in a violent car accident, leaving behind their child. His brother was drunk and lost control of the car and hit a tree. His brother's wife had flown of the window. She had not worn her seat belt. Mitch's father ended up smashing his head into the steering wheel. Mitch was left all alone.

And just like that, as if fate was playing a cruel joke on him, Charlie reappeared in Mitch's life. The sight of his nephew stirred up a whirlwind of emotions in Mitch, bringing back memories long buried in the recesses of his mind. He hated how Charlie made him feel, the guilt and regret washing over him in waves.

When tragedy struck and Mitch's brother passed away, leaving his teenage son Charlie behind, with no money to his name, Patty insisted that they take him in. Reluctantly, Mitch agreed. He never wanted the responsibility of having kids or taking care of his brother's kid, but he felt guilty for leaving his younger brother behind all those years ago, and so he let Charlie move in.

He made it clear that Charlie was to work, pay rent, and stay out of his way. Charlie was to mind his own business. Mitch was a private man, and he valued solitude. He was not allowed to ask questions. Mitch had no plans on getting to know him, and luckily, Charlie kept to himself for a while. Mitch knew he could get away with paying him on the low side, and the money that went to Charlie would be reapplied back to Mitch's expenses. The plan wasn't so bad if Charlie stuck to the rules.

Charlie was a quiet boy, still grappling with the loss of his parents and adjusting to his new life with Mitch and Patty. The days turned into weeks, and Mitch put Charlie to work in the shop, teaching him the value of hard work and responsibility. At the beginning, Mitch let Charlie do some minor work on cars, sweep the floors, organize the shelves, and assist customers. Mitch thought to himself, "This isn't too bad." It was less work for Mitch to do.

Patty found Charlie's presence comforting. With him around, she found herself in brighter moods, and her smiles came more easily. But for Mitch, Charlie was like a shadow from the past that he desperately wanted to forget - a past that haunted him.

As Mitch grappled with his inner turmoil, he couldn't help but feel the brewing anger beneath his skin. The constant reminder of his past, the wounds so fresh yet so old, threatened to consume him once again.

I've come too far. I won't allow Charlie to be a threat. I'll see to that, he thought. Mitch said to himself with determination. Mitch dialed the number. It went straight to voicemail. "Shit!"

He slammed his phone down on the desk. The unanswered calls and texts drove him mad. What started as a playful chase had now become a game of annoyance for him.

At first, the thrill of the chase excited him. The flirtatious banter, the subtle hints of desire - it all fueled his passion. But now, all he craved was release. The tension building within him begged for an outlet, and she was the one who occupied his thoughts.

For Mitch, there was a carnal satisfaction in the act of sex when tension ran high. It was like a primal energy coursing through his veins, awakening his inner beast. In those moments, he felt like a conqueror, a master of his desires.

In his mind's eye, Mitch saw himself as the ultimate seducer, a man who commanded attention and lust in equal measure. He was the embodiment of every woman's fantasies, a magnetic force that drew them in.

He set his sights on a mysterious woman who exuded an air of elegance and grace. At first, she played coy, her mysterious smile giving nothing away. But Mitch wasn't one to back down from a challenge. With each encounter, he laid on his charm and humor thick, slowly breaking down her walls. What started as small talk turned into deep and meaningful conversations that kept them up late into the night.

Mitch couldn't help but fantasize about the woman, her slender figure haunting his every thought. She was delicate yet full of untapped passion. The mere idea of touching her sent shivers down his spine, igniting a fire within him that he hadn't felt in ages.

As their connection grew stronger, Mitch found himself entangled in a web of desire and longing. He yearned to possess her, to make her his in every sense of the word. The thought of her surrendering to him, willingly and completely, consumed his every waking moment.

No woman had ever captivated Mitch in such a way before. He was willing to do whatever it took to make her his, to unlock the secrets hidden behind those enigmatic eyes.

Mitch couldn't believe how quickly everything unfolded between them. As days turned into weeks, he noticed her walls slowly crumbling down, allowing him to see a vulnerable side of her that he found endearing. He approached their budding relationship with caution, savoring each moment as if it were a precious gift waiting to be unwrapped.

In the quiet intimacy of their shared moments, Mitch felt a surge of desire coursing through him, igniting a vital flame that consumed them both. She mirrored his wild passion, matching his fervor with a hunger of her own, proving to be an equal in every sense.

"Where the fuck is she?"

CHAPTER 15
Resentment

HER HEAD WAS POUNDING. Sarah groaned and reached over to her nightstand. Her hand

Fumbling around until it found the familiar shape of a bottle of aspirin. With a sigh of relief, she managed to open the cap and shake out three pills into her palm.

She tossed them into her mouth and chased them down with a gulp of water. But as she swallowed, one of the pills seemed to have a mind of its own and got stuck in her throat. The bitter taste of the pill's coating seeped into her mouth, making her grimace in disgust.

Hastily, Sarah took another swig of water, hoping to wash away the awful taste. The last pill went down smoothly this time, but the bitter aftertaste lingered, reminding her of the ordeal she had just endured.

As she lay back against her headboard waiting for the aspirin to kick in and relieve her pounding headache, Sarah couldn't help but sigh at the unexpected drama of the past few days.

Her eyes scanned the room, taking in the disarray that had taken hold of her since she got home. With a heavy heart, she realized that even her safe space was not immune to the chaos that had been seeping into her life lately. Clothes were scattered haphazardly, books and papers were scattered about, and her once neatly made bed was now a jumble of blankets, with several pillows on the floor. Schoolwork, responsibilities, and worries had all piled up. It was as if her room had transformed into a reflection of the cluttered thoughts swirling in her mind.

As she lay in the midst of the disorder, a sense of overwhelming washed over her. She was second-guessing her trip home. It hadn't helped her stress levels at all. The familiar urge to escape to the water beckoned; a nice, hard swim would be good for her and help her relieve some stress.

"No wonder I want to leave here," she thought.

Margaret seemed withdrawn and had disappeared. Charlie had been acting so weird, keeping secrets, losing his temper, and now hanging up on her. Her father was completely losing it on Charlie, and now her mom was having an affair with a psycho. What else could happen?

Choosing the school farthest away from home, Sarah believed that distance would bring clarity. She longed for a life beyond the confines of her overbearing father and the constant comparisons to her older sister, Margaret. Margaret was the epitome of perfection in their parents' eyes, overshadowing Sarah at every turn.

As Sarah packed her bags and bid farewell to familiar streets and faces, a mix of excitement and nervousness swirled within her. The road ahead was unknown, but she welcomed uncertainty with open arms. Perhaps in the vast halls of the university, she would find her own voice, free from the endless echoes of Margaret's achievements. It was so hard for Sarah to be seen; she felt like she was invisible. Though at times, Sarah wished she was more like her sister. So, when Margaret announced that she would be studying under the famous artist Emily Martin, Sarah's jealousy reached new heights. It seemed like Margaret always got opportunities that Sarah could only dream of.

"Why couldn't I have been the one with the artistic talent?" Sarah often grumbled to herself. She couldn't help but compare herself to her sister and wonder why she hadn't been blessed with the same skills.

As Margaret flourished under Emily Martin's tutelage, Sarah's resentment grew. She found herself saying things she didn't mean, wishing secretly for her sister to stumble and fail. "It would make me so happy if she didn't succeed," she whispered to herself in moments of bitterness.

But when Margaret faced a setback and had her breakdown, Sarah's heart sank. She realized that her jealousy and ill-wishes had only brought her guilt and regret. She couldn't take back the words she had spoken in a fit of envy.

Margaret was a brilliant painter with a unique vision that captured the beauty of the world in vibrant hues and intricate details. But one day, Margaret made a decision that shattered her world. She walked out of her studio, leaving behind her painting supplies, her unfinished masterpiece, and a broken-hearted Emily. Her parents were devastated, their disappointment turning to anger as they struggled to make sense of her sudden departure.

Her father's voice was harsh with the sting of betrayal. "You had it all, Margaret. The world was at your feet, waiting for you to paint it with your dreams. How could you throw it all away like this? You're a fool to walk away from your talent, from everything you could have been."

And their mother, once the wellspring of their family's love and warmth, now sat in sorrow, her tears a silent lament for the daughter who had lost her way. She whispered brokenly, "Margaret, my child, why did you give up such a gift?" Their mother cried. "Why have you done this to yourself, Margaret? I've always regretted giving up my dream. You could have done it differently."

It was as if a dark cloud had settled over their once happy home, casting a shadow over everything they did. Their arguments had become a daily occurrence, with her parents finding fault in just about everything. From the way they cooked breakfast to the color of the curtains, there was always something to fight about.

Initially, disagreements centered around Margaret's choices. But soon enough, the fights began seeping into every corner of their lives. Back and forth, the two of them pointed their fingers at each other. It was all Robert's fault. He was always working, too preoccupied to be present for his family.

Gwen found herself overwhelmed with the endless demands of managing everything on her own. Robert, on the other hand, saw Gwen as inadequate and lacking in toughness, especially when it came to their daughters, Margaret and Sarah. He believed they were spoiled, never having worked for anything they wanted.

In the midst, of their heated arguments, Sarah couldn't shake off the thought – was her mom's affair a result of this dysfunction in their family? As she checked the time on her phone, realizing how late it had gotten, concern grew for Margaret, who still hadn't returned home. Where could she be off all this time? The moon's glow illuminated the room as Sarah stared out the window, her head throbbing with a dull ache.

"Where are you, Margaret?" Sarah said to herself.

Feeling a mix of worry and curiosity, Sarah contemplated seeking solace in her mom's company. Maybe she could gain some insight into Mitch. Perhaps talking things out with her mom would provide some clarity amidst the chaos. Of course, she couldn't come out and ask directly. Maybe she could find some answers to the questions swirling in her mind. Amidst the tense atmosphere at home, Sarah hoped for a glimmer of understanding and connection to ease the growing sense of unease within her.

CHAPTER 16

Gwen

MARGARET LAY ON HER BACK, her thoughts wandering aimlessly as the man she had been seeing traced patterns on her stomach with his tongue. His usual charm that had always been able to ignite a fire within her seemed to fall flat tonight.

"Put your finger there while you're doing that," she murmured absentmindedly, her mind disengaged from the moment. His touches felt distant, his caresses failing to evoke the usual shivers down her spine.

"Yeah... that's sexy," he replied, his voice carrying a hint of uncertainty as he tried to gauge Margaret's reaction. Her small, firm breasts were exposed to the dim light in the room, casting shadows that danced across her skin.

The slow rotation of the ceiling fan above provided a hypnotic backdrop to their tryst, the cool breeze creating a stark contrast against their heated bodies. Margaret's mind, however, remained elsewhere, disconnected from the passion that usually coursed between them.

"Do you like that?" he asked. "Keep doing that."

She wasn't even feeling it. She pretends to get into it. She moved her body back and forth.

"You like that? I know how to make you feel good."

"You're so good." Margaret's thoughts were miles away.

Margaret suddenly pushed him away and abruptly stood up, her legs still a bit shaky from their impromptu exchange. She made her way to the bathroom, needing a moment to collect her thoughts. The cool tiles under her feet provided a brief respite from the intensity of the moment. She hated motels.

As she splashed cold water on her face, Margaret couldn't help but replay the scene in her mind. His proximity, his energy—it was all so overwhelming. She wasn't sure if she was ready for this level of intimacy, even if it was just a casual encounter.

Taking a deep breath, Margaret composed herself and returned to the room. He was sitting on the edge of the bed, looking contemplative.

"Hey, what's up with you?" he asked, his tone laced with curiosity.

She looked at him, meeting his gaze with a mixture of vulnerability and determination.

"I just have a really bad headache. I need to get home."

* * *

SARAH WALKED INTO HER PARENTS' bedroom. Her mother had just taken a bath, and she was wrapped in her white, fluffy bathrobe, which hung just below her knees. It looked soft and warm. Her hair was still pulled up and clipped. She was sitting on her parents' bed rubbing lotion into her legs. The bed was a beautiful wilderness, bristlecone pinewood, four poster bed, with luxurious white soft linens, accented with Icelandic white sheepskin fur.

Sarah stood by the doorway. Her mom looked up.

"Hey, Mom. Do you have a minute?"

"Sure, sweetie. You, okay?"

"Yeah, I was kind of hoping that we could talk."

"Of course. Come in here while I brush my hair."

Sarah followed her mom into the large bathroom. The moment she stepped inside, Sarah couldn't help but take in the grandeur of the space. The room felt like it belonged in a fancy hotel, with its oversized dimensions and slightly chilly ambiance.

The floor was a striking Statuario luxury tile, with its veining patterns and pristine white color, which exuded sophistication and classical beauty, under soft lighting. The cabinets, painted in a white finish, looked sleek and modern. The countertop was a smooth expanse of white quartz, seamlessly molded with matte, stainless-steel sinks hanging beneath it. Three large, framed mirrors adorned the walls, reflecting the opulence of the room. Modern sconces added a touch of sophistication, their sleek designs complementing the overall aesthetic.

The shower area was a study in opulence. The walls were adorned with white linear glass tiles, creating a contemporary and inviting feel. A long white marble bench ran along the inside of the shower, complete with two, his and her, matte stainless steel shower-heads that promised a lavish showering experience. Besides the shower stall, a spacious ball-foot bathtub beckoned, positioned elegantly beneath a circular window that let in the soft glow of natural light.

As Sarah's gaze swept across the room, she couldn't help but wonder at the beauty and elegance of the space. It was a sanctuary of grandeur, a place where one could unwind and pamper themselves in style.

Her mom sat in her oversized makeup chair. Even though there was a wooden bench with white faux pillows positioned against the wall, Sarah sat on the bathroom countertop where she oddly felt more comfortable.

"How's your headache, Mom?"

"I'm better after I get some sleep. I haven't had a migraine in a long time. Did you get something to eat, sweetheart?"

"Yeah, I'm fine."

"I slept so long, I'm probably not going to sleep very well tonight. It's already 11:30."

Sarah felt like the day seemed to last forever.

"I meant to make dinner tonight, but...I realized I needed to go get some groceries. I just didn't have the energy."

"It's okay, Mom."

"I was thinking about making something special for dinner tomorrow night. What do you think?"

"Sure, that sounds great."

Her mom took out the clip from her hair. Her hair dropped down below her neck.

"I've been thinking I need a change. I've had my hair this way forever. I was thinking about getting it cut shorter."

"Really?"

Since Sarah can remember, her mom has always had her hair long. Even in her mom's younger pictures, she had long hair.

"So, do you think I would look good with shorter hair?"

"Absolutely."

"I wonder if your father would like it?"

"Why should that matter? It's what you want, not what he wants."

"Your father always told me that it was my hair that first caught his eye."

"Well, now you've got him, and besides, you're still the prettiest mom around. I hope I look half as good as you when I'm your age."

"Sweetie, you're too kind to me."

"All those guys checking you out, I've seen them, Mom, when you aren't looking. They're always pointing you out to their buddies."

Her mom smiled at Sarah in the mirror. "Is that so?"

"Mitch thinks you're pretty."

"Who...?" Gwen hesitated. Her mom's voice suddenly sounded different.

"You know, Mitch, Charlie's uncle?"

Gwen kept brushing her hair.

"Charlie said that Mitch thought you were pretty. He's really cute, like Charlie. Don't you think?"

"Sarah, I'm sure he didn't say that."

Sarah could tell she wanted to drop this conversation. Sarah pushed harder. "I'm just saying that you could still get any guy if you really wanted to."

"Sarah, stop this nonsense. I'm married to your father."

Gwen brushed her hair harder. This discussion seemed to be making her very edgy. Her mother wasn't making it easy. Sarah knew that her mom wouldn't just confess to having an affair. She decided to back off. Sarah picked up her mom's bottle of perfume. "It smells nice, like vanilla."

"Your father got that for me."

Sarah sprayed some on herself. Sarah sniffed the air. "I've heard you and Dad fighting a couple of times since I got home."

"You have?"

"Is everything all right between you two?"

"Of course, your dad and I are just having a rough time right now."

"About what?"

"Sweetie, it's complicated."

"Margaret told me you fought all the time."

"Sometimes things aren't always what they seem. People change."

"So, you're changing?"

"It's not just me, your dad too."

"So, what? You don't love him anymore?"

"No Sarah, I love your father, but..."

"Well...I don't understand."

"Is it because of us? I know Margaret and I haven't always lived up to your expectations and... me not graduating..."

"Sometimes we fight about the two of you. You two are our babies. We only want what's best for you both, besides, we worry about you."

Her mother took out a jar of night cream and scooped some out with her fingers. "Margaret worries me the most. She's been extremely distant from us and her friends. She seems very depressed at times. She won't talk to either of us, and you know how your father is... he refuses to let her continue to take advantage of this."

Gwen rubbed the cream into her face. "He wants both of you to be strong on your own two feet. That's why it's important for you to graduate and to be able to take care of yourself."

"You and dad are worried about me?"

"Sweetie, yes, we are concerned. We hope that you will graduate."

Her mother looked at Sarah in the mirror. Sarah felt ashamed. She looked down at the floor.

"I will. I promise."

"Of course you will."

Her mom's face looked shiny under the lights after applying her cream. Sarah always hated the feeling of cream on her face because it made her skin feel greasy.

"Your father is also concerned about Charlie."

Sarah wondered if her mom knew that her father had called his lawyer.

"What else did dad tell you about Charlie? Never mind?" Sarah didn't want to tell her about her dad calling Harry.

"Sarah, nobody has the right to hit you. It can get far worse. This could just be the beginning. Charlie has told us things about his past that have been pretty awful. It's hard to separate yourself from those kinds of trauma."

"Charlie is different. He isn't like his dad," Sarah thought to herself.

"I do like Charlie... I always have. I think what Charlie did to you was wrong, and he has to deal with some things and get his life together."

Her mom wiped the remaining cream on her towel.

"Mom, Charlie knows he made a mistake. He feels really bad," Sarah said.

"Maybe so. But it is our job to protect you."

"So, are you going to hold this against him?"

"Sarah... Ultimately, this is your decision, not mine, but I'm afraid your father might stand in your way."

Sarah sighed loudly. "I know. Will you help me change Dad's mind?"

"Sweetie, I'll try... only because you seem to think he really regrets what he did, but I can't promise you anything."

"Thanks, Mom." Sarah headed for the doorway.

"Sarah, one more thing. You know whomever you choose to marry will have access to all your money. That's why it's important that you marry someone you can trust."

* * *

MARGARET HAD JUST GOTTEN HOME. It was late. She wanted to crash, but she thought she might have to talk to Sarah first. Margaret felt exhaustion in her legs as she walked up the stairs. Margaret could hear voices coming down the hall. She walked towards her parents' bedroom.

Her mom was talking about her. Margaret's ears perked up. "Margaret worries me the most."

Margaret strained to hear each word.

"She's been extremely distant from us and her friends. She seems very depressed at times. She won't talk to either of us, and you know how your father is... he refuses to let her continue to take advantage of this."

"Dad is definitely losing patience with me," Margaret thought. "I know that's why he's been avoiding me."

"He wants both of you to be strong on your own two feet."

"He can't even say this to my face," she thought. Margaret felt anger surge in her body.

"You won't get one dime." Her father belted out those words the last time they had a really big fight. He always threatened her using money.

"You plan to be a receptionist your whole life? Don't expect anything from me."

Maybe her father was right, she thought. How far would $16 an hour make her? Moving out seemed almost inevitable now. She imagined herself in a small, cramped apartment, surrounded by cheap, used furniture instead of the luxurious pieces she was accustomed to. Her sleek car, a symbol of independence and success, would have to go too. She grimaced at the thought of driving a beat-up old car, practical but far less glamorous. And her clothes! Margaret's heart sank as she thought about her designer wardrobe, filled with expensive outfits that now seemed out of reach.

She had always had everything she wanted, but now she would have to give it all up. Her father would not just hand the money over to her. She had let him down by not finishing her apprenticeship. It was his money, and he made the rules. She could have everything she wanted if she only asked to go back to Emily, but that idea weighed too heavily on her mind.

"I can't do it again. I won't do it again. Doesn't he get it?" she said to herself. This had been the problem from the very start. "I don't want to be an artist, and I don't want to be famous. I never wanted any of this." Her gift had become her oppression.

Once under Emily, Margaret strived for perfection in her art. Every stroke, every shade had to be flawless in her eyes, yet the more she pursued this ideal, the more it eluded her. The pressure to achieve greatness weighed heavily on her shoulders, like an invisible burden that grew heavier with each passing day.

In Emily's secluded studio, Margaret poured her heart and soul into her paintings, each one a reflection of her inner turmoil. The more she tried to perfect them, the more flawed they appeared to her. She couldn't escape the feeling that nothing she created was ever good enough. The colors seemed too dull, the lines too crooked, the composition off-balance.

Margaret was a perfectionist to the core. She strived for flawlessness in every brushstroke, every hue, and every detail. However, her pursuit of perfection became her greatest downfall. No matter how hard she tried, she could never quite reach the lofty standards she had set for herself.

To the outside world, Margaret's artwork was breathtaking, a symphony of vivid hues and intricate patterns. But to Margaret, it was a mirror reflecting her insecurities and fears. She saw only imperfections, flaws, and inadequacies in her work. Her inner critic, relentless and unforgiving, never missed an opportunity to point out every supposed mistake and misstep.

If someone took the time to look beyond the surface, they would glimpse Margaret curled up in a ball, her eyes filled with unshed tears, her heart heavy with unspoken pain. But most passersby never noticed, captivated by the allure of her artistry, blind to the silent cries for help hidden in plain sight.

And so, Margaret continued to paint, to create, to pour her heart and soul onto the canvas, hoping that someday, someone would see past the colors and shapes to the vulnerable soul that lay beneath. But until then, she remained trapped in a whirlwind of self-doubt and perfectionism, unable to break free from the chains of her own making.

One fateful night, as a storm raged inside Emily's studio, Margaret found herself face to face with her inner demon. She saw the monster of perfectionism staring back at her in the reflection of her half-finished painting. It sneered at her, mocking her efforts and tearing apart her creations with its sharp claws.

Every stroke of the brush, every splash of color on the canvas, revealed her secret - her lack of authenticity. Guilt weighed heavily on her shoulders as she looked at the paintings spread out around the room, each one highlighting her flaws and insecurities.

But she couldn't bear to let them down. She couldn't bear to admit defeat. So, she painted on, day after day, hoping that somehow she could fool them all. Maybe today would be the day she finally created something worthy of their trust and admiration.

Margaret's anxiety grew with each passing day, causing her to lose sleep and her appetite. Her once healthy frame became too skinny, and her face lost its natural color. It seemed as if the weight of the world was on her shoulders, pushing her to the brink.

Feeling cornered and alone, Margaret knew she had to make a decision - one that no one would understand or accept. It was a choice that she never thought she would have to make, but the circumstances had left her with no other option. Margaret felt like she was slowly fading away, losing not only her physical health but also her sense of self. The once vibrant girl now felt empty, as if she had lost everything that mattered to her - her future, her family, her identity.

Sitting amidst judgmental eyes and whispers of disapproval, Margaret felt like a ghost of her former self. She was no longer the carefree girl everyone knew; instead, she was a shadow of a person, struggling to find her place in a world that seemed to have turned its back on her. Margaret knew deep down that she had to stay true to herself, even if it meant facing rejection and isolation. She may have lost everything she once held dear, but she refused to lose herself in the process.

Margaret pulled herself back to the present moment. Sarah and her mom were still talking. Margaret tiptoed into her parents' bedroom, daring not to be seen. Margaret took her gold necklace off her neck. The ruby pendant sparkled in the dim light. Margaret had always felt a deep connection to the necklace, a symbol of her family's bond. She placed it on her dad's nightstand.

As she stared at it on the nightstand, a wave of determination washed over her. She had let others control her for far too long, letting their expectations and opinions dictate her every move. "I won't be weak anymore," she whispered to herself, her voice filled with resolve.

With a newfound sense of empowerment, Margaret made a decision to break free from the chains that had bound her for so long. Margaret knew that a new chapter was beginning in her life. No longer would she allow others to hold sway over her choices and decisions. She was ready to embrace her own strength and independence, to carve out a path that was truly her own.

She tiptoed out of her parents' room, feeling her tension release. With each step into her room, her confidence grew. As she settled into bed, Margaret closed her eyes, feeling a sense of peace wash over her. She drifted off to sleep.

* * *

Gwen put the jar of cream away and paused, pondering Sarah's mention of Mitch. Was it just a coincidence or was something more at play? How could Sarah have known about Mitch? Gwen prided herself on being careful, so this revelation shook her to the core.

Perhaps her guilt was playing tricks on her mind. She gazed at her reflection in the mirror, dissatisfied with the tired, puffy eyes staring back at her. Her skin had lost its glow, sporting a dull ash tint, with dark circles haunting her gaze. Grey hairs sprouted from her crown, a harsh reminder of her sleepless nights and waning interest in life.

Amidst her battle with depression, Gwen struggled to find solace in the things she once loved. The weight of her secrets bore down on her, leaving her questioning everything she thought she knew.

Her anxiety attacks had become more frequent, like uninvited guests that overstayed their welcome. Sometimes, it felt like a storm was raging inside her, threatening to consume her whole. Panic attacks would grip her at the most unexpected moments, leaving her gasping for air like a fish out of water.

With each passing day, Gwen felt like she was drowning in a sea of responsibilities, overwhelmed by the weight of her failing relationships with her daughters and her husband, Robert. She knew she needed to make a change, but the fear of the unknown held her back, trapping her in a cycle of unhappiness.

Every morning, Gwen would wake up with a heavy heart, the weight of her worries pressing down on her chest. She longed to escape it all, to retreat into the comforting embrace of sleep and forget about the mess her life had become. But deep down, she knew that running away was not the answer.

Gwen knew she had to confront her feelings for Mitch, who now represented everything that was wrong in her life. She was torn between holding on to the past and facing an uncertain future without him. The thought of letting go filled her with dread, as if she would lose a part of herself in the process.

She never meant to take it this far. It all started innocently enough when they met accidentally at the local bar. They bumped into each other. They played pool. Their conversations just flowed naturally.

Mitch was the kind of guy who could make her laugh like no one else could. His jokes were corny, but they always brought a smile to her face. He had this silly sense of humor that just seemed to match perfectly with her own.

One thing Gwen admired about Mitch was his passion for cars. He would talk for hours about engines, horsepower, and all sorts of automotive jargon that she barely understood. But the sparkle in his eyes whenever he talked about cars was contagious.

As they continued to meet up, Gwen and Mitch began to open-up to each other about their struggles in their respective relationships. It was as if they were two lost souls finding solace in each other's company. Mitch was a good listener, always lending a sympathetic ear and offering advice that came from a place of genuine care.

Before they knew it, Gwen and Mitch had formed a bond that neither of them had expected. They found themselves confiding in each other more and more, sharing intimate details of their lives that they hadn't shared with anyone else.

Gwen couldn't deny the growing feelings she had for Mitch, feelings that went beyond friendship. She knew she was treading dangerous waters, but his charm and understanding were just too irresistible to ignore.

Little did Gwen know that their innocent chats and shared moments would lead them down a path neither of them could have foreseen. Companionship had a funny way of showing up when you least expected it, turning the lives of two strangers into something neither could have imagined.

Their connection was immediate, intense, and oh so passionate. It was as if they had known each other for a lifetime, yet this was just the beginning of something new and exhilarating. Gwen felt like she had been wandering through life in a daze, going through the motions but never truly living. But with him, it was different. With him, she felt alive, awakened, as if a dormant part of her had suddenly been stirred from its slumber.

The more time they spent together, the more Gwen craved his presence, his touch, his words. She found herself hanging onto his every syllable, his every promise, his every whisper of affection. He showered her with attention, with compliments, with declarations of love that made her heart skip a beat. She wanted to believe every word he said, to trust in the sincerity of his feelings, to hold onto this blissful bubble they had created together.

As the days turned into weeks and the weeks turned into months, doubts began to creep into Gwen's mind. Was it all too good to be true? Was she letting her heart run wild, blind to the reality that lurked beneath the surface? She questioned his intentions, his motives, his true emotions towards her. Was he just a master of words, a charmer of hearts, a player in the game of love?

Gwen remembered that night when she sat across from Mitch, her heart racing as she processed his unexpected words. She had not been prepared for this conversation, for this ultimatum that he had placed before her. Mitch had always been a wild card, but even she didn't expect him to be the one to suggest leaving her husband, Robert, for their love to flourish.

"I... I don't know, Mitch," she stammered, her hands trembling slightly. She had fallen for him, there was no denying that. But to leave her family, her life with Robert and their kids, it just seemed impossible. How could she even consider breaking apart her family?

Mitch's frustration was visible, evident in the way he clenched his jaw and ran a hand through his hair. "Gwen, we can't keep living this way. I want to be with you fully and completely. But I can't do that if you're still tied to him. Tell me, would you ever leave him for me?

Guilt washed over Gwen, a heavy weight settling in her chest. She knew that her relationship with Robert had grown distant over the years, but she still believed in the love they once shared. Now, torn between two men, she felt the burden of her own emotions.

"I... I just can't, Mitch," she finally admitted, tears welling up in her eyes. "I love you, but I can't bear the thought of tearing my family apart. I'm sorry."

Mitch became increasingly frustrated. "You're never going to leave Robert."

"I don't understand. You're still with Patty."

Mitch became angry and distant, even jealous of every person who came near Gwen. He would pick fights for no reason, causing Gwen to feel like she was walking on eggshells. But Gwen, ever patient and full of love, assured him repeatedly that she chose him, and Robert wasn't an issue.

Despite Gwen's constant reassurances, Mitch's behavior grew worse. He would ignore Gwen's calls, leaving him voicemails filled with pleas and declarations of love. Each time he threatened to leave, Gwen's heart shattered into a million pieces, yet she held on tight to him, hoping things would eventually go back to the way they were. And they did, every time Mitch decided to come back. But with each return, Gwen's confidence crumbled a little more, like a sandcastle being washed away by relentless tides. She allowed Mitch to control her actions, her thoughts, and even her own self-worth. Gwen found herself losing more of herself to the toxic cycle of their relationship. She was tangled in a web of love and pain, unable to break free.

Mitch played with Gwen's emotions like a skilled puppeteer, manipulating her feelings with his words and actions. He made her believe that she was the center of his universe one minute, and then treated her like trash the next. But deep down, Gwen knew the truth. She sensed that Mitch's attention was being distracted.

Gwen's intuition grew stronger, whispering in her ear that Mitch was not the prince charming she had imagined him to be. She caught glimpses of him with other women, his eyes lingering a little too long, his smiles a little too bright. And in those moments, a seed of doubt took root in Gwen's heart. She knew he was sleeping around, but she couldn't prove any of it, and even if she could, she didn't have the right to ask him to only see her when she was still married.

She focused on herself in the mirror. She looked tired, her blonde hair sparkling under the light, a slight flutter in her heart once more. She reached into her bottom drawer and grabbed a pill container, twisting the white child-proof lid effortlessly. In her palm, a single green pill found its place. With a deep breath, she knew she would need strength. As she swallowed the pill, she whispered to herself, "One step at a time, you've got this."

CHAPTER 17

The Bar

THE NIGHT HAD FLOWN BY. Charlie and John had ended up at the bar down the street after the basketball game. The bar would close in fifteen minutes and it was the last call.

"What will you gentlemen have?"

"Nothing more for me."

"Shit, Charlie come on, one more drink."

"No, I'm through."

"I'm going to get us one."

John motioned his hand to the bartender as if he were the conductor of a symphony.

"Some whiskey, no ice." John slurred his words.

Charlie shook his head at the bartender.

"Like I said, none for me."

As the clock ticked closer to closing time, the dimly lit bar seemed to hold a sense of nostalgia with every laugh and every clinking glass.

John took a slow sip of his whiskey, savoring the burn as it traveled down his throat. He glanced around the bar, his eyes lingering on the old jukebox in the corner playing a tune that seemed to echo the sentiments of the night.

Charlie leaned back in his chair, a faint smile tugging at the corners of his lips. The weight of the day seemed to lift off his shoulders in that moment, replaced by a sense of contentment that only the company of a good friend could bring.

The bartender wiped down the counter, her movements slow and deliberate as if she, too, was savoring the final moments of the night. The last call bell rang out, its sound a bittersweet reminder that all good things must come to an end.

As the two friends sat in silence, lost in their own thoughts, the bartender approached them one last time.

"Well, gentlemen, it's closing time. Time to head home," she said with a smile.

Charlie and John had been downing the heavy stuff all night long. While Charlie managed to maintain some semblance of sobriety, John was teetering on the edge of a drunken stupor. Charlie prided himself on being able to hold his liquor better than most, but even he could feel the effects creeping in.

As he watched his buddy stumble around, Charlie couldn't help but think about his old man. His father, a chronic alcoholic, was a cautionary tale that haunted Charlie every drunken night. He vowed never to end up like him, never to lose control of his life to the bottle.

His father's routine was etched into Charlie's memory like a bad dream. Every night, he would drink until he passed out, usually slumped in the lounge chair in front of the blaring TV. His head would drop forward, emitting a symphony of snores and gasps, his hand still clutching a half-empty glass. The ashtray on the end table overflowed with cigarette butts and ashes, a testament to his father's reckless disregard for his own well-being.

Charlie and John walked down the street, heading back to John's place. As Charlie watched John stumble and slur his words, he knew he was at a crossroads. He could see two paths stretching out before him: one leading to the same fate as his father, drowning in a sea of alcohol and regret, and the other leading to a different, brighter future.

"What made you hit her anyway?" John asked.

"What?" Charlie was taken aback by John's comment.

"Sarah?"

Charlie felt a churn in his stomach.

"I mean, she's a girl. You aren't supposed to hit a girl. Shit, Charlie. I've known Sarah since ninth grade. She's a nice girl."

"Look, John, I don't need any crap from you right now."

"I just don't understand what happened."

"I don't know. It all happened so fast. She pissed me off."

"Enough to hit her. Shit, if I were her old man, I would never let you near her either."

"Could you just shut the fuck up?" John walked on quietly.

"Look, John, I'm working on a plan."

John swayed and laughed out loud. "I don't know, Charlie. It doesn't... look good." Spit flew from John's mouth. That last drink definitely went to his head. "Hey, man, forget about it. Who needs women anyway? Women are too much work, if you ask me." John turned around suddenly and waved at someone who wasn't there. He stumbled to his feet.

"John, let's get you home."

John put his arms around Charlie and almost knocked the two of them over. "Hey dude, why are we leaving? The night is just getting started!"

"John, they're closing up. It's time to go home. You've had way too much to drink, and you're not going to be feeling very good in the morning."

"Man, I'm not drunk. I can drink way more than this."

* * *

As the conversation on the pay phone continued, the man leaned against the graffiti-covered wall of the gas station.

"Hey, it's me. Are you alone?" he asked. His voice tinged with a hint of nervousness.

"Yeah. Where have you been?" came her calm voice through the crackling phone line.

"It's a long story." His voice was heavy.

"Are you at the gas station?" she asked.

He glanced around the dimly lit parking lot. "Yeah."

"It's late," she said, a touch of concern evident in her tone.

"I know. I wanted to see if it was okay to meet. "I'm thinking about you," he confessed, twirling the quarter in his hand.

"Yeah, okay," she said after a moment's hesitation, her voice soft yet filled with warmth.

"I'll see you in a few," he promised, a sense of relief washing over him as he hung up the phone.

CHAPTER 18

Nightmares

She stood amidst the dense woodland, the moon casting its ethereal glow through the canopy above. She shivered, realizing the frosty bite in the air was seeping through her thin, long white cotton nightgown. A perplexed expression crossed her face as she glanced down at herself, puzzled by the unexpected attire.

Her eyebrows furrowed in confusion as she noticed her bare toes peeking out from the hem of the gown, causing a shiver to run up her legs. "What on earth am I doing here, dressed like this?" she murmured to herself, the whimsical air of the night adding an eerie touch to her predicament.

With a curious mix of apprehension and curiosity, Sarah's gaze darted around the shadowy woods, the silhouettes of trees dancing in the moonlight. As a sense of unease crept upon her, she knew that unraveling the mystery of her nocturnal escapade would plunge her into an unpredictable nightmare in the heart of the mysterious forest.

She found herself lost in the depths of the woods. Her body trembled, not just from the biting cold that nipped at her skin, but also from the creeping unease that crawled its way into her mind. Wisps of her tangled hair fluttered in the sharp gusts of wind, obscuring her vision as she frantically scanned her surroundings.

"Where am I?" she whispered to herself, the sound barely audible against the canvas of rustling leaves and the distant hoots of an owl. The familiar woods, which she thought she knew like the back of her hand, now seemed shrouded in an eerie darkness that unsettled her to the core.

With each passing moment, a sense of foreboding gripped her heart, making her pulse quicken and her breath come in short gasps. A chill slithered up her spine like icy fingers, sending shivers throughout her body. Her eyes darted from tree to tree, her senses on high alert. She felt it then, a prickling sensation on the back of her neck, as if someone's gaze bore into her soul. The shadows offered no answers, only the haunting symphony of the night.

As she took a cautious step forward, a twig snapped behind her, making her heart leap into her chest. She whirled around, her heart pounding in her ears, only to be met with silence. Every rustle of a leaf, every whisper of the wind, seemed to hold a sinister edge, amplifying her fear.

Despite the overwhelming dread that threatened to consume her, she gathered her resolve. With shaky determination, she trudged slowly forward, drawn by an inexplicable pull, guided only by the flickering light of the moon above.

In that moment, as she navigated the labyrinth of shadows, more crackling and crunching sounds followed, echoing through the quiet night. Her heart raced as she stood frozen in place, hoping that whatever was out there wouldn't notice her. But then, she felt the moon's rays gleaming on her white nightgown, making her an easy target in the shadows.

Realizing she might be seen, she quickly dropped to the ground, huddling close to the earth, trying to make herself as small as possible. The sound of her ragged breaths filled her ears as she waited, fear coursing through her veins. As she wandered aimlessly, the tranquility of the woods was shattered by a sudden noise that pierced the stillness of the air.

Her eyes widened in fear as a loud thumping, followed by a sound of pounding, echoed through the forest, sending shivers down her spine. A large mass appeared to be crashing through the layers of leaves and pine needles, creating a cacophony of chaos in the serene surroundings.

Startled, she spun around on her heels, searching frantically for the source of the mysterious noise. Was it a wild animal, a fallen tree, or something even more ominous lurking in the shadows? Her heart raced with each thunderous beat, threatening to burst out of her chest in a desperate bid for escape.

As the unsettling sounds grew closer, a sense of urgency gripped her senses, urging her to flee from the impending danger. Without a moment to spare, she made a split-second decision to trust her instincts and forge a path through the tangled maze of the forest, guided only by the distant light filtering through the dense canopy above.

With adrenaline coursing through her veins, she pushed herself to run faster, her feet pounding against the forest floor as she raced against time itself. Branches whipped past her face, and twigs snapped beneath her hurried footsteps, creating a frenzy that mirrored the tumultuous beating of her own heart.

She glanced up at the only source of light in the darkness, a small break in the canopy where the moon cast its eerie glow upon the forest floor. With a deep breath, she continued her resolve to keep pushing herself forward through the tangled branches, her bare feet numb and bloody from the twigs sticking up from the cold ground.

The branches seemed to conspire against her, scratching at her skin and tearing at her gown as she thrust ahead with all her might. Each step was a painful reminder of her predicament, but she refused to give up, fueled by fierce determination to escape the suffocating embrace of the trees.

As she raced through the forest, she could feel adrenaline coursing through her veins, her senses heightened by the urgency of her situation. Every sound and every shadow seemed to whisper of hidden dangers lurking in the darkness, but she was propelled onwards, her fear swallowed by the fervor of her escape, under the silent gaze of the moon, her spirit as untamed as the wilderness around her, determined to find her way back, no matter the obstacles in her path.

As the horrifying sound grew louder and closer behind her, she shuddered. It was as if a stampede of a hundred hooves was thundering towards her, their echoing beat resonating in the night.

She didn't dare look back, fearing what monstrosity might be chasing her. With her heart thrashing in her chest, she urged her legs to press further, the cool air burning her lungs with each desperate gasp. Her nightgown was streaked with blood, a grim reminder of the terrors she had faced.

Despite the fear gnawing at her, she couldn't shake the feeling that the malevolent force was right on her heels. With every step she took, the sound seemed to grow louder, closer, almost as if it were breathing down her neck.

But she refused to succumb to the panic rising within her. She knew she had to keep moving, to keep running, no matter what lurked in the shadows behind her. The night was her only ally now, its cloak of darkness offering her both sanctuary and peril, but she couldn't out-run them.

"Oh my God, what are they?" she thought, her heart racing. They were large and towering. She saw large shadows, but unlike before she heard no noise, just the rustling of the trees. And then she saw them clearly. Horses. Twenty-five of them. "No, it couldn't be." She screamed in her head.

She tried to steady her trembling hands as she watched the majestic creatures approach. The horses moved with a grace that seemed almost unreal. Their hooves barely made a sound as they glided closer.

As they surrounded her, she noticed their eyes, big and intelligent, gazing at her curiously. She couldn't help but feel a sense of calm wash over her. These horses were not here to harm her. They were here for a reason.

One of the horses, a beautiful black stallion, stepped forward and snorted. Sitting on top of the dark horse was a commanding woman who seemed to be the leader. The commander of the herd seemed to communicate with the other horses with her eyes. The other horses stood around the menacing figurehead, forming a protective circle

On top of the black horse sat someone who looked like her sister. Her blonde hair was flowing in the wind, looking all ethereal and spooky. Sarah's heart raced as she stared up at her sister, or whatever was masquerading as her sister. "That can't be Margaret," Sarah thought to herself. She was wearing black, adding to the whole mysterious vibe. Her head seemed to be floating in a weird, otherworldly way. The eerie sight of her red eyes gave Sarah major goosebumps. The imposter spread her arms outward like she was some kind of mystical being, making Sarah's skin crawl even more.

The leader lifted her head towards the sky and opened her mouth. The sound that came out was bone-chilling - it was like the wails of the damned echoing through the moonlit night. Sarah's mind raced with fear and confusion. Was this really her sister? Or was this some kind of nightmarish vision playing tricks on her? Either way, one thing was for sure - she needed to find a way out of this surreal and terrifying encounter before it was too late. Then the imposter who looked like her sister looked directly at her.

Sarah sat straight up on her bed, shaking uncontrollably. She frantically reached over to her side table and turned on the lamp, knocking her book off the table. She looked back and forth around the room, and everything looked calm, except for the mess of things sprawling across her room. Her heart pounded against her chest. Her body was moist with sweat. "It was only a dream, thank God." Sarah looked down at herself, just to make sure.

The dream seemed so real. Maybe the moon was all-powerful and had cursed her and her family. She thought about all that had happened since she had gotten home. First, Charlie, who came out of nowhere and hit her, then her mother who was having an affair with Charlie's crazy uncle, and now her paranoid father who was desperate to find some sort of evidence to destroy Charlie's life. It will be a full moon tomorrow. "How can things get any worse?" She thought about the several dreams she already had about werewolves.

These scowling animals, no longer recognizable as humans, would make their way to a secluded spot known only to them. It was a place of shadows and whispers, where the moonlight cast eerie patterns on the ground. Only when they became beasts would they know of this secret place, under the shimmering moon. The place where Charlie took her, Sarah thought to herself.

As the creatures gathered under the watchful gaze of the moon, they would begin to howl in unison, a mournful sound that pierced the night air. They were no longer restrained by their human emotions, no longer burdened by the complexities of their former lives. In this moment, they could run free and wild, becoming one with the untamed spirit of nature itself.

There was a strange beauty in their primal dance, a haunting grace as they moved beneath the moon's luminous glow. They had no rules to obey, no laws to follow, except for the ancient rhythms of the natural world. In that moment, they were truly alive, truly free, truly themselves.

"Why am I dreaming about this?" Sarah muttered to herself, trying to shake off the thoughts that filled her mind.

Sarah knew she wouldn't be able to go back to sleep. She looked at the time on her phone, 4:25 AM. She decided she would go downstairs to make herself an espresso. It was one of those chilly mornings when a warm drink was exactly what she needed after her bizarre nightmare. As she walked down the stairs, towards the kitchen, she noticed the light was already on. Margaret was sitting at the table, lost in her own world with a bowl of cereal.

Margaret was startled when she heard Sarah's footsteps, causing her to jump and accidentally spill her cereal all over the table. Sarah couldn't help but chuckle at Margaret's reaction.

"Crap," Margaret said with a sheepish grin, grabbing a napkin to clean up the mess.

"I didn't mean to startle you," Sarah replied, walking over to the pantry to grab a cup.

"What the hell Sarah? Why are you sneaking around?"

"Sneaking around?"

Margaret continued to wipe up her mess. As Sarah prepared her espresso, Margaret finally joined her at the counter, intrigued by the idea of a warm drink on such a cool morning. Their father had finally bought their mom a super fancy plumb-only, dual boiler expresso machine. Sarah thought it made the best expressos ever.

"Mind if I make myself a cup too?" Margaret asked, flashing a hopeful smile.

"Sure." Sarah exclaimed, happy to have some company for her indulgence. "You can't sleep either?" Sarah asked.

"Sleeping isn't the problem. I woke up hungry. I only had a bagel today. I guess I forgot to eat lunch and dinner."

"You forgot to eat? How do you forget to eat?

"I don't know. I didn't think about it until my stomach started grumbling."

Sarah rolled her eyes. Sarah loved to eat, but unlike Margaret, she always had to watch what she ate. She wasn't fat, but she knew she could gain weight easily if she didn't keep a close eye on herself. Margaret, on the other hand, could devour anything and everything without a single worry about her weight. It frustrated Sarah to no end, especially when Margaret would absentmindedly skip meals and still look perfectly fine.

"So, why are you up so early?"

"I couldn't sleep. I had a bad dream. I'm kind of glad you are down here. It was pretty scary."

Margaret took a sip of her expresso. "What was the dream about?"

"Werewolves."

Margaret yawned. "What? Werewolves?"

Sarah poured more agave into her coffee. "Yeah, I don't really want to talk about it."

"Why werewolves?"

"I don't know."

"You must have watched a scary movie."

"Maybe. Where were you all day? I haven't seen you since we washed your car."

"I spent the day shopping and met up with a friend."

"Who's that?"

"You don't know him."

"A guy?

"Yeah."

"Nice. Do you like him?"

"No, not really," Margaret said frankly.

"Oh. Maybe it's because he doesn't buy you anything to eat."

Margaret smirked.

"I looked for you when I got in, but you were talking to Mom. I didn't want to disturb you two, so I went to bed."

Sarah wondered what Margaret had heard. She stirred her espresso with a spoon.

"I heard what had happened between you and Charlie."

Sarah looked at Margaret.

"Did you hear us talking?"

"No, I actually heard mom and dad talking about it earlier. I just didn't want to get involved."

"I see."

"No wonder you're having nightmares," Margaret insisted.

"Yeah, I guess."

"It sounds bad. Dad's not too happy about it."

"It's not what you think." Sarah stopped herself.

"Why didn't you tell me Charlie hit you?"

"I don't know. It's not something I want to talk about."

Margaret didn't say anything.

"Sorry, Margaret, I should have told you. I was going to, but..."

Margaret pulled her hair back and held her hand around it, as if she was putting it in a ponytail. She let go, and her hair fell forward over her shoulders.

"So, now that you know, what do you think?"

Margaret looked puzzled. "Now, you're asking for my opinion?"

"Yeah."

"Did you deserve it?"

"What?"

"Just joking. You should be careful." Margaret filled a glass halfway with water. She drank it all and put the glass and the expresso cup in the dishwasher.

"That's it? You don't have anything more to say?"

"Not really. I'm going back to bed. It's only 4:50 AM. I'm exhausted." She headed into the hallway and then turned around.

"Hey, Sarah? Sweet dreams."

* * *

THE LIGHTS WERE on when he arrived. He walked in the back door and looked around the room. This room always reminded him of her. The kitchen was small and cozy. The walls were painted a sea green with white oversized subway tile. The appliances and stove hood were stainless-steel and the cabinets were accented by stainless steel liner door pulls. A large white porcelain farm sink was accented with a stainless steel modern faucet. A vase of wild flowers sat on the roughhewn round wood dinette table. His shoes made a sound as he walked on the tile floor.

He opened one of the white upper cabinet doors and took out a tall glass. A plate and a coffee mug were placed next to the sink. He filled his glass with water. The countertops were sparse of decoration except for a coffee maker and three white farmhouse canisters. He saw a note.

"I'm waiting for you upstairs."

He shoved the note into his pocket, gulped his water, and walked upstairs.

He was highly excited as he looked at her. He was bulging under his jeans. She saw desire in his eyes. He was breathing hard. She would taunt him, playing into his lust. He watched her as she touched her body, sliding her hands over her round breasts and down her stomach and around her hips. He wanted her, all of her. She moved closer to him and picked up his right hand and sucked on his finger, arousing him. He felt as if he was going to lose it right there, but he would try harder to hold on.

She slowly unbuttoned his jeans and pulled down his zipper. He grabbed the back of her head and pulled her toward him. She yanked at his jeans, pulling them down to his knees. He excitedly stumbled out of them, trying to get them off fast as fast as he could.

He stood hard and erect. She pulled her body into him smashing her breasts against his muscular chest. He moaned with pleasure as he felt her warm body against him. His heart was racing. He held her hair as she pressed her face into his chest licking him. She moved her hand downward and grabbed his penis. She squeezed her hands around it. It was warm and it throbbed beneath her fingers.

"Oh ..."

He wanted her now. He pushed her against the bed. She fell onto her back. Her breasts were large. He grabbed them. They were soft and firm. She softly moaned. She was now ready for him. She rolled onto her stomach and pulled herself to her knees. He slid into her and pulsed back and forth. Her breasts hung and moved with her body.

He held firmly to her waist. His movements became faster and harder. Her voice made a whimpering sound. Sweat dripped off his forehead onto her back. Her hair was wet with sweat and wrapped around her fair shoulders. He glided his hands down her back and to her butt. She moved with him in rhythm until at last he surged into her. She felt him tense and then finally he released. He groaned in pleasure.

* * *

He woke up satisfied after their fiery sex last night. The sun was shining brightly through the white colored half shutters casting horizontal bands across her smooth back. Her head was buried beneath her pillow. Last night he was worked up and he wanted her badly. He knew she liked knowing he desperately wanted her. It made her hot. Their sex was better when she felt this way. Last night he could tell she was excited. Her nipples were hard beneath her top. They tore at each other. Grabbing and pulling each other's clothes.

He lay back against the pillow. She was just starting to wake up. "Hey, what time is it?"

"It's almost 9:30."

She pulled herself up from the bed and uncovered herself. Her full breasts hung free.

"You got a great set of…"

She smiled. "I could tell you liked them last night."

"I like them right now."

"Hey, calm down tiger, I'm still half asleep."

She dropped her legs over the bed and bent forward to pick up her T-shirt. Her hair fell forward. She pulled the T-shirt over her head.

"What are you doing?"

"I have to go to the bathroom."

He heard her walk down the hallway and close the bathroom door. He saw his bulge beneath the covers. He looked around the room. It was a medium-sized room. It only had five pieces of furniture, a queen bed, a large armoire, two night tables, each accented with a table lamp, and an oversized chair. A large picture hung over the bed with pale blue colored walls as the backdrop. It was an abstract painting with sail boats. There was a closet door in the corner of the room, which opened into a walk-in closet. It was jammed with clothes. Her shoes lay on the floor of the closet. Sweaters, pocket books, and boxes covered the top shelf.

He didn't notice her standing in the doorway until she cleared her throat. She had nothing but a smile.

"So, does this do anything for you?"

She placed her hand on her hips. Again he felt the blood pulse in his penis.

"Turn around. Let me see the back."

She slowly turned around. He smiled.

"I don't know. You might have to try harder."

* * *

SHE HAD BEEN WAITING NEARLY an hour for her father. He had been in his study doing business on the phone all morning and Sarah was starting to get impatient. Sarah's father had seen her standing outside his door. He motioned several times that it would only be a few more minutes. I just want to get this over with she thought. She had decided that she needed to have a conversation with her father about Charlie. She needed to know why he had called his lawyer. Her father would be furious to learn that she had been spying on his conversation last night. She would have to phrase the questions carefully. Her patience grew thin. Sarah peeked her head into his office once again.

"Hold on a moment, will you Nick?" Her father cupped the phone.

"Sarah, this is an important phone call. Go to the other room and wait for me there. Close the door."

"But dad..."

"Sorry about that Nick."

Sarah closed the door. She placed her ear on the door and tried to listen but she couldn't make out any words. Sarah sulked and walked into the family room. She would wait here for him.

It was a beautiful morning. Sunshine was beaming through all the windows in the family room. Sarah lay back on the sofa. She felt tired. She hadn't gotten enough good sleep since she arrived home. She was already deprived of her long hours at school. After her nightmare last night, she couldn't go back to sleep. She stayed up most of the morning thinking about Charlie. Talking to my dad is the only way to sort all this mess out, she thought. Sarah felt her body sink into the sofa, her eyes were getting heavy.

Sarah thought about Charlie. Charlie had always been untrustworthy of people. His father was mean to him. Charlie said he always had to watch his back. Charlie kept all his pain inside. He never had anyone to talk to about his problems until he met Sarah, but even then, it took him a while to open up to her.

Sarah could tell that it made him uncomfortable to talk about his past, but when he got started his memory was as vivid as the day he left. He had grown up poor and his family had struggled to pay the bills. Alcoholism and the abuse that he endured had been very painful. He showed her a scar where his father had hit him with a stick. Charlie would say the abuse made him stronger. Sarah wondered. Maybe it's made him more violent.

Sarah had never been around this kind of abuse before, and she found it hard to believe. She had only known about such things happening in movies. But for Charlie, it was as real as day and night. He had endured this torment for most of his childhood years until his parents' tragic car accident. Even then, he admitted that it was his lucky break and felt no remorse for their death. Sarah couldn't help but feel conflicted about his lack of grief. Shouldn't one cry and grieve when they lose the two people closest to them? But she understood that they had hurt him repeatedly, their only child.

The thought of how parents could mistreat their child in such a manner left Sarah feeling a mix of sadness and disbelief. Her own family had experienced its share of struggles, but never like that. Her heart went out to

Charlie; he had been through more than anyone should
have endured.

As Sarah waited on her father to finish his phone call, she
couldn't shake off these heavy thoughts. Her mind
wandered, and before she knew it, her eyes closed, and she
drifted off.

* * *

"I'M STILL HAVING THAT DREAM."

"You are interesting."

"Yeah, I'm starting to get annoyed."

"I see. So is it the same dream?"

"Yep, but each night something new happens."

"Something new?"

"It's weird. It's subtle."

"What's subtle?"

"The changes."

"Try and tell me."

"Okay... Um. It's like before. The same room."

*I find myself in this same large room that always seems so
familiar. With a crackling fireplace just barely smoldering, the
room feels inviting and comforting. The scent of wood burning
fills the air, adding to the cozy atmosphere.
I glance around the room, taking in the old world style
furniture, a plush rug underfoot, and beautifully framed
pictures adorning the walls. However, my gaze always lands on*

the wood door tucked away in the corner of the room, mysterious and intriguing.

Without fail, I walk over to the grand fireplace, drawn by its warmth and flickering flames. I reach for the box of matches resting on the mantel, feeling the cool strike of the match against my fingertips. With a swift motion, I light the match and watch as it dances before me, illuminating the room in a soft glow.

But the match always burns out too quickly, leaving me in semi-darkness. Frustrated, I turn around to search for something to ignite a better flame. My eyes land on the large envelope on the shelf. I pick it up, expecting to find something in it.

To my surprise, the envelope was filled this time with a note. Excited to finally find something I pulled the note out and read the words. "You painted it on my face," written in a vivid red jagged fingerprint. A chill runs down my spine as I drop the paper to the floor, a sense of unease creeping over me.

Something feels off, out of place in this familiar room. The silence is deafening, the absence of words unsettling. With a sense of foreboding, I realize that the room is not as it seems, and the mysteries hidden within its walls may be darker than I ever imagined.

I feel myself getting really anxious. I look towards the door but I already know it won't be there. It's gone. Just disappears and then everything else in the room just goes away. One by one, until it is void of anything but a light bulb hanging from a light socket in the middle of the rectangular room. My shadow cast eerily across the floor. I'm panicking because I know the light is about to go out.

"Does it?" a voice asks.

"Um... Yes."

"Well?" the voice prompts casually.

And in that moment, the light bulb flickers, casting long shadows that dance across the room. The room is suddenly plunged into darkness, enveloping me in a black void. My heart races, my breath quickens, and then... silence.

I find myself in a strange and eerie situation. I stand alone in the dark, my heart pounding in my chest. The darkness envelopes me like a thick curtain, making it impossible for me to see anything. It felt as if I had been plunged into a world of oblivion, my senses deprived of their usual sharpness.

As I stand frozen in the darkness, a sense of unease comes over me. I can't shake the feeling of being completely blind, lost in a void of nothingness.

Time seems to stretch out endlessly, each moment feeling like an eternity.

After what feels like a lifetime, I muster up the courage to take a step forward. Slowly and cautiously, I inch my way towards what I hope is a wall. The sound of my shoes echos eerily against the hard floor. Despite the fear creeping up within me, I persist, counting each step in my mind.

Twenty-two steps later, my outstretched hands meet a solid, unyielding surface—the wall I have been seeking. With a mixture of relief and trepidation, I run my hands over the rough surface, searching for any irregularities, any signs of a hidden escape.

Maybe my eyes are playing tricks on me, but there it is - a faint light coming from a crack in the wall. My heart starts racing with excitement. Could this be a way out? Without hesitation, I rush over to the light and press my hands against the crack. The surface feels different beneath my touch - it's not just a wall, it's a door. My frantic search leads me to the familiar wooden door hidden in the corner of the room. I fumble for the handle, my fingers tracing its cold hardness until I find it. With a deep breath, I turn the handle and push open the door with all my strength. A blinding brightness fills my eyes, making it hard to see at first.

The intense light burns, but slowly I manage to open my eyes. The room beyond the door is small yet cozy, filled with warm wood, shelves of books, and a captivating painting hanging on the wall. The painting was familiar. Something about the painting strikes me, but I can't quite place it.

As I step further into the room, the coziness envelops me like a comforting hug. The mysteries hidden within this newfound space beckon me to explore further, and the enigmatic painting whispers a tale waiting to be unraveled. I can't help but wonder - why does it feel like I've been here before? I saw something. There is a person in the room.

As I cautiously approach the person in the leather chair from behind, my heart races with a mix of anticipation and dread. "Hello?" I call out, but the figure remains eerily still, not even acknowledging my presence. With trembling steps, I inch closer, my mind running wild with possibilities.

"What's going on?" I whisper, my voice barely above a breath. I finally muster the courage to circle around the chair. As I caught sight of the person's arm, my breath stops in my throat - it was a stark, vivid red, feeling almost unnatural against the dimly lit room.

A chilling realization creeps over me as I notice the pool of crimson at the chair's base. Panic surges through my veins, sending a wave of dizziness cascading over me. The walls seem to sway, my surroundings blurred as the gravity of the situation sinks in.

I stare down at my hands, now stained with the same scarlet hue that seemed to have consumed the room. Was this a dream, a twisted nightmare that refused to release its hold on me? I struggle to distinguish reality from the terrifying figments of my imagination.

"Are you okay?" A voice pierced through her thoughts, pulling her back to the present.

She blinked rapidly, her gaze snapping at the doctor seated nearby. "Oh... yeah, I'm okay" She managed to utter, her voice strained with unease. "I don't want to experience that nightmare again."

The doctor's expression softened, a gentle understanding in her eyes as she reassured her. "It's alright. Dreams can be unsettling, but they aren't reality."

With a deep, steady breath, she tried to shake off the lingering dread that clung to her subconscious. "I'm so tired of this dream."

"I'm sure you are, but you have this dream for a reason. It is your mind's way of dealing with an issue, something that must be bothering you."

"I want it to stop."

"The only way it will stop is when you have come to terms with it. Maybe the dream will work itself out."

"God, is this the best you can do?"

"Tell me, did you see who the person was in your dream?"

"Um... No."

"Could you tell if it was a man or a woman?"

"No."

"I see."

"What should I do?"

"There really isn't anything you can do. It will go away eventually. Don't work yourself up about it. It will only increase your anxiety."

"Shit. I'd rather have anxiety than have that dream."

"Has anything happened in your life?"

"Not that I can think of."

"You must try to think about it. See if you find anything that could bother you. Work, family, friends, anything."

"Keep taking your medicine. Don't miss any days. Let's see if anything changes in the next couple of days. Call me in two days."

The doctor opened her notebook and wrote in her book. "You think you'll be okay until then?"

"I guess so."

* * *

SHE FELT horror creep up her spine as she stood beneath them, surrounded by a chorus of eerie howls that echoed through the night. The moon, a spotlight in the ink-black sky, cast shadows of the massive trees that towered over her like brooding giants.

As the moonlight filtered through the dense branches, Sarah could make out their silhouettes in the darkness. Cloaked in black, they sat proudly atop their horses, their figures illuminated by the ethereal glow of the moon. Their mouths hung open in unison, releasing a haunting melody that sent shivers down Sarah's spine. It was as if the very forest itself was responding to their eerie call.

Their voices carried through the night, a symphony of gratitude for the newfound power that coursed through their veins. Sarah felt a sense of dread wash over her, realizing the magnitude of their presence and the ancient magic that fueled their howling ritual.

Frozen in place, Sarah dared not challenge them, for she knew that in the presence of such supernatural beings, her mortal self stood no chance. She watched in awe and trepidation as they continued their ritual, their voices reaching a crescendo that seemed to shake the very foundations of the earth.

Once the cacophony of wailing had finally subsided, an eerie silence settled over the group, broken only by the whispering of the wind. Sarah squinted in an attempt to make out the faces of the other people gathered around her, but the moon seemed intent on playing a cruel game of shadow puppetry, distorting their features beyond recognition.

However, when her gaze landed on someone who looked like her sister, there was no mistaking that familiar face - a face that had shared countless secrets and mischievous grins with her over the years. The moonlight seemed to illuminate her sister's look alike, her features like a spotlight on a stage, highlighting the mischievous glint in her eyes.

She couldn't help but let out a disturbing chuckle, breaking the tension of the moment. "Well, well, well," she exclaimed in a playful tone. "If it isn't my dear sister, the drama queen herself, stealing the spotlight once again!"

Her sister shot her a playful glare, the corners of her mouth twitching in a suppressed smile. Margaret's eyes stared right at Sarah. Sarah immediately regretted her words. "Please, I'm frightened." I don't understand what's happening. What do you want? What do you all want?"

Margaret laughed and the sound echoed through the woods. Her sister seemed so weird.

"I want you to help me."

"Me, why me?"

"I've been waiting for this for a very long time."

"Wait for what?"

"Mmm..."

She looked at all the other huge shadows in the background. She returned her gaze to Margaret. Margaret clenched her teeth. They sparkled under the moonlight.

"You will soon find out."

Her stomach dropped. Everything around her was spinning. She turned and tried to run. The horses kicked their hooves up and let out a whine as she came towards them. One almost came down on her. It could have surely killed her. She could feel the horses' distress as they moved about.

"Where are you going?" There is no place to run." Margaret's voice sounded raspy.

"You're crazy. What is wrong with you?"

"It's you that's wrong. You'll see that soon enough."

As Margaret's babbling grew more intense, Sarah could sense an eerie presence looming over them. Her heart pounded in her chest as she watched her sister's hands tremble and her head slowly turn to face her. What came next was beyond Sarah's wildest nightmares.

A low, guttural growl erupted from Margaret's throat, sending chills down Sarah's spine. It was a sound unlike anything she had ever heard before, a sound that seemed to carry the weight of centuries-old secrets and untold mysteries. Sarah's mind raced as she tried to make sense of the situation, but her rational thoughts seemed to vanish in the face of such unexplainable phenomena.

"Oh my God."

Margaret opened her mouth wide. Sarah could see large teeth protruding, almost like those of a dog.

She hissed and brought her hands down. Then the others slid off their horses one by one. They moved slightly forward, their faces still covered with shadows.

"I don't understand."

"Because we chose you."

"Please, I'll do anything."

"You're making it harder on yourself."

In a panic, she tried to make a run for it, but fate had other plans for her. Just as she leaped forward, a mysterious force gripped her with an iron grasp. She winced in agony as she felt an excruciating, sharp pain shoots up her arm. Margaret, with a sinister glint in her eyes, had delivered a blow that cut through her skin and spilled crimson rivers of blood.

As Sarah struggled to resist an overwhelming nausea threatening to overcome her, she couldn't help but notice Margaret's twisted laughter echoing in the eerie silence. It sent chills down her already trembling spine. The others, under Margaret's command, closed in on Sarah like dark shadows in the night.

CHAPTER 19

Answers

"Hey Robert, it's Harry."

"Harry, I didn't expect to hear from you so soon."

"I got some information that I thought you would want to know. It's on that Mitch Connors guy you asked about, except his name used to be Mitch Parker. It shows here that he changed his name when he was twenty-two."

"That would explain Charlie Parker's name," Robert stated.

"He must have changed his name after some of these complaints. There's a series of them filed by young women, and he beat up someone pretty badly."

"Whoa. A woman?" Robert asked.

"Yes, women too." Harry replied

Robert heard Harry rustling through papers over the phone.

"Let's see... this report is from the bartender that night. This particular report shows he beat up a guy in a bar fight.

"Interesting."

"It seems Mitch and this guy Pete Taylor got into a fight over a bet on a pool game. Mr. Taylor couldn't pay up after their game. People in the bar that witnessed this exchange said that Mitch was drunk. He lost his temper."

Robert listened as Harry told the story

"He was playing pool and winning all night. Pete had been sitting in the corner watching him play and decided to challenge Mitch. Apparently, Pete is good at pool. He said he could beat him. He wagered a large bet. The game took longer than usual. Mitch finally won. The guy said that he had cheated. Now, there is no eyewitness of him cheating. Pete refused to pay. The notes say Pete picks up his beer and walks away. Mitch followed him and poked him in the shoulder.

The atmosphere was thick with tension as people gathered around Mitch and Pete, their voices cutting through the buzz of chatter. A large crowd had formed around the two men in the center of the room, their eyes locked in a standoff that crackled with energy. Pete shifted nervously, beads of sweat forming on his forehead as he realized that Mitch, a burly figure with arms like tree trunks, was not going to let him get out of paying what he owed. Pete's voice was gruff as he demanded, "Hey man. It's cool, I'll get you the money. My friend Jim over there will give you the money."

But Mitch was having none of it. With a sarcastic smirk, he retorted, "Little Jimmy to the rescue." Mitch glanced around the room. He could hear the crowd talking about him which revived him up even more. "No asshole, that's not the point. You thought you could play me for a fool. Well, I can't let you get away with that."

The guy's apology fell flat as Mitch's patience wore thin. "Hey, I'm really sorry dude. I was just playing around," he stammered, hoping to smooth things over.

But Mitch's icy glare was unwavering. "Look asshole, I don't have time for your bullshit. Get your fucking ass outside," he growled, his words slicing through the air like a sharpened blade.

The bartender described Pete as shaking and pleading with him. "Jim, give him the fucking money," Pete demanded, but Jim simply turned the other way.

"Fuck Jim, are you listening?" Mitch retorted.

Pete's desperation was palpable as he tried to salvage the situation, but it was too late. Mitch intervened and decisively pushed Pete through the doorway, causing him to fall to the ground. On his knees, Pete began to beg, "Please man. I said I was sorry."

But Mitch, fueled by anger and a thirst for justice, was not having any of it. "Shut the fuck up. You should have thought about that before you pulled this crap on me," Mitch growled, his voice dripping with disdain.

Without further ado, Mitch unleashed a flurry of punches and kicks on Pete, leaving him battered and bloody on the floor. The sound of the blows echoed throughout the bar as onlookers gasped in shock. The situation escalated quickly, with Mitch's boots repeatedly meeting Pete's head with brutal force.

As the chaos unfolded, a bystander finally took action and called the police. The paramedics arrived shortly after, tending to Pete's injuries amidst the chaos of the bar.

"Did he go to prison?"

"Hell no. Mitch spent the night and the next day in jail. He paid his fine and got off easy. His lawyer got him two years' probation with twenty-five hours of community time. He attended alcohol and anger mangement classes. He checked in with a social worker from time to time."

"God. That man is crazy."

"Yeah, but that's just the beginning."

* * *

"Fuck." What the fuck is happening?"

His drinking binge only numbed him for a few hours. Now reality was back in full motion. His stomach growled, yet he felt slightly nauseous. He was on a quest for a satisfying meal. Charlie found himself caught in a whirlwind of emotions and thoughts. The rumbling of his empty stomach was harmonizing with the roaring engine of his truck, creating a symphony of hunger and determination.

As the sun peeked through the dense branches of the pine trees, casting playful shadows on his face, Charlie's mind wandered to Sarah. The memory of her words from last night weighed heavily on him, adding fuel to the fire of frustration burning within him. Then having more bad luck, when Sarah was talking about her father and looking into his past, John's phone died, surely solidifying Sarah's mistrust of him.

"She thinks I'm a bad guy. Her father thinks I'm a criminal. Ha! That old man has no idea what he's talking about," Charlie muttered to himself, his jaw clenched in defiance. With a sudden burst of determination, he pressed hard on the accelerator, unleashing the full power of his truck.

The tires screeched in protest as they struggled to keep up with Charlie's need for speed. The wind whipped through the windows, tousling his hair in a wild dance. Despite the slight headache nagging at the back of his skull, fueled by the lingering effects of the night before, Charlie found a sense of liberation in the rush of adrenaline. "I need food," Charlie pressed on.

* * *

SARAH SUDDENLY AWOKE WITH A START, her heart racing from the vivid nightmare that had gripped her in its terror-filled clutches. "What's up with these nightmares?" she mumbled groggily, rubbing her bleary eyes. "They seemed so real... They just got worse and worse." She glanced at her phone, squinting at the bright screen through the haze of sleep. "I slept for over an hour. Seriously?"

With a sinking feeling, Sarah realized there were no missed calls or messages from Charlie. Her heart sank like a stone in her chest. Jumping off the sofa, she muttered to herself, "Surely he would have called by now. He did hang on to me though." Sarah felt that common pit in her stomach return.

As she made her way through the house, checking her father's office, Sarah couldn't shake off the lingering unease from her nightmare. "Dad?" she called out. Her voice was tinged with a hint of sarcasm. "Are you hiding from me or something?" It was empty. The silence in the house seemed to amplify the eerie feeling that something was amiss. Sarah's wit and humor were her coping mechanisms in times of distress, but deep down, she couldn't shake off the nightmare that clung to her like a shadow.

"Okay, seriously, Dad," she called out, her voice bouncing off the wall.

As she entered the kitchen, she paused for a moment, glancing around in frustration. "Where did he go now?" she muttered under her breath. Her brows furrowed in annoyance. She had been looking forward to discussing Charlie.

Just then, she heard the faint murmur of familiar voices drifting from her parents' bedroom. Curious, Sarah followed the sound and found herself standing outside their half-closed door. Through the door, she could hear the heated exchange of words between her parents as they argued about something about Charlie. Their hushed talks were becoming more commonplace these days.

"I'm telling you that's what he told me."

"What is your problem in the first place Robert? Do you like spying on people? Do you think you have the right because you make more money than them?"

"Yes, Gwen, I do. People assume we have a lot of money. Of course, they would like to get their hands on it. I'm just looking out for all of us. I've worked hard. No one is going to take that away from us."

"So, Charlie is after our money?"

"And maybe Mitch."

"Mitch. What's this got to do with him? He has always been nothing but polite and helpful."

"Charlie lives with Mitch, so there is reason for concern."

"Well, that information is wrong. I have never heard anything about Mitch."

"Look, I'm just telling you what I've heard … assault is a bad thing."

"Assault, is that what you're calling it?"

Sarah could hear it in her mother's voice that she was trying to control her emotions in front of her father.

"There had been suspicions surrounding this young girl. She swore he tried to rape her in her father's car. Nothing ever came of it. They couldn't find enough evidence against him. It was her words against his."

Sarah knew her mother was overwhelmed, as she overheard her mother talking to her father in hushed tones. It was as if her mother was trying to bottle up her emotions while keeping up a facade of normalcy. Sarah could read between the lines - her mother hadn't disclosed the truth about her relationship with Mitch to her father, and now it seemed like she never would.

Sarah's heart sank as she realized the reason behind her mother's silence. Mitch's violent outburst had changed everything. It was a side of Mitch she never thought existed, and now it seemed her mother was now hearing about it for the first time.

Sarah felt a knot form in her stomach as she overheard her father exposing Mitch. She had always known he was no angel, especially with the way he treated Charlie, but this was a whole new level of deceit. It was shocking to think that he could be using his own mother to get their family's money.

Sarah tried to process the information she had just stumbled upon. She remembered all the moments Mitch seemed 'too good to be true,' always charming everyone with his smooth talk and witty jokes. How could she have been so blind to his ulterior motives?

As the reality of the situation sank in, Sarah's mind raced with questions and doubts. How long had Mitch been planning this? Was he really capable of manipulating her own family just for financial gain? And most importantly, what would happen to Charlie once everything came to light?

"Gwen, people hide who they really are all the time. Several young women have filed reports against him accusing him of violent behavior."

"Then it has to be a different Mitch Connors." Gwen's voice was defensive.

"No Gwen, he has a record under the name Parker. He changed his name from Parker to Connors. He's been hiding under this new name. I always wondered why Charlie had a different last name. His family was a real mess. Mitch left home at fifteen and never went back."

"God, I don't want to hear all this. I don't understand why you're doing this. It would hurt Sarah so much."

"It's for her own good."

Gwen's voice was defensive. "Do what you need to do Robert."

Her mom fled the room, holding back the tears that finally burst and were now running down her face. Gwen ran into Sarah in the hallway.

Oh Sarah, you startled me."

Her mom looked fragile and pale. Her face was red and blotchy.

"Mom, are you okay?"

"Did you hear our conversation?"

"Um... no mom, Sarah lied. I was just coming to find dad.

"It just sounded like you and dad were arguing. Are you guys alright?"

"We're fine sweetie. Don't worry."

Her mom walked off. She knew her mom was upset about Mitch. Charlie was right, it wasn't her place to tell her dad about Mitch and her mom. But somehow Sarah was glad that her mom now knew that Mitch was not the great guy that she had thought. She wouldn't have to tell her father. This would surely end their relationship and maybe she could convince her dad that Charlie had been under a lot of pressure dealing with Mitch. Charlie wasn't after their money. That couldn't be true. But maybe Mitch was somehow brainwashing her mom to get her to leave her dad.

Sarah walked into her parents' room, her dark blonde hair swaying with each determined step. She found her father sitting on the edge of the bed. His eyes were fixed on the floor, lost in a world of his own thoughts.

"Dad? Dad, I heard you and mom talking," Sarah's voice cut through the heavy silence, breaking the spell that enveloped the room.

Her father slowly raised his head, his expression clouded with an emotion Sarah couldn't quite place.

"Oh."

"Are you okay?" Sarah asked, her concern evident in her voice.

"I'm fine, Sarah," her father replied, his tone soft but guarded.

"Why is everyone so mad at everyone in this house?" Sarah blurted out, unable to contain her frustration.

Her father remained silent, his silence hanging heavily in the air like a thick fog.

"Dad, I heard you talking about Charlie," Sarah continued, determined to get to the bottom of things.

"I see," her father replied cryptically, his eyes betraying a hint of sadness.

"It's Mitch's fault. Not Charlie's," Sarah argued, her voice firm with defiance.

"There is something not right about them," her father said, his words laden with a weight that Sarah couldn't comprehend.

"Why are you doing this?" Are you punishing me for not graduating on time?" Sarah prodded, her frustration bubbling to the surface.

"What? Of course not, Sarah. You just can't know what it means right now at your age. Your life is different from his," her father explained, his tone tinged with wisdom and understanding.

"How, dad?" Sarah pressed further, her curiosity piqued.

"You come from money," her father stated matter-of-factly, a touch of wittiness in his voice.

"So, you think our money makes a difference?"

Her father sighed. "Yes, to those who have never had money. There will be some people that are just your friends because you are rich. They will try to attach themselves to you. Some of these people think that money gives them power. They will want your money. They will try to get it anyway they know how."

"So, are you saying Charlie is one of those people?"

"No, Sarah, I'm not saying that."

"Then what?"

Her father looked down at the floor.

"I know you called your lawyer."

"I see."

"You've never trusted Charlie, have you?

"That's not true.

"It's because his father was a drunk and he came from a poor family."

"Sarah."

"I know it's true. This was your chance to finally get rid of him. You never really wanted me to date him."

"He hit you, Sarah. He scared me the other night. I saw him Sarah, the way he was looking at you. So much anger and hatred. If I hadn't come in he might have..."

"I hit him first. I provoked him."

"Why would you do that?"

"I don't know. I have been frustrated with him for a while."

"Hmm... Still he has no right to hit you."

"No, but I slapped him. It was my fault."

"Do you just want me to forget about it?"

"Yes, I want you to trust me. I love him."

"Trust. He may be using you Sarah. What if he only wants our money?" "Why because he's poor?"

"Yes and because his father was violent."

Sarah felt her father's concern. His need to protect her was strong.

"Sarah, I just don't want you to ever get hurt and especially by someone you love and trust."

"Dad, I'm a big girl now and you are going to have to let me make my own decisions."

"I know. I know." He looked tired. His body slumped forward. "Are those things true about Mitch?"

Her father's eyebrows lifted. "You heard that?"

Sarah lifted her shoulders. "Yeah.

"Yeah, Harry faxed me the documents. Mitch is a bad guy."

"I know he is. I think Mitch might have hit his wife. Charlie is afraid to leave her alone."

"Did he tell you this?"

"Yes. He hit Charlie too. Charlie has been trying to protect Mitch's wife."

"I had no idea he was abusing her."

"Charlie says he isn't the bad guy."

"Well, this sure sheds some light on things."

"So, what are you going to do?"

Her father looked at her. His body weight shifted and he sat up straight.

"For starters I'm going to get this family back together."

Sarah's face suddenly lit up for the first time since she got home.

"Maybe I should give Charlie another chance. Against my better judgement I might add."

"Really?"

"Yes, really."

As Sarah hugged her father, she couldn't help but notice the familiar scent of his freshly laundered golf shirt. It was a comforting smell that brought back memories of lazy Sunday mornings spent practicing putting in the backyard.

The silence between them was filled with unspoken words and shared understanding. Sarah glanced at her father, noticing the many more gray strands of hair that had appeared on his head since the last time they had seen each other.

Finally, Sarah broke the quiet moment with a sly grin on her face. "Thanks Dad," she said in a sweet voice.

CHAPTER 20

Confrontation

CHARLIE STROLLED into Mitch's house, balancing his sandwich, a coke and a sandwich for Patty. Mitch wouldn't be gracing them with his presence today — a blessing in disguise considering the never-ending chaos at the shop.

He had tucked John in after getting in late last night from the bar. John had immediately passed out, his snoring echoing through the small apartment. Charlie realized that he had only gotten about 6 hours in the past two days. He had barely slept.

Feeling utterly exhausted, Charlie yearned for a nap after devouring his roast beef sandwich. With anticipation, he settled on the edge of the sofa, leaning over the coffee table. The room's two windows were slightly ajar, allowing a gentle breeze to waft in, carrying the distant hum of a lawn mower.

As he savored each bite, his hunger gradually waned, and his thoughts wandered to Sarah. "I wish Sarah would just give me a call." Charlie muttered to himself. He was honestly worried that her father was watching her phone.

He realized how scarce their time together had been since her return. Instead of enjoying her company, he allowed his pent-up frustration to rear its ugly head.

Lamenting his own actions, Charlie thought about how he had failed to control his anger and missed out on precious moments with Sarah. With a sigh, he vowed to mend his ways and make the most of the time he had left with her, hoping for a chance to set things right.

He wished he could pretend, like Mitch, that his childhood had never even happened. Mitch managed to do well for himself. He was handsome, he had his own business, and he had the prettiest wife in town. He looked around the room. Mitch lived in a nice neighborhood and his house was the nicest on the street. He had it all. No one would ever know that he came from poverty and that he had hit his wife.

Charlie was eating the last bite of his sandwich when Patty walked into the room.

"Hey, I didn't know you were back."

"Yeah. I parked down the street. Just in case. I need to crash for a bit."

"Yeah, you look tired."

"I got you a sandwich. It's on the kitchen counter."

"Thanks."

Charlie took a sip of his coke.

"Mitch called. He's looking for you. He told me I wasn't allowed to let you in."

"Maybe I should leave?"

"Nah... you're safe for a while."

"But what if he caught us?"

"He's too busy."

Charlie chewed with his mouth full, as he spoke, "I don't like you being here by yourself."

"I can take care of myself."

"I'm gonna figure something out."

Patty sat down next to Charlie on the sofa. Her hair was pulled back in a ponytail which highlighted her green eyes. She didn't have any makeup on.

"I don't know if I'm ever going to work for him again."

"But Charlie. You need that job."

"I don't need it that badly. I can get another job."

"He owns the only shop for mechanics in town."

"Well, I guess I'll have to move then."

Patty's eyes shifted. "You can come with me."

"What? How?"

"I don't know, but I'm working on a plan."

Charlie's eyebrows lifted. "What plan?"

"I'm gonna get the fuck out of here."

"Well, we can come up with a plan together."

"Hmm."

"He doesn't even love me yet he won't let me leave. "

"His bullshit ego." Charlie retorted.

"We'll figure something out." Patty said with determination.

"Fucking asshole. He better not touch you." Charlie reached over and kissed the top of her forehead. Charlie saw Patty's cheeks flush.

"It will be okay. I won't let him hurt you."

"Promise?"

"I promise."

* * *

SARAH COULDN'T STOP SMILING, feeling light as a feather. Her heart was practically doing cartwheels in her chest after her talk with her father. The news he had shared with her had lifted a weight off her shoulders and filled her with a newfound sense of hope and excitement.

After her refreshing shower, Sarah stepped out feeling rejuvenated, with her hair bouncing in soft waves around her shoulders. She practically radiated the scent of fresh laundry, making her feel as cozy as a warm blanket straight out of the dryer. She couldn't help but hum a tune as she got dressed in her favorite white crisp shirt and khaki capri pants that hugged her curves in all the right places.

As she slipped on her favorite pair of sneakers, she couldn't wait to share the good news with Charlie. She dialed his number eagerly, only to be met with the dreaded voicemail greeting. "Typical Charlie," she muttered under her breath, rolling her eyes playfully. "Probably knee-deep in work as usual."

Sarah decided to drive to the shop. She thought it would be much better to tell him in person this time. The whole situation with Mitch was getting way too complicated for text messages. It was about a twenty-minute drive, but Sarah didn't mind. As she pulled up, she parked around the corner just in case Mitch was lurking about. She had no plans on running into him.

She scanned the parking lot for Charlie's distinctive red truck. It was nowhere to be seen. "Well, well, well. Where in the world is Charlie?" Sarah thought to herself, raising an eyebrow.

Unfazed, Sarah made her way into the reception area. The bell above the door chimed as she entered, announcing her presence. The receptionist looked up and gave her a warm smile.

"Hey there, Sarah. What can we do for you today?" the receptionist asked cheerfully.

Sarah flashed a quick smile before answering in her usual witty manner, "Oh, you know, just looking for Charlie as usual. Is he around?"

The receptionist chuckled at Sarah's playful banter. "He didn't show up for work."

"Oh."

"Yeah. He was scheduled but I hadn't heard from him."

"Is Mitch here?"

"Yeah, he's back in his office."

"You want me to get him for you?"

"Oh, that's okay. Did Mitch say anything?"

"About?"

"Charlie not coming in?"

"No...nothing to me." Wonder why he's not shown up the past two days. I tried calling him."

"Yeah, me too," Sarah replied. He's not answering his phone."

"You think something happened?" The receptionist asked politely.

"Oh no. He's probably not feeling well."

"Is John here?"

"No, he has the day off."

"Oh, I see. Okay I better get going." She wanted to get out of there before Mitch saw her.

"I will tell him you're looking for him if he comes in."

Sarah turned and looked back over her shoulders. Thanks, I would appreciate it."

Sarah should have guessed that Charlie wouldn't show up at work after Mitch assaulted him. She called John when she got back to the car.

"Yelloooo?"

"Hey, John, it's Sarah."

"Hey Sarah, how are ya?"

"You sound sick, are you okay?"

"Yeah, just a bit hung over."

Sarah laughed. "John, you're always nursing a hangover."

"Yeah... Charlie and I hit the town last night. Had a few too many. I've been lying on the couch all morning. Don't even know how I got home. Charlie must have put me to bed."

"So, Charlie isn't there?"

"Nope. He must've left earlier this morning before I rolled out of bed. He probably went to the shop. He had to work today."

"Yeah, I know. Okay, well thanks."

"Oh, Sarah." "Yeah?"

"I probably shouldn't be telling you this but Charlie feels bad... He didn't give me much detail but..."

Sarah could tell John knew more than he was letting on.

"He was really down on himself."

"Thanks for letting me know. If you talk to him let him know that I'm looking for him."

"Will do."

Without thinking, Sarah drove her car immediately to Mitch's house. She pulled in front of his house. Charlie's truck wasn't in sight. She looked around the surrounding area and then back to the front of the house. Where is Charlie? His phone was still going straight to voicemail. Maybe Patty was home. Sarah parked her car and walked up the sidewalk. It was a cute bungalow-style house. It was painted in a driftwood colored grey accented with a red door. A small porch was attached to the front of the house which made it feel very welcoming. Too bad a crazy man lives here she thought. She rang the doorbell twice before the door opened.

"Ah, Sarah. Nice to see you."

Patty looked like she had just crawled out of bed. Her hair was pulled back in a messy ponytail, and she didn't have any make-up on. Her eyes were red and she squinted at the sun.

"Hey Patty."

"How are you? Sarah?"

"Good, thanks." Sarah smiled.

"You must be looking for Charlie?"

"Yeah, I am. Is he here?"

"Sorry Sarah, he's not here. I haven't seen him."

"Do you know where he might be?"

"Did you try him at work?"

"Yeah. He didn't show up today."

"He didn't come home last night."

"Yeah. He was with John." Sarah responded.

"That makes sense. Maybe he is still with John."

"Tried him there already."

Sarah wondered if Patty was lying. She sensed an awkward tone in Patty's voice.

"If I see him, I'll tell him you stopped by."

"Tell him to call me right away."

"Yeah okay. Nice seeing you again."

"You too."

"Shit. Where is he?"

* * *

GWEN SAT IN HER KITCHEN, fidgeting nervously as she replayed her conversation with Robert in her head. Her anxiety levels were shooting through the roof, leaving her feeling hot and sticky - a stark contrast to the cool and collected facade she usually wore. She knew she couldn't bring herself to confess about her affair with Mitch, especially not now. Could Mitch really be capable of all those things? Sure, he had his moments of jealousy that manifested in bursts of anger, but he had never crossed the line before - at least not towards her.

Reflecting on her encounter with Mitch, Gwen couldn't deny the thrill that coursed through her when he was rough and dominant in bed. It awakened a side of her that felt young and alive, igniting a fiery passion that left her feeling sexy and desired. Comparing it to her more vanilla, yet stable, relationship with Robert only made the differences more glaring. With Robert, their intimacy was pleasant and comfortable, yet lacking the raw intensity that she experienced with Mitch.

As Gwen pondered her situation, a wry thought crossed her mind - it seemed life had a way of throwing unexpected twists and turns, leaving her entangled in a web of desire and deceit. How would she navigate through this mess of tangled emotions and conflicting desires?

Gwen felt sweat drip down her back. "Is this what it feels like to be premenopausal?" She muttered sarcastically as she turned the temperature down, hoping to cool not just the room but her racing thoughts as well. Gwen couldn't help but wonder how she had let herself drift so far from her true self. The thrill of riding horses competitively used to make her feel alive, but now it was just a distant memory buried under piles of responsibility and unfulfilled dreams.

As her head throbbed with frustration, Gwen couldn't help but dwell on her relationship with Robert. The man she had once thought would be her partner in crime had slowly but surely become more like a roommate who was always too caught up in work to notice her slipping away. She couldn't help but wonder if he ever saw the woman she used to be, or if she had become just another fixture in the background of his busy life.

Her wandering mind couldn't help but drift to her whirlwind romance with Robert. The man who had swept her off her feet and whisked her away into a life of luxury and excitement. Sure, she loved him dearly, but with his frequent travels leaving her solo in their vast abode, a pang of loneliness crept in.

As she absentmindedly rubbed circles around her temples, Gwen couldn't help but ponder the what-ifs. What if she had dated more before Robert came along? Would she have found someone who didn't leave her with an echoing house as her best friend?

When Mitch began showing interest in her, she experienced a heightened sense of self-awareness. This newfound attention made her feel youthful and desirable, reigniting a sense of vitality within her. However, it also presented her with a challenge that had been absent from her life. As she reflected on her marriage to Robert, she began to question if she had rushed into their union too hastily. Feeling vulnerable and uncertain, she started to doubt the foundation of their relationship, introducing additional strain into an already troubled partnership.

As the tension between Robert and Gwen escalated, Mitch found himself inadvertently caught in the middle of their marital strife. To Gwen's amusement, Mitch's knack for clever quips and his infectious charm became her solace in the storm of disagreements with her husband. Gwen couldn't help but think about whether perhaps Mitch was the missing puzzle piece in her life that she never knew she needed. And as fate would have it, the more she found herself drifting towards Mitch, the more she questioned whether Robert was truly the man she was meant to be with.

As Gwen surmised the possibility of tying the knot with Mitch, she couldn't help but imagine the rollercoaster of love and chaos it might bring into her life. Would he be the key to unlocking a new level of happiness, or would he turn out to be a walking disaster zone? It would most definitely bring drama, to not only her, but also to her daughter's lives.

"Was Mitch really after their money?" Gwen thought to herself. Why would he do such a thing when he seemed to have it all - a successful career and a marriage? Gwen's stomach churned with jealousy towards Patty, who Mitch claimed was merely nothing more than his roommate. I thought I loved her, he once said. But let's be real, Patty was stunning - curves for days, and sex appeal oozing from every pore. Mitch swore he wasn't into Patty, vowed to divorce his wife, and even urged Gwen to do the same with her husband. Yet, there was something fishy about him that Gwen just couldn't shake. Maybe it was his smooth talk or his perfect smile. She wanted to believe his every word, but deep down, her intuition was screaming red flags. She had to admit, though, that she fell for his charm and even professed her love for this man.

What have I done? Is my judgment that bad? Am I crazy? She had known him for a year and a half now, and it never once occurred to her that he might be dangerous. He had assaulted young women. What if he had hurt me? The idea was crazy, but how crazy was it? She had risked losing everything in her life for a demented person.

He had deceived her from the beginning. She could see that now. Her emotions were exposed. He found her when she was weak and vulnerable. He was charming and he had fooled her. She felt violated and gutted. How did I not see the person for who he truly was? Gwen felt sick to her stomach and her head was pounding.

With a theatrical sigh, she fetched a bottle of Advil from the depths of her kitchen cabinet. Ah, the elixir of life for all her relationship-induced headaches. Plopping four tablets into her mouth like they were pieces of candy, she washed them down with a swig of water, as if hoping it would wash away her doubts and uncertainties along with them.

She needed to deal with Mitch, the soon-to-be ex-lover. He wouldn't take the news well. It didn't matter, she had to cut the cord. Mitch must've thought she would never catch on. She'd face the music later, but for now, Mitch's membership in her life was expiring, pronto. Her hand was shaking as she reluctantly dialed his number. Just her luck, her arm decided to play dominoes with her glass of water, sending it crashing down onto the ground, pieces of glass displaced everywhere.

Shit."

She dialed his phone number, waiting for him to answer. It rang several times.

"Mitch, it's Gwen."

"I was just thinking about you. A lot has happened and you're just the person that I need to see.

"No, Mitch, I can't do that."

"Maybe later then."

"No, I mean never."

He laughed. "Shit, Gwen, don't be silly. Sounds like you're just having a moment like usual.

Gwen heard Mitch rustling in the background. "Are you even listening to me?"

"Barely."

"You never listen to me."

"It's just the same bullshit over and over."

"Not this time. We are finished."

"Yep, overreacting as usual. It's always something with you."

Gwen felt anger surge through her body. This was so typical of Mitch. He never cared about her feelings. "You are such an ass. It's over between us. I should have never let this happen in the first place."

"Let's not make any rash decisions right now."

"I'm going to hang up now. It's over."

"Don't you fucking hang up on me? Let's work this out before you do anything stupid."

"I've already done something stupid and I'm trying to make things better." Gwen sighed and was silent. "You manipulated me."

"Quit pretending that you're the victim here. You wanted this too."

"Maybe, but I don't want it anymore."

"Oh please."

"I can't keep doing this to my family. I was wrong. I know that now. Mitch one more thing, leave Charlie alone."

"What's Charlie got to do with this?"

"Mitch, I'm not going to talk about this anymore. I just called to let you know that we are done. If you can't accept that, then that's your problem."

"You'll come back."

"I wouldn't count on that. It's over, I'm sorry."

"You're just a drama queen."

"Don't call me again."

"You think Mr. Hotshot can give you what you need?

Gwen hung up the phone.

You'll be back."

* * *

SHE WATCHED her mom as she threw the phone onto the counter. It made a loud clunking sound as it hit the quartz.

"Shit."

Her mother was now sobbing, her hands on her hips, as if she had just finished a marathon. She leaned her weight against the counter, her legs giving way to the heaviness that she must have been feeling. She didn't mean to overhear the conversation that her mother was having but she knew it was serious. Her mother's voice sounded abrasive and absolute, but she also sounded weak and timid.

Suddenly, she felt a pang of empathy for her mother, realizing that she was dealing with something beyond her understanding. She tentatively started to approach her, then hesitated. She knew that this wasn't the right time. Her mom would have to start putting the pieces back together again, one piece at a time. She watched her mom for a moment longer and then quietly walked away. She would leave the house, giving her mom much needed space.

CHAPTER 21

Kissy-Kissy

"Fuck."

Mitch hated not being in control especially with a woman. No women dumped him or turned him down. He had Gwen wrapped around his fingers.

"God damn bitch hung up on me,"

He paced back and forth in his office. He was furious, and it made him even angrier that she could provoke him like this. He pushed his books and his coffee mug to the floor. Amber, the young receptionist, stood outside his office door.

"Is everything all right, Mitch?"

Mitch was startled and looked over at the door. Amber's black hair framed her fair skin. Her freckles looked more pronounced than usual under fluorescent lights.

"What do you think?" he snapped back, the edge in his voice unmistakable. Amber flinched slightly, her eyes widening in surprise. Despite his frustration, Mitch couldn't help but notice how vulnerable she looked in that moment.

"Can I get you anything?"

"No. I'm fine, go back to work."

Mitch had a reputation for being a player. He was always surrounded by a bevy of beauties, and he knew Gwen couldn't help being jealous every time she saw him talking to another woman. At time times he suspected that Gwen thought he was cheating on her, but whenever she confronted him, he would spin tales of love and fidelity that would make even the most cynical hearts swoon.

"You're the only one for me, Gwen," Mitch would say with a convincing sincerity that left her breathless. And like a puppet on strings, Gwen would nod in agreement, letting herself be pulled further into his tangled web of deceit.

As the days turned into weeks and the weeks into months, Gwen's suspicions would ebb and flow like the tide, but Mitch's hold on her remained unyielding. She would beg him to stay, to never leave her.

But little did Gwen know that Mitch's affections were as shallow as a puddle in the summer sun. His promises were mere whispers carried away by the wind, leaving Gwen grasping at the shadows of a love that was never truly hers.

Mitch had always told himself he was done with her. Her drama and complications weren't worth the trouble most days. Yet, there was something about her that kept pulling him back in. He found himself missing the way she understood his body, even when he was with other women. It was frustrating how vulnerable she made him feel.

Why should he remain faithful to her when she is still married to a rich man? The fancy lifestyle her husband provided - a lavish house, expensive cars, horses in a barn, luxurious vacations - was something Mitch could never compete with. It irked him to his core.

And yet, despite all the reasons to walk away, he found himself longing for her touch, missing her presence next to him in bed. Mitch couldn't escape the magnetic pull she had on him, no matter how hard he tried to resist.

Fucking bitches, all of them. All women were liars. Mitch's anger intensified. Mitch couldn't help but be reminded of his childhood.

Young Mitch sat at the dinner table, a frown creasing from his brow as he watched his mother devour her meal like a hungry bear in the wild. The sight of her polishing off a whole bucket of fried chicken, a quart of mashed potatoes, and a quart of baked beans made his stomach churn. It was a wonder how she could eat so much without bursting at the seams.

Back then, his mother was always the one who made sure he had enough to eat, who cooked his favorite meals with love and care. But now, seeing her indulge in her own gluttony, he couldn't shake off the feeling of disappointment. As she leaned back in her chair, his mom let out a contented sigh.

"Momma, are you sure you should be eating so much?" Mitch finally spoke up, unable to contain his disgust.

His mother looked up at him, a twinkle of mischief in her eyes. "Oh, don't worry about me, Mitchy. I've always had a healthy appetite, you know that."

Mitch sighed, knowing that arguing with her was futile. He pushed his plate away, suddenly feeling full just from watching his mother's feast.

His mom sat in her chair and took a deep breath.

"Mighty good. Yous boys helps momma up," she said, her voice soft yet firm.

"Yes, Momma," the two boys chorused obediently, a sense of responsibility in their young eyes.

"Tonight's family time," their mother added with a smile, signaling the importance of their bonding moments.

The two boys, with determination in their hearts, approached where she was sitting and gently assisted their mother out of the chair to the couch. Their mother's weight enveloped them like an unrelenting heaviness.

"Now, clean them dishes. When yous through, come sits by momma," she instructed, her orders for them evident in every word.

Mitch felt a twinge of frustration. He despised these moments when his mom's mood was unpredictable. He wanted to rebel, to say no, but he knew that defying her would only lead to more trouble. He knew that his actions could affect not just him but also his younger brother.

Reluctantly, Mitch began washing the dishes, the warm water soothing his conflicted thoughts. He knew that the simple act of cleaning up after dinner was a way for him to show his submission for his mom.

As the last dish was dried and stacked away, Mitch and his brother joined their mother on the couch.

"Tells momma yous love her."

"I love you, momma," said Mitch's brother.

"Mitchy, tells momma."

Mitch was starting to feel worse at this point. "Same with me momma." Mitch barely choked out the words.

"Is that the way yous tells your momma thats yous love her?" His mom sounded mad. "You best be meanin it boy."

He was having a hard time. He didn't want to be anywhere near her. He just wanted to run and never come back. Mitch suddenly started coughing. He felt a powerful urge to throw up.

"Boy, don't you be pretending to be sick?" Her voice was loud.

"Please, I feel..." Mitch was looking down at the floor trying not to move too much in fear of throwing up. His mother grabbed a handful of Mitch's hair and yanked his head upward. He stared into her dark eyes.

She was mad. "You pretendin?"

"No, momma."

"That's a good boy." She still had a chunk of his hair in her palm. "I likes it when my Mitchy is a good boy."

Mitch felt vomit in the back of his throat.

She stared into his eyes. "Yous my good boy, Mitchy. Give your momma a kissy kissy."

"Please..."

She puckered her lips up tight, determined to plant a wet one on Mitch. He squirmed, trying to free himself, but his mom's grip was surprisingly strong. Just as he thought he could escape, her purple lips made contact with his, and before he knew it, her tongue was in his mouth. His younger brother cringed, feeling secondhand embarrassment for his brother.

The taste of greasy chicken lingered on his mom's tongue, making the whole situation even more revolting. His younger brother watched in horror as she swirled her tongue around inside Mitch's mouth, oblivious to his discomfort. It was like a scene straight out of a B-movie horror flick.

Unable to contain his revulsion any longer, Mitch felt his dinner making a reappearance. In a sudden and violent upheaval, the contents of his stomach spewed forth, propelled by a primal instinct to purge the unthinkable image before him. Chunks of food flew out of his mouth and into his mom's lap, painting a grotesque picture of culinary chaos.

The room fell into stunned silence as the aftermath of Mitch's involuntary regurgitation sank in. Mitch, now free from his mom's grasp, looked equal parts horrified and disgusted. At this point his mom, unfazed by the unexpected turn of events, simply wiped his dinner off her lap and wiped it onto the floor.

As Mitch tried to compose himself, wiping the remnants of his dinner off his clothes, he stood there in shock, his mind trying to process what had just happened. His mother's reaction was beyond anything he could have imagined. He could still feel the sticky remnants of his dinner clinging to his skin, sticking to his face, neck, body, and legs. Mitch's attempt to rid himself of the horrible food had only resulted in his mother's fury.

The transition from her initial sweet, gross demeanor to intense anger was jarring. Her eyes, once filled with love, were now burning with rage. Mitch could see disappointment etched into her features, and it cut him to the core.

As he continued to cough up bits of his dinner, his mother's voice cut through the air like a sharp knife. "You, boy, made yourself throw up." The words pierced his heart, and before he could react, her hand made contact with the side of his face. The force that sent his head spinning.

The pain was excruciating, the sting of her slap echoing in his ears. Another blow followed, and Mitch felt his eyes begin to swell. Tears welled up in his eyes, a mix of pain and confusion clouding his vision. His mother's heavy breaths filled the room, a stark contrast to the eerie silence that now enveloped them.

Mitch remained frozen, his gaze fixed on the mess that surrounded him. He could feel his mother's presence looming over him. The weight of her disapproval hung heavy in the air, suffocating him in a cloud of shame and regret.

"Father, come here. Now!"

He came quickly from the kitchen.

"Take our boy outside, ins the back. Yous make sure he stays put." Mitch felt fear.

Her husband did as she asked. Mitch shivered as he followed his father outside. The weather man had said it was only 40 degrees. It was dark except for the porch light. The two of them waited without coats in the cold. The sticky vomit felt like it was freezing on his clothes. His father and Mitch were both silent except for their cold breath. Mitch was growing steadily nervous. He had no idea what his mother was going to do. Finally, his mother made her way outside.

"Mitchy, move over there."

Mitch was afraid to move but he was more afraid not to. He did what he was told.

"Get ready," she said with a smirk. "Mitchy, yous might wanna holds your breath. It's gonna be cold. Father, use your watch. Tells mother whens two minutes are up."

His mother walked over to the water spigot where the hose was attached. She turned on the nozzle. The hose spurted and choked as the cold water traveled through the snake-like tube. Mitch watched in confusion, wondering what his mother had planned. As the water sprayed out, Mitch's mother grabbed the hose, a mischievous glint in her eyes.

Before Mitch could react, his mother aimed the hose at them and unleashed a powerful stream of icy water. Mitch yelled in surprise as the freezing water drenched him to the bone. Mitch's teeth chattered uncontrollably as he tried to shield himself from the onslaught. His mother laughed heartily, enjoying the chaos she had caused.

To this day, this memory made Mitch feel weak and disgusting, a raw ache deep in his chest that he couldn't shake. All women were the same, he thought bitterly. Like his mom, they all wanted to control him, just like his mom controlled his pathetic father. The memories of her sharp words and piercing gaze haunted him, a constant reminder of his own helplessness. No woman is going to control me again, he vowed silently, clenching his fists in determination.

Was this Gwen's new game, he wondered, his mind racing with suspicion and uncertainty? Was she trying to manipulate him, toying with his emotions like a puppet on a string? She was always so good at finding ways to get him to react, a master of deception and subtle manipulation.

Or did her husband find out somehow? He mused, his thoughts spiraling down a dark path of paranoia. No, they were careful, he reasoned. They were never seen in public by anyone who might talk. It's something else, he concluded, a knot of dread forming in the pit of his stomach.

Gwen mentioned something about Charlie, he recalled, his brow furrowing in confusion. What was that she said? He wondered, "Leave Charlie alone." The pieces of the puzzle slowly came together in his mind, the pieces of a puzzle that he was hesitant to solve, knowing that the truth might shatter everything he thought he knew.

"What had Charlie said?" Mitch muttered to himself, worry evident in his voice. He replayed the conversation in his mind, trying to decipher any hidden meanings behind Charlie's words. It didn't seem possible that Charlie could know about Gwen, but paranoia crept in nonetheless.

As the pieces came together, Mitch couldn't shake off the nagging feeling that Charlie was up to something. The way Robert showed up at the shop unexpected visit made Mitch's stomach churn with unease. Robert now seemed like a potential accomplice in Charlie's schemes.

"Robert seemed normal," Mitch mused, attempting to rationalize the situation. But deep down, he knew that something was amiss. The sudden realization hit him like a ton of bricks - Charlie had betrayed his trust, weaving a tangled web of deceit that threatened to unravel his carefully constructed life.

Mitch cursed himself for ever confiding in Charlie, for letting his guard down and allowing someone to manipulate his vulnerabilities.

"Shit." Mitch said it out loud. The words resounded throughout his office.

During their fight the other day Charlie said he would get help. Is that what he meant? "Fuck."

Taking a deep breath, Mitch tried to push aside the panic threatening to consume him. He needed to stay calm, think clearly, and come up with a plan. It was clear that he was in the middle of a dangerous game, one where the stakes were higher than he had ever imagined. He loved women wanting him, desiring him and controlling their hearts. Now he felt the stabbing pain that maybe she was serious this time and that Charlie most certainly had something to do with it.

Mitch looked at the stack of paperwork in front of him. He was so behind. He was too busy working in the garage because Charlie had not shown up and he hadn't been able to focus on getting this done. Charlie had left him stranded. That boy is gonna pay.

CHAPTER 22

Patty

CHARLIE WAS asleep when the doorbell rang. The bell sound lingered in his ears as his brain felt like it was a boat drifting in the fog. His eyes were heavy as he looked around the room. He felt a throbbing in his head. He knew the headache was from partying too much the night before. He closed his eyes and slowly drifted back to sleep. He didn't hear her come into his room.

"Charlie?"

"What?" Charlie lifted his pounding head from the pillow.

"Charlie?"

He squinted his eyes. "I thought I had heard the doorbell."

"Yeah."

"Who was it?"

"Who do you think?"

"Shit if I know, as long as it's not Mitch."

"It was Sarah."

"Sarah?"

Charlie sat straight up. He felt his body want to collapse back into a deep slumber, but he forced himself to jump out of bed. He reached for his shirt on the floor. His muscles were strong and leaning along his six-foot-one frame.

"Patty, why didn't you get me? I need to talk to her."

"God, why do you think?"

"Shit. I don't have time for this." He pulled his shirt over his head.

"You haven't told her yet have you?"

He stopped what he was doing. He looked at Patty. "She was so pretty with her red hair and light eyes," he thought to himself. He sat on the edge of the bed.

"No."

"I thought we agreed that you would tell her this time no matter what."

"I know. It's just..."

"It's just what?"

Charlie looked at the floor.

"What's wrong?"

"I'm not sure."

"You told me you..."

"I'm sorry I don't know if I can. It's complicated."

"Why are you making it complicated?" Patty asked.

"Listen Patty, I've been thinking about a lot of things. Maybe this is my chance to be more than a bum mechanic. I've never had anything like that in my life. My parents weren't worth shit. Maybe Sarah is my answer to having a better life."

"So, you've changed your mind?"

"No, I don't know. Maybe. I keep messing everything up. I'm even messing things up with you. I'm not sure if it can work between us, not the way you are thinking."

She turned away and walked towards the window. "Why, because I'm not going to be rich like Sarah?"

"Don't you understand? I don't want to struggle anymore with my life. Do you know what it's like to be really poor?"

She just stared out the window.

"Patty, are you listening to me?"

"Yes."

"This is a hard decision for me."

"Why have you been leading me? It sucks."

"I'm not trying to. I know I can't have you both. I've been confused about my feelings. I want to protect you too."

"Protect me...you just care more about money."

"Yes, I will protect you, but I don't want to be a loser."

"Is that what it's going to take to make you truly happy?"

"Money sure makes things a lot easier." Charlie walked over and picked up his shoes. He sat on the edge of the bed next to Patty who had now moved to the bed. Patty watched him as he put his socks on and then tied his shoes. "I wonder why she stopped by. Maybe she has news about her father."

"Her father?"

"Sarah and I had a fight the other night and her father saw part of it. He was pretty mad."

"What did you do Charlie?"

"I was a jerk."

"What did you do?"

Charlie was fidgeting. Patty sensed he was nervous.

"Never mind," He continued to tie his boots. "Her dad is looking for excuses to make me out as the worst person."

"Huh?"

"It doesn't matter."

"That doesn't make sense."

Charlie walked over to the mirror. He looked at himself. His hair hung free. His face looked paler than normal. His blue eyes sparkled. "It could be different for me with Sarah. I can't let what I did mess things up. I must figure this out."

Patty watched as Charlie seemed to be talking to himself. She saw angry frustration in his eyes. She stayed quiet.

"Why do I always screw things up? First Sarah and then her father and now with you."

"You can still be with me."

"I know we talked about getting out of here, but Patty thought about it."

"I have."

"We could never be together." Mitch would never accept it. You know that. He's crazy. Fuck, he scares the shit out of me. If he finds me in this house after what has happened... shit, I might as well dig my own grave."

"We would just go where he couldn't find us."

"No, we can't just run away forever."

"So, you're just going to leave me with him?"

"No. I'm gonna help you get away from him."

"How?"

"I don't know yet."

"I'm scared."

"I won't let him hurt you Patty, but first I need to deal with Sarah and her father right now. I'm not going to let all this ruin my life."

"Charlie, are you sure that's what you want?" Her eyes looked up at Charlie.

He leaned over and kissed Patty on her head. He smiled and ran his hand through her long wavy hair. Then Charlie walked out of the room.

* * *

MITCH KNEW Charlie would be sneaky. He drove around the surrounding streets near his house. He saw Charlie's truck parked down the street around the corner. Mitch drove past the truck.

"Fuck, I knew he would be here."

"I should come home more often," he thought. Mitch felt his body tense. He had warned Patty not to let him into the house. She would pay. His heart pumped faster as adrenaline raged through his muscles. "I will show them."

He too parked down the street. He turned off his engine. Mitch could hear several kids playing in the distance. No more mister nice guy, fuck that. No one's taking me for a ride any longer. He opened his glove compartment and took out his gun. Mitch sat in his truck for a minute. The shiny gun felt smooth and heavy in his hand. He then took out a slender cylinder. He screwed the silencer on the tip of the gun. He double checked the chamber. It was loaded. He took a deep breath so that he could pull himself together. He tucked his gun into the side of his jeans underneath his shirt. Mitch quietly got out of his truck. He wanted his arrival to be a surprise.

* * *

HE THOUGHT about Patty as he walked out of the bedroom. Her red hair cascading like waves around her face as she looked up at him with sadness in her eyes. The memory of her touch sent a shiver down his spine, and he felt himself growing excited beneath his pants. Hastily adjusting himself, he tugged at his shirt, suddenly feeling the heat of the moment wash over him.

With a determined effort, he tore his gaze away from Patty and forced himself to focus on the task at hand – finding Sarah. He knew he had a mission to accomplish, and he couldn't let his thoughts stray. He walked down the hallway to the bathroom.

Grabbing his phone, he punched in Sarah's number, his heart pounding with anticipation. As the phone rang on the other end, he couldn't help but wonder what Sarah's reaction would be when he finally reached her.

It hit hard. He fell flat on his stomach. His phone flew across the hallway, hitting the wall and then falling to the ground. Still confused and out of breath, he pulled his upper body to his knees. His lungs were gasping for air. What happened? He felt blood drip from his forehead. The intense pain shot down his head, neck, and back.

When he realized what was happening, the gun came smashing down again on the same spot of his head. Charlie felt more blood trickle down his face. As he touched the warm spot on top of his head, something pounced on him like a cat. His weight was heavy on Charlie's neck and back.

Patty was already standing in the hallway. "What the hell are you doing?" she screamed.

As Charlie struggled under Mitch's grip, he frantically tried to make sense of the chaos surrounding him. Pain pulsed through his body, each heartbeat a reminder of the danger he was in. With all his strength, he pushed against Mitch, trying to break free from the suffocating pressure on his neck.

Mitch lunged forward, but Charlie ducked just in time, feeling a rush of air as the assailant's hand grazed his shoulder. Patty's presence in the hallway sent a jolt of hope through Charlie.

"Help me get him off me!"

Mitch turned quickly and gazed into her eyes. "Stay back. You're next." She saw rage. "Have you gone crazy?"

He turned away and continued to beat Charlie. Patty leapt on top of Mitch. Out of desperation she tried to pull the gun out of Mitch's hand but his grasp was tight. "Get off him you asshole." Patty screamed the words into his ear and pounded on his back.

"Fucking bitch." Mitch slapped Patty hard across her head with his arm and pushed her across the hallway.

She screamed and bent to her knees holding her hands on her head. Tears were pouring out of her eyes.

"Leave her alone."

"Shut the fuck up!" Mitch focused his energy back on Charlie. He put his gun into his left fist and pounded his right fist into Charlie's upper back. Charlie struggled like a worm, but Mitch would not budge. Charlie leaned over and grabbed a hold of Mitch's right leg and bit his thigh.

"Fucking prick." The words echoed throughout the house. Charlie rolled from under him and pulled himself off the floor. Mitch, losing control of the gun, trying to keep up with Charlie, put his gun in his right hand, the gun was pointed at the floor. Patty took a step forward. Mitch lifted the gun and pointed it at Charlie.

"Patty, stay back." Mitch's eyes darted from Charlie to Patty and back to Charlie. Charlie stood still watching Mitch's every move. They were all breathing heavily. Charlie waited. The seconds felt like minutes. Patty took a baby step forward and Mitch shifted his eyes to Patty. That was his moment. Charlie lunged forward toward Mitch's gun hand.

"No!" Charlie threw his weight onto Mitch's right arm, but he somehow held on tight to the gun.

Charlie and Mitch's bodies were locked. He pushed Mitch up against the hall wall. As his body made a loud thumping sound, Mitch kicked Charlie in the shin. Charlie buckled and he pulled Mitch with him to the floor. The two of them rolled on top of each other, pounding and kicking, down the hallway towards the stairs. The two of them were hanging desperately on to the gun pointing it away from their bodies. Patty waited until Mitch rolled to the top so she could get a piece of him. She reached down and pulled Mitch's hair. His head lifted and he groaned in pain. Trying desperately to rid himself of Patty's grasp, both still holding onto the gun, neither of them about to let go of it, rolled down the stairwell.

The bodies impacted each wood step as they rolled like barrels down to the bottom and then suddenly a weird sound echoed through the house. The noise was quiet but high pitched. The smell of gunpowder filled the space. Patty was still standing at the top of the stairs.

"Oh my God. "Charlie?"

Patty's heart was racing. She froze. She didn't want to know. She moved to the edge of the top step and looked down below her. Her eyes widened as she saw a puddle of blood pooling on the floor, and next to it lay Charlie, unmoving. Mitch was nowhere to be seen.

"Oh my god. Was this real?" Patty muttered to herself, knowing it wasn't a prank, trying to make sense of the bizarre scene before her. She took a deep breath to calm her nerves, slowly descending the staircase to get a closer look.

As she reached the bottom step, without hesitation, Patty stepped into the unknown, guided by a sense of urgency to save Charlie.

Charlie was lying on the floor surrounded by blood. He wasn't moving. Patty's legs were frozen. She didn't see Mitch.

"Charlie, Charlie?" She rushed towards him. Mitch was surely in the other room waiting to shoot her. She quickly looked around. No sign of Mitch. Charlie?" She shook him. He didn't answer. She could hardly see. Tears were rolling down her face. "Please, Charlie, answer me!" What if he dies? It was all her fault. She should have stopped Mitch. "Please God, don't let him die."

* * *

MEMORIES OF CHARLIE flood her mind.

Charlie had an aura of kindness and understanding that instantly put Patty at ease. From the time he came to live with Mitch and Patty, he listened attentively to Patty's story, offering a comforting presence that she had long forgotten. With each passing day, Charlie became a beacon of light in her life, gently guiding her towards self-discovery and healing.

Together, they embarked on a journey of self-love and acceptance, unraveling layers of pain and hurt that had weighed heavy on their hearts. Through laughter and tears, shared moments of joy and vulnerability, Patty began to see herself in a new light – not as Fatty Patty or an ugly reflection in the mirror, but as a resilient woman deserving of love and respect.

As the days turned into weeks and the weeks into months, Patty's transformation was nothing short of miraculous. With Charlie by her side, she found the courage to confront her demons, to stand tall in the face of adversity, and to reclaim the beauty and strength that had always been within her.

And so, with Charlie's unwavering support, she learned that happiness was not just a distant dream, but a reality waiting to be embraced. She emerged from the depths of despair, a radiant soul reborn, ready to face the world with a newfound sense of purpose and self-worth.

Years before Charlie arrived, Patty had fallen head over heels for Mitch, a charming and much older handsome guy who had swept her off her feet with his words and promises of love.

But as time passed, Patty started to notice inconsistencies in Mitch's stories. Little white lies here and there, adding up to a web of deceit that she couldn't ignore. She tried to confront Mitch, to make sense of it all, but he evaded her questions with a smile and a kiss.

The more she dug, the more lies unraveled before her eyes. Mitch's late nights at the shop turned into late nights with other women. His excuses fell apart like a house of cards, leaving her heartbroken and lost.

She blamed herself at first, questioning her worth and wondering what she had done wrong. But as the truth became clear, she realized that Mitch's lies were not her fault. She deserved better than someone who couldn't be honest with her, but she felt trapped knowing Mitch would never let her go even though he didn't want her.

"Won't be home till late tonight. Way behind on work. Don't wait up." Was Mitch's usual excuse.

When she called his phone, he didn't answer. She texted him but he ignored them too. After months of this behavior, frustrated and depressed, Patty decided to drive to his office one night to talk to him. The lot was empty. His truck wasn't there. Furious and sad Patty drove her car back home and she waited up for him until 3:30 in the morning, when he finally walked in the door. She confronted him. He said an old friend had stopped by and they went out and had some drinks. She knew he was lying.

Patty tried to confront him, but Mitch brushed it off, saying to mind her own business. The tension between them grew, and their once happy home became filled with arguments and mistrust.

"You're a fucking liar. You're fucking someone else."

"Get the fuck away from me. I'm going to sleep."

"Tell me who you're fucking!"

This was the first time that he hit her.

As the days passed, Mitch's late-night escapades became more frequent, leaving Patty feeling neglected and broken-hearted. She couldn't understand why Mitch couldn't see how much she loved him and how much his actions were hurting her.

Despite her pain, Patty held on to the hope that Mitch would come to his senses and realize what she meant to him. But as time went on, things only got worse between them. Mitch's affairs continued, and Patty's trust in him slowly crumbled.

Patty, in some ways, convinced herself that it was okay what he was doing. Men need different things than women. It was only sex. He didn't love these other women. Besides, Patty was the one he chose to marry. They lived in a nice house in a nice neighborhood. They had nice things in their house.

The real problem came when Mitch couldn't pretend to be nice anymore. Patty often found herself a victim of his temper. He was often jealous and controlling. He forced her to stay at home. He didn't want her to have friends around and eventually he didn't want her to have any friends at all. Over time, Mitch had little or no patience for Patty. He would barely notice her or even talk to her. She felt isolated and alone.

She had gained a bit of weight since the two of them first met and Mitch reminded her of that every day.

"Look at you. How do you expect me to still be attracted to you?"

She looked down at herself. Her body was fuller beneath her clothes. "What am I supposed to do? You don't want me to be fat, but you won't let me workout."

"You're gonna end up like my fat mom."

Mitch was mean. He hated fat people. Patty never saw a picture of Mitch's mother, but she knew that she must have been a very large person. Mitch always made comments about fat people and how it disgusted him. He didn't hesitate to call her fat names every time he saw her. He would look in the trash for evidence to see what she had eaten. He held each item up as if he was taking inventory. "A bag of chips, three cans of soda..."

"I've only gained fifteen pounds."

"It looks more like 50."

Mitch poked her hard in the belly. Patty felt embarrassed and flinched.

"Just seeing if you can still feel anything with all that fat hanging on you."

"Mitch, if you would let me do something maybe I wouldn't sit here all day and eat. Let me get a job?"

"No wife of mine needs to work."

Patty couldn't help but compare herself to the women around her, thinking that she would never measure up. She believed that no one would ever want to be with someone like her when there were plenty of other beautiful and confident women out there.

As she spiraled deeper into despair, Patty turned to food for comfort. The more she ate, the more weight she gained, and the more her confidence plummeted. She felt like she was becoming one of those "overweight people" which only fueled her self-loathing even more. But the truth was that Patty was too thin and the fifteen pounds only added to her beauty.

Patty had wished so many times that she had never met him. Every day, she prays for Mitch to leave her alone. "Please just let Mitch go away," she thought to herself. If only he wasn't in her life, things would be better.

What had she seen in him? He was so charming when they first met, telling her that she was beautiful and that he would never love another woman as much as he loved her. The horrible truth was that he never cared about her, and now he was just embarrassed by her. Now he could control her, and in some way, she needed to be controlled. It seemed as if by putting her down, it fed his ego to see her suffering. He was quicksand pulling her slowly in. The sand was imploding on her, sucking her down bit by bit until her head went under. She was too weak to defend herself.

Amidst the shadowed room, she lay there, cocooned in the embrace of darkness. The weight of her depression had settled in like an unwelcome guest, refusing to leave. Days blurred into weeks, which merged into months, now years had slipped by unnoticed not even by the ghosts themselves. In the midst, of this never-ending struggle, there was one particular day that stood out. The memory remained etched in her mind.

The room was enveloped in darkness, with blinds closed and heavy drapes drawn shut. The absence of light felt like a comforting shield, protecting her from the harsh reality outside. Neglect had become her daily companion, with days passing without a shower or a change of clothes. She remained still, lying on her side, covers pulled up to her neck, lost in the patterns of the wall she stared at endlessly.

The cracks and tiny flecks on the wall formed intricate patterns that captured her attention for hours on end. Each imperfection became a story of its own, a distraction from the overwhelming weight that burdened her soul. Every passing moment felt like an eternity, yet she found solace in the familiarity of the room that had become her sanctuary.

As darkness embraced her, she drifted into a state of numbness, a place where time stood still. The outside world faded away. In that moment, she found a fleeting sense of peace, a respite from the turbulent emotions that threatened to consume her. And so, she lay there, a solitary figure in a room filled with shadows, waiting for the light to return and illuminate the path towards healing.

Once again, the morning sun peeked through the curtains, gently coaxing Patty out of her slumber. She had promised herself that today would be different. Today, she would get out of bed, or at least journey from her bed to the front door. But as she attempted to swing her heavy legs over to the side, she was met with resistance that felt insurmountable.

"Why am I always so tired?" she wondered. Her voice barely a whisper in the quiet room. It seemed like an eternity since she had last felt truly alive. Everyday blended together in a haze of exhaustion and apathy.

In a moment of clarity, she realized that maybe she was truly unwell. Perhaps there was a reason for this persistent fatigue that had taken hold of her like a vice. She needed to see a doctor, get some answers, and maybe a magical pill to lift this heavy burden off her shoulders.

That day the darkness was heavy. The need to break this cycle was overwhelming. It felt like a wave that crashed into the shore. Patty's insides were burning. A gaping wound grew in the middle of her chest. The pain within her was eating her like cancer. Her breathing was shallow. She felt jittery. She cried, but her tears became sobs of pain. Her body buckled as her sobbing enveloped her. Did anyone care? Couldn't anyone see that she was slowly dying?

"Please, I don't want to feel this way," she whispered into the void.

On one particular day, as the sun dipped below the horizon painting the sky in shades of crimson and gold, Patty found herself at the edge of a cliff. The cool breeze whispered secrets in her ears, tempting her with escape. The world below stretched out before her, the distant lights twinkling like lost stars in the vast night sky.

Wouldn't it just be easier to just die? She thought, her mind a battleground of dark thoughts and whispered doubts. The weight of her existence pressed down on her chest, suffocating her with its cruel embrace. But she couldn't do it. A glimmer of hope still held fast to her.

Maybe an angel was watching over her? She did believe in love once.

What had happened to her, she wondered, as tears mingled with the salt of the sea breeze? Why had this darkness settled in her soul, a specter haunting her every waking moment? Still, something made her turn, walking away from the cliff.

Parry closed her eyes, trying to drown out the noise of her thoughts, to silence the relentless whispers in her mind. She needed a lifeline, a beacon of hope in the storm of despair.

"Please, God," she whispered into the wind, her voice lost in the expanse of the night sky.

Then it happened. This day someone had finally heard her pleas. "Was it an angel?" Her door opened and light entered the room with its full force. He pulled back all the drapes and turned up the blinds. Her eyes burned. Drops of tears escaped her eyes. She turned away from the light. She looked pale. Her hair was matted.

"You're not staying in this room anymore."

"Get out." Patty forced out the words.

"You're not an angel."

"Nope. Just a regular dude."

"I'm not going anywhere. Leave me alone."

"I'm going to help you."

"I don't want your help."

"That's too bad. I'm not leaving. I'm not going to watch you rot in this room anymore."

"What do you know?"

"I know you're feeling sorry for yourself."

"Get out of my room."

Charlie didn't listen. He reached into her bureau and pulled out a green T-shirt, jeans and a pair of socks. "Get dressed."

"No, I'm too tired."

"Then I'll help you."

"You can't dress me."

"It's either you or me. You choose."

He laid a stack of her clothes on her lap. She looked down and then up at Charlie.

"I don't think these jeans will fit me."

"They're yours, aren't they?"

"Yes, but those won't fit."

Charlie rustled through her drawers. He found a pair of her sweat pants. Pants that looked cozy. He tossed them towards Patty. "These will fit you."

"Yeah... sweats."

"Then I guess I'll have to take you shopping so you can get some new clothes."

That fateful day, Charlie came into her life like a ray of sunshine breaking through the clouds. He reached out when she needed it the most, pulling her out of the depths of her despair. Patty couldn't help but wonder why he would care enough to come to her rescue. Was he after something? Those thoughts flitted through her mind, but she pushed them away. All that mattered was that he was there, offering his kindness without asking for anything in return. He must be her angel.

As time passed, Charlie became Patty's beacon of light in the darkness. He showed her kindness and compassion, making her feel good about herself once again. With his support, Patty began to find the strength to face her demons and to believe in herself.

Through their shared laughter and tears, Patty realized that Charlie wasn't just a savior, but a true friend who saw her for who she truly was. And as they walked along the path of their intertwined destinies, Patty knew that she would always be grateful for the day Charlie saved her life and brought her back into the light.

"Look at yourself, you're beautiful. Stop listening to him. He can only hurt you if you let him."

Charlie was right. Patty tried hard not to listen to Mitch. Why should she care about what he thinks?

Everyday Charlie encouraged her. "You need to start taking control of your life. You need to start working on yourself so that someday you can leave Mitch."

How was that going to be possible? Mitch controlled her. He would never just let her leave.

"Patty, you need to start saving some money."

"How Charlie? He never lets me near money except for a few dollars here and there."

"We'll find a way."

Charlie had no idea how this was going to happen, but he just believed they would figure something out.

"Patty, we need to get you a job."

"You know he won't let me. Besides I don't have any experience. No one is going to hire me."

"Yes, they will. I know just the person to help us out."

Margaret worked at a day spa for a while. He would ask Margaret to help Patty out. Charlie called Margaret one afternoon.

"Why don't you have Patty stop by on Friday? The other girl just quit with no explenation. My manager is looking for a part-time receptionist. The hours she'll need you to work will be between 9:00AM and 2:00PM."

Patty was nervous. She had never done anything like this before. Charlie drove her there for the interview.

"I can't do this. Mitch will never let me."

"Don't worry. We will figure something out. The hours are perfect. He won't even know you were gone."

Margaret put in a good word and Patty got the job. Patty would keep her job a secret. It should be easy. Her husband was never around. She would leave after he went to work. He usually left the house around 7:00 AM. She would be home way before him. He would never know. For once she felt happy.

Patty got away with it for a little over eight months. When he found out, Mitch went crazy.

"How dare you deceive me, you bitch?"

Mitch was like a venomous snake slithering through Patty's life, leaving behind a trail of chaos and heartache. Mitch unleashed his fury upon Patty, leaving her battered and bruised, a shadow of her former self. As she lay in bed, nursing her wounds and nursing a grudge against the man who had once promised her the world, her phone rang shrilly, breaking the silence of the night.

It was Margaret, her co-worker with a heart of gold. "Patty, let me help you. Charlie told me that Mitch hit you pretty bad." Margaret's voice was tinged with a mixture of concern and righteous anger.

Patty's face, swollen and bruised, bore the marks of Mitch's cruelty like a twisted work of art. She felt a surge of shame wash over her, mingled with a sense of helplessness.

"Margaret, there is nothing you or Charlie can do for me. I knew I couldn't get away with it. "He took all my money," Patty confessed, her voice barely above a whisper.

But Margaret was having none of it. With a fire in her eyes that could rival the flames of hell itself, she declared, "Don't worry, you still have a job here." They think you had a bad accident. No matter what, don't give up. Don't let him bully you around. I'll call you in a few days to see how you're doing."

Patty found herself in a situation that made her rethink her priorities. Working at a job she loved opened up a whole new world, one where she felt important and fulfilled. No longer did she rely on the toxic words and actions of Mitch to define her self-worth. She had made a true friend, Margaret who helped her through all of it.

As soon as Patty was able, she eagerly returned to work, determined to make the most of her life. Mitch was furious at her decision, but Patty had reached a point where his opinions no longer held sway over her.

As days passed, Patty found herself growing stronger and more confident, thanks to the support of her friends

Charlie, Margaret and even the other girls at the salon. Despite Mitch's attempts to sabotage her job by making it difficult for her to get to work on time, Patty's colleagues, especially Margaret, always had her back, ensuring that she could continue doing what she deserved. And more importantly, Patty no longer let him take advantage of her financially, realizing that her happiness and well-being were more important than his power games.

With each passing day, Patty felt a shift within herself, a sense of empowerment that came from standing up for herself and taking back control of her life. She knew that change was on the horizon, and that Mitch's hold over her was slowly but surely slipping away.

Mitch was losing his power over her.

* * *

PATTY WAS LEANING OVER CHARLIE. Her heart sank. Blood was everywhere. His breath was shallow.

"Oh my god."

She hadn't realized she was sobbing.

"Do you hear me, Charlie?"

As Patty gazed at the scene before her eyes, her heart pounding in her chest, she couldn't believe the sight of blood that surrounded him. Mitch had shot Charlie and disappeared into darkness, leaving her alone with the horrifying aftermath.

Frantically, she dashed to the kitchen, her footsteps echoing in the empty house. Without sparing a second thought, she located her purse hanging on the edge of a chair and upended its contents onto the floor. Coins clattered and keys jingled as her trembling hands searched desperately for her phone. Sweat beaded her forehead as she finally located it beneath her coin purse.

With shaking hands, Patty dialed 911. Her casual tone betrayed the chaos that enveloped her. "Please help, he has been shot... I'm not sure... Charles Parker. Yes... Mitch..." Her voice faltered as she struggled to convey the urgency of the situation to the emergency operator.

As sirens wailed in the distance, Patty felt a shiver run down her spine. What had started as a seemingly ordinary day had spiraled into a nightmare beyond her wildest imagination. With her world turned upside down in a matter of seconds, all she could do was wait for help to arrive and pray that Mitch would be brought to justice.

And as the first responders rushed into the house, their voices mingling with the sound of approaching sirens, Patty stayed close to Charlie. There was a sense of orderly chaos around her. The team of paramedics and police officers roamed in and out of each of the rooms.

In the mist of confusion, Charlie grabbed her arm.

"Patty...," his voice was a whisper.

She jumped. "Charlie, you're okay. I thought you were..." Patty leaned over and kissed the top of his head. Blood was smeared on her top.

"I'm okay."

"Thank God." God had answered her prayer. He was alive. The gun wound to his arm had only done minor damage. He would be all right.

"Looks to be mainly okay. He's bleeding badly though." The paramedic remarked.

"Mrs. Conners, we need you to come down to the station and answer some questions."

"But I want to go with him."

"I understand. We need you to help us find your husband. We don't want him hurting any more people. We need you to fill out some paperwork."

"But Charlie needs me."

He is in good hands Mrs. Connors. Now just please cooperate. It's going to be a long day."

* * *

PATTY HAD JUST ABOUT ENOUGH of the police station by the time she finished her round of questioning. She couldn't believe how much of her day had been spent recounting the details of what had happened. It felt like a never-ending cycle of going over and over the same things.

"Did you know your husband has a record for assault under the name of Mitch Parker?

Patty nodded her head no. "You don't seem surprised."

Patty could believe anything after living with his violent behavior these past years. It somehow all made sense.

As she glanced around, her eyes landed on the odd assortment of items scattered across the room. There was a rather overwhelming pinup board adorned with notes and newspaper clippings, a dry erase board boasting red scribbles in a language she couldn't quite decipher, and a schedule for a softball game pinned neatly nearby. The walls, looking neglected and bare, begged some love and attention.

The windows, framed in deteriorating wood, were hardly doing any better. Covered with dusty metal blinds drawn mostly closed, they let in only slivers of light, adding to the room's lifeless atmosphere. A lone American flag stood proudly in one corner, the only touch of color in the otherwise drab space.

Seated at the table was a stoic male officer. A sink and a tiny refrigerator occupied one corner of the room, with a tired-looking coffee pot perched on the counter, emanating a faint aroma of stale brew.

The officer saw Patty looking at the coffee pot. "Would you like some coffee?"

"Yes, thank you."

As Patty watched the officer get up to make them coffee, she felt a sense of anticipation building in the air. The modest room held secrets of the past waiting to still be unraveled, weaving a tale of intrigue and unexpected twists in the most unlikely of settings.

The officer poured two cups of coffee, one for her and one for himself. He opened six packets of sugar and poured it into the hot dark brown liquid. Patty's stomach rumbled. She realized she was starving. "May I have some sugar in my coffee too?"

"How many?"

"Six please."

"You like sugar with your coffee too?" He chuckled.

"Yeah, I guess so."

The officer sat back down and continued with the questioning. "We also have a report here filed by your parents.

Patty looked at him. "My parents?"

"You didn't know about this?"

"Your husband was called in by your parents for questioning. Nothing came of it."

"Why wasn't I asked to come in?"

"Your parents didn't want to involve you at this particular time."

"I don't understand."

"It appears that they were very concerned about your welfare. They believed that he had been abusive. They saw bruises on your body. Your husband denied it of course. He said you had fallen. Your husband stated that you asked your parents to leave you alone or you would call the police. Your parents did not deny this. Is that a correct statement?"

Patty sat on the hard metal seat, feeling the weight of her thoughts pressing down on her. She stared blankly at her coffee, her mind replaying the events that brought her to this moment. How did she end up here, feeling so lost and alone?

Her husband, Mitch, had a way of making her doubt herself. His words were like silk, weaving a web of manipulation around her. She thought back to the time when she first introduced him to her parents. Their eyes were filled with pride and hope for her future. They saw him as the perfect match for their only daughter – handsome, successful, and charming.

But as the years went by, Patty's fairy tale romance turned into a nightmare. Mitch's true colors began to emerge, revealing a controlling and abusive side that Patty never imagined existed. She tried to shield her parents from the truth, putting on a facade of a perfect marriage whenever they visited or called.

She yearned for the comfort of her parents' embrace, their words of wisdom and love that seemed like a distant memory. Patty's parents, concerned about her well-being, reached out to her one day after noticing a few bruises on her arm. Mitch's reaction was unexpected and intense. He demanded that Patty cut off all contact with her parents, claiming that they would never understand their relationship. Deep down, Patty knew that something was wrong, but the fear of losing Mitch clouded her judgment.

"They will never understand us. You and I are different. That scares them." Mitch retorted.

As Mitch continued to manipulate Patty, planting seeds of doubt and resentment towards her parents, she found herself torn between her love for him and her desire to reconnect with her family. Each day became a battle between her loyalty to Mitch and her longing for the familiar warmth of her parents' love.

"You and I have to stick together, or they'll try to destroy everything we've worked for." Mitch demanded.

The last time Patty saw her parents Mitch made her lie to them.

"You don't know anything about us. We are happy. Stop trying to ruin our marriage." Believing her words to be true at the time.

Patty told them she would call the police the next time they tried to intervene again. After that Patty's parents stopped calling. She knew that her betrayal of her parents must have hurt them badly. Patty felt ashamed. She believed she could never face them again.

"Yes, that part is true." Tears rolled down her face.

The officer handed her a box of tissues. "Your parents believed that Mitch had convinced you to turn against them, but there was nothing anyone could do until you came forward."

"Yes, he convinced me that they were against us."

The officer typed something on his laptop.

"What about his past assault charges?" Patty asked softly.

"It seems, at the time of these charges, there was not enough hard evidence to convict him of any crime. When he changed his name, nothing more became of him until now, said the officer."

"I see."

"You're lucky that you and your nephew didn't get seriously hurt."

"My nephew, oh you mean Charlie?"

"He is your nephew?"

"Yes, I'm just tired."

"Well, maybe we should wrap things up so that you can go home and get some rest Mrs. Connors. You've had a very stressful day. We might need you to come back down in a day or two to answer some more questions."

"I've told you everything.

"We understand, but sometimes it helps move the case along. You want to catch your husband?

"Of course."

"We appreciate your help Mrs. Connors. If you think of anything else, give us a call. Here's my card."

Patty reached out to grab it. "I will."

"I'm sure one of our patrol officers will pick him up tonight."

Patty nodded. She walked out of the room and shut the door behind her.

By the time the questioning was over, Patty felt mentally and emotionally drained. She hoped that her cooperation would help the police find Mitch and have him arrested.

The day was completely gone. She was exhausted. Patty noticed the clock on the wall. She couldn't believe how long it took at the police station. No wonder I'm so hungry, she thought to herself. The clerk behind the desk called out.

"Mrs. Connors, if you could wait a few more minutes, Officer Smith will drive you home."

"Oh yes, thank you." Patty said in a relieved voice.

She was glad that the police were on the lookout for Mitch. "Serve you right, Mitch," she muttered under her breath, a sly smile playing on her lips. She knew he was cunning and could slip through anyone's fingers like sand, but she didn't care anymore. "Maybe he was on his way to Mexico in his fancy truck, trying to escape the mess he had created." She thought, if he was far away from her, she was content. Patty's thoughts drifted to Charlie. Maybe now Charlie will see things differently. Maybe, just maybe, she could change his mind about going back to Sarah.

On the drive home with Officer Smith, Patty's mind raced with thoughts of her endless to-do list. She glanced out the window at the passing city lights, dimmed by the darkness of night. The faint hum of the radio filled the silence in the car.

Turning to Officer Smith, she broke the quiet, "Thanks for the ride, Officer. I appreciate it."

He nodded with a kind smile. "No problem, Mrs. Connor. Just doing my job."

Patty nodded back, grateful for his help in this chaotic situation. As they approached her house, she couldn't help but feel a sense of relief washing over her. Maybe things were finally looking up for once.

CHAPTER 23

Dinner

AFTER SEARCHING FOR CHARLIE, and having no success, Sarah decided to head back home. Her mind was elsewhere. She couldn't shake the feeling of unease that had settled in the pit of her stomach. Her mom stuck to her word and made that nice dinner, a rare occurrence in their busy household. It seemed like the perfect opportunity for the whole family to gather together and share a meal, something that hadn't happened since Sarah had returned home. She had promised her mom that she would be home for dinner, but all she really wanted was to find Charlie, to make sure he was okay

Sarah's thoughts weren't on the delicious smells wafting from the kitchen or the warmth of her family's presence. No, all she could think about was her handsomw boyfriend who was MIA. Charlie, the one who always knew how to make her laugh and who had been strangely absent for the past few days made her body boil.

With a heavy heart, Sarah entered the kitchen. The aroma of her mom's cooking enveloped her like a warm hug. She found her family gathered around the dining table, yet no one seemed to be eating much on their plate.

"We thought you had forgotten," her mom stated.

"Sorry mom. I'm just running behind. I didn't realise what time it was."

"I hope you saved an appetite."

"It looks delicious."

The four of them sat quietly picking up their food. Her parents both appeared to be extremely preoccupied. Margaret scrolled through her phone.

Sarah forced a smile, but inside, she was seething with frustration. He wasn't answering his phone. Why did he hang up on me? She thought again to herself. No number of texts or calls seemed to reach him.

As the meal progressed, Sarah's restlessness grew. She pushed her food around her plate, her mind a whirlwind of worry and anger. How could Charlie be so inconsiderate, so careless with her feelings? Didn't he know how much she needed him, especially at a time like this? Time was running out and there was nothing she could do.

"I'm flying out Sunday evening." Only two more nights, Sarah thought to herself.

Sarah took another bite out of her salad and talked with her mouth full. "Who's taking me to the airport?" Sarah couldn't believe she had to go back already.

Sarah's father gave her one of those looks about talking with your mouth full.

"Oh, sorry."

Margaret stabbed a tomato. The insides squirted across the table and tomato guts landed on her father's white golf shirt. Margaret smiled. No one seemed to notice.

"What time does your flight leave?"

"I need to double check, but I think around 7:00 PM."

"I can take you."

"Thanks Margaret."

Robert looked at Margaret. "I want you to come straight home afterwards. We need to have a talk."

Margaret looked down at her dad. "Really, can you for once just give me a break?"

"Margaret don't even start with me. My patience is running out."

Gwen gave Robert a dirty look. Robert seemed to ignore her. Margaret scooped a chunk of her mashed potatoes up with a fork. She turned the fork over and the potatoes fell to her plate, making a splatting sound.

"Something needs to be done around here. Margaret stop playing with your food." Robert was seemingly becoming more annoyed.

"Why are you trying to ruin a nice dinner, Robert?" Gwen said firmly, but calmly.

"By the way, I'm pretty sick and tired of the two of you fighting all the time," Margaret retorted.

Robert leaned into the table. He was trying to remain calm. "Margaret, if it weren't for your mother, you would have been out that door a lot sooner."

Margaret chewed on her squashed tomato. She looked over at her mom. "Thanks mom. I owe you one."

Robert's face was reddened. "Margaret, not another word or..."

Gwen interrupted him. "Robert stop it."

"Whatever. I'm not hungry." Margaret stood up and tugged at her shorts. She then pointed to her father's shirt.

He looked down. "Shit. This is a new shirt. I just got it last week."

Margaret smirked and walked out of the kitchen with a big smile on her face.

Gwen stared at Robert. "What is your problem?"

Sarah sat in her chair quietly, feeling extremely uncomfortable. This was an issue that she didn't want to get involved in. Glancing over at her father, she noticed the red stain dominating his once pristine white shirt. He sat there, staring at his plate with a look of agitation. Their earlier talk was meant to improve things between them, but it seemed to have had the opposite effect.

Her father's tired eyes had dark circles under them, and his skin looked pale. Sarah could see that he was still dealing with a lot of anger and stress, causing him to act edgier than usual. She knew that her parents' relationship would take time to heal, just like she needed to figure out her own situation.

In some ways, Sarah couldn't blame her father for his behavior. The once happy and content family he knew had fallen apart, leaving him struggling to cope.

Sarah's mom sat quietly at the table, picking at the remnants of her dinner. Her eyes glistened with unshed tears, desperately trying to hold back the flood of emotions threatening to spill over. Her father, on the other hand, sat at the table, his back rigid with anger.

"Mom, dinner was great!"

The two of them looked at Sarah.

"Let me clean the dishes since you spent so much time making us a nice dinner."

"Thanks sweetie. That would be a great help." Gwen smiled and she handed Sarah her plate.

Robert walked out of the room. Gwen sat in her chair and started crying.

"Mom, are you okay?"

Her mom nodded her head that she was okay, but she continued to cry.

"Mom, you don't seem okay."

Gwen wiped the tears from her eyes. "I just don't understand your father. He seems so distant from everyone lately. I just wish..."

"You just wish for what, mom?"

"I just wish things were like they used to be."

"Yeah, like when we all got along?" Sarah said softly in an emotional way.

Gwen looked at her daughter and chuckled lightly. "Yes. Things have been bad for a long time, haven't they?"

"Margaret says the two of you constantly fight."

"Your father can make me so mad at times. He never compromises on anything. I'm always the one to give in.

He's tearing this family apart and I'm sick and tired of it."

"He's tearing up the family?" Sarah replied.

Gwen looked at Sarah.

"I mean, can't you and dad just try to work things out?"

"I'm trying, but I'm just so sad and I don't know what to do anymore." Gwen's words wavered.

"Don't you think it will work out between you two? It wouldn't be right for the two of you to just end it after all these years."

Her mom still didn't know that Sarah knew about her relationship with Mitch. She knew she might be giving away too much information, but she hated what her mother was doing to her father and the family by having an affair.

"Sarah, I'm tired and I really don't feel like discussing my marriage with you." Her mother seemed frustrated.

Sarah had hit a sore spot. "I'm part of this family too, aren't I?"

"Of course, Sarah, but this is difficult for me right now and I'm just too mad to talk about it."

"But mom..."

"Sarah, I appreciate your concern, but I said I wasn't talking about it. This is between your father and I and I will handle it. I'll make things right or how they should be. I'm going upstairs. Thanks for doing the dishes."

"No problem mom, that's the least I can do."

As Sarah scrubbed at the stubborn pots, her thoughts swirled around her parents like a whirlpool. Her mom's strange behavior and her dad's recent outbursts have been more than a little unsettling. It was like they were dancing on the edge of a storm, trying to keep their balance amid the chaos.

She couldn't help but feel a pang of satisfaction in the knowledge that her father had finally seen through Mitch's façade. The guy had always given off shady vibes, and Sarah had always been wary of him, especially now after learning how he had been treating Charlie and his own wife. Now, seeing her dad realize the truth made her feel a strange mix of vindication and worry.

Her mind wandered to her older sister, Margaret, and the way she seemed to bounce from one relationship to another, never staying with one guy long enough to put down roots. Sarah had always thought it was just Margaret's flighty nature, but now she couldn't help but wonder if there was something deeper at play.

Was their mother's unhappiness in her marriage casting a shadow over the way her daughters viewed relationships? Sarah mulled over the idea, feeling a weight settle in her chest. Maybe Margaret's reluctance to commit stemmed from a subconscious desire to avoid the kind of pain their mother seemed to be in.

And then there was Sarah herself, navigating the murky waters of dating with her own set of challenges. She couldn't help but shake her head at her own choices, wondering why she always seemed to pick guys who carried their own baggage of issues.

Sarah realized she had been washing the same glass for several minutes. She looked over at the clock. It's already

6:30. Sarah checked her phone. Charlie still had not called. Her father had made it clear for Charlie to stay away so maybe that's what he was doing, respecting his wishes, but why couldn't she find him?

Sarah wiped the kitchen table and placed the bowl of fruit in the center of it. God, I just wish I could make these last few days just disappear. Maybe coming home wasn't such a good idea.

CHAPTER 24

The T-Shirt

Sᴀʀᴀʜ ɢʀᴀʙʙᴇᴅ her cell phone and walked outside onto the deck. She lay in the lounge chair and looked up at the sky. "I'll relax for a while and hopefully Charlie will call. He'll call. I know he will," she murmured to herself, feeling a mix of anticipation and exhaustion. The past semester at school has been a complete blur, with late nights and endless assignments that seem to never end. Despite her efforts, she hadn't made it through the semester unscathed.

Closing her eyes, Sarah let out a long exhale, feeling the weight of stress slowly melt away. She couldn't remember the last time, except for the past day or so, that she had taken a few moments to just breathe and enjoy the quiet moments of life. "I could sleep for a week straight," she thought, a small smile forming on her lips.

Sarah's mind drifted to the sunset. A full moon tonight, promising a night of magic and mystery. Tonight, its full beauty would light up the darkness, casting a silver glow over everything it touched. As she lay there, bathed in the warm glowing sun, Sarah felt a sense of peace wash over her.

The gentle rustling of leaves in the evening breeze, the distant sound of crickets chirping, and the soothing rhythm of her own breath filled the air around her. For the first time in what felt like forever, Sarah allowed herself to simply be in the moment, embracing the tranquility of the night.

As she gazed up at the sky, Sarah felt a sense of gratitude for the beauty of the world around her. With a contented sigh, she drifted off to sleep, feeling a sense of calm and renewal wash over her tired soul.

* * *

SARAH WOKE up face down on the ground, coughing as she tasted the remnants of twigs, grass, and mud in her mouth. With a grimace, she spat to rid herself of the gritty taste. Her body ached as she slowly lifted her head and surveyed her surroundings. All she could see were layers of trees and ancient, ghostly branches stretching into the fog-covered forest ground.

Blinking dazedly, Sarah pushed herself up onto her hands and knees, feeling the damp earth beneath her palms. The forest was eerily silent, save for the distant calls of unseen birds and the rustling of leaves in the gentle breeze. Where was she? How did she end up here?

As she tried to piece together the events leading up to her current predicament, Sarah's heart began to race with a mixture of fear and confusion. She couldn't remember how she got to this mysterious place or why she was alone in the heart of the dark, foreboding forest.

Shaking off the fog of sleep and disorientation, Sarah slowly rose to her feet, wincing at the soreness in her muscles. The forest seemed to loom around her, its ancient trees casting long shadows that danced in the shifting light. With a deep breath, she took a tentative step forward, her senses on high alert.

As she walked deeper into the forest, each step crunching on the forest floor, Sarah felt a sense of unease creeping over her. The air was thick with the scent of moss and damp earth, and she couldn't shake the feeling that she was being watched.

As she stumbled through the dense forest, the rustling leaves and eerie silence made her heart race even faster. Every step was a struggle, as if the very ground beneath her was resisting her movements. The chilly night air sent shivers down her spine, making her wish she had some clue as to how she ended up in this nightmare.

Her mind was a blank canvas, void of any memories or hints as to what led her to this desolate place. The torn nightgown clinging to her skin felt like a cruel reminder of the chaos that must have unfolded before she found herself in the darkness of the woods.

The branches of the trees clawed at her exposed arms, leaving red welts in their wake. She tried to call out for help, but all that escaped her lips was a hoarse whisper lost in the vast expanse of the forest. Her only companion was the pounding in her chest, a steady rhythm that matched the urgency of her predicament.

As she pushed forward, each step bringing her closer to an unknown destination, a sense of dread settled deep within her chest. What horrors awaited her beyond the trees, lurking in the shadows just out of sight? She had to stay strong, had to keep moving despite fear gripping her every fiber.

Nothing seemed to filter through the dense canopy above. Every shadow seemed to contain a lurking terror, a threat she couldn't quite define but could feel in the very marrow of her bones.

With shaky determination, she forced her aching feet to carry her farther into the unknown. She may not know where she was going, but she knew that she had to escape this place, this nightmare that had become her reality.

She pressed on, her heart pounding in her chest, her torn nightgown fluttering in the cold night breeze. Though the path ahead was shrouded in darkness, she knew that she had to keep moving forward, but which way? Sarah was lost in the middle of a dense forest with no clear path to follow. Every step she took seemed to bring her deeper into the maze of trees and branches. She could feel the panic rising in her chest, urging her to keep moving, to keep running away from whatever lurked behind her.

The fog seemed to thicken around her, obscuring her vision and making it even harder to find her way. She felt like she was trapped in a repeating bad dream, chased by unseen forces that threatened to swallow her whole. But Sarah refused to give up. She forced her tired legs to keep moving, to keep pushing forward no matter what.

Suddenly, a glimmer of light caught her eye through the dense trees. It was a faint flicker of hope in the darkness, a sign that there was still a way out of this incubus. With renewed determination, Sarah ran towards the light, ignoring the burning pain in her legs and the chill in the air.

As she burst out of the forest into an open meadow, Sarah collapsed to the ground, gasping for breath. She had made it out, escaped the clutches of the dark and menacing woods. Looking back at the trees that had nearly consumed her, she shuddered at the memory of what could have been.

She sensed the moon. She felt it would guide her to safety. She followed the moon's rays. The light became her path, bright and white. It gave her energy too. She could now feel a sensation on her feet. They felt warmer and her body felt rejuvenated somehow. Could it be the moon that was making her feel better? She thought to herself. She could outrun anything as long as the moon was with her.

In the distance she saw a road. It was familiar. Could it be? Yes she knew this road well. It heads east. This road should take her right to her house. Her battered feet pounded against the pavement.

* * *

SARAH WOKE UP TENSE, her hand tightly gripping her phone. As she slowly sat up, she realized that she had fallen asleep again. Why couldn't she shake off this recurring dream that left her feeling uneasy every time? The chilly wind outside made her shiver, prompting her to glance at the wood patio table where a spider was slowly crawling over the wooden slats.

Checking her phone, she saw no new notifications, and she noticed that it was already 8:10 in the evening. Pushing herself up from the lounge chair, she stretched her stiff arms, feeling the tension slowly dissipate. Despite that, her legs still felt shaky, and the strange feeling of the dream lingered.

Deciding that she no longer wanted to be outside alone, Sarah made her way through the French doors into the warm embrace of the family room. The sense of anger and tension still clung to her like a heavy cloak, making her feel on edge even in the familiar surroundings of her home. Where is Charlie?

"The least you can do is call." She said out loud.

As soon as I get back to campus, I need to swim some laps, she thought to herself. It was the only thing that really relaxed her. This stress is killing me. I'm going crazy.

Sarah picked up her phone and called all the places she could think of looking for Charlie, but still no one had seen him. Nervously Sarah paced back and forth. Maybe something had happened between Charlie and Mitch. Sarah suddenly had a strange feeling that something bad had happened. Charlie wouldn't just ignore her, or would he?

Maybe she should drive over to Charlie's house again and see if everything is alright. Was she being paranoid? No, it was the right thing to do. If Charlie was there, well then she had good news for him. He would definitely want to know that her father had agreed to give Charlie another chance. Sarah suddenly felt nervous and didn't want to go alone. I'll ask Margaret to come with me, she thought as she ran up the stairs.

* * *

MARGARET THOUGHT to herself as she looked through all her things. "Where is it?" I know it's here."

She wore it last at the river. She was sure of it. Her mind wandered off to that hot day last summer.

On a scorching summer day in the Northwest, the air felt like a thick blanket wrapping around everything and everyone. The sky was a blur of pale white, with no relief in sight. People were wilting in the heat, not accustomed to this kind of weather in their usually cool region.

Central air was a luxury most didn't have, and those without it were feeling the full force of the relentless sun. Complaints filled the air like buzzing bees, each person a chorus of discomfort. News reports told of heat-related incidents, with some unfortunate souls succumbing to the unforgiving temperatures. The sun showed no mercy, claiming even the lives of those who dared to defy its scorching power.

The only respite from the oppressive heat lay in public places, like bustling malls, air-conditioned restaurants, and cool movie theaters. Families flocked to the public pools, seeking solace in the refreshing waters, while kids splashed and played, oblivious to the intensity of the heat.

Margaret, once a child who frolicked under the sprinklers, was now too old to partake in such simple pleasures. Instead, she found herself seeking refuge in the cool corners of her home, yearning for a breeze that never came.

When they were younger, Margaret and Sarah found refuge from the sweltering heat by playing in the backyard, where their trusty sprinkler faithfully sprayed cooling mist all around. As the droplets danced through the air, the two young girls spun and twirled, imagining themselves on the edge of a majestic waterfall, feeling the thrill of danger in their make-believe adventure.

In their imaginary world, the edge of the great cliff was a precarious spot, where one wrong step could send them tumbling into the abyss of roaring waters below. The girls giggled and squealed as they carefully navigated the edge, pretending that the spiral current would whisk them away to a land of ancient mysteries and fearsome creatures.

"Watch out for the monsters!" Sarah would shout, her eyes wide with excitement.

Margaret would play along, her heart racing with the thrill of the unknown. "We must be brave and smart, or we'll be stuck in this place forever!"

In this savage land of their imagination, Margaret and Sarah faced terrifying beasts and treacherous challenges. They survived on strange fruits and bitter vegetables, their thirst quenched by the pure rainwater that fell from the sky. Every moment was an adventure, every day a fight for survival in a world where danger lurked behind every shadow.

These fearless sisters decided to build a cool treehouse high up in a gargantuan tree with gnarling branches that seemed to dance in the wind.

The gnarling branches intertwined with each other, creating a perfect spot for the girls to build their dream hideout. Being up high in the treehouse not only gave them an amazing view of the jungle but also kept them safe from the prowling predators lurking below.

Of course, living in the treetops wasn't all fun and games. There were giant snakes that slithered around and wrapped themselves around the branches of the trees. These massive reptiles were always on the hunt for their next meal, and they could easily swallow a person whole, especially a small child like Margaret and Sarah.

Despite the lurking danger, the girls were undeterred. They kept a lookout for giant snakes, making sure to stay safe in their treehouse hideout. Armed with their creativity and resourcefulness, the girls turned their treehouse into a cozy haven, complete with a makeshift bed, a tiny kitchen, and even a swing made from vines.

As the days went by, Margaret's and Sarah's treehouse became the envy of the jungle. Animals would come by to marvel at the girls' handiwork, and birds would chirp happily in the branches above. And when the sun sets, casting a warm glow over the treetops, the girls would snuggle up in the cozy treehouse, safe and sound in their little piece of paradise.

And so, high up in the gargantuan tree with gnarling branches, two brave girls lived out their wildest adventures, proving that with a little courage and a lot of creativity, anything was possible in the magical jungle they called home.

The most dangerous time was when torrential rains came suddenly. As the black-green clouds loomed overhead, the girls would hurry to their tree house, hoping to seek shelter from the impending storm. But no sooner had they settled into their sanctuary, the sky would open its jaws, unleashing pounding pellets of rain that turned the ground below into a raging river.

Margaret and Sarah would hold on tightly to the branches of their tree house, their hearts pounding with fear. The quarter-size drops would sting their skin, and the force of the rainfall threatened to tear their tree house apart.

With each passing moment, the river of rain below would rise higher and higher. The girls clung on to their treehouse, their knuckles white with exertion. But the slippery branches proved to be treacherous, and one by one, they began to lose their grip.

First Margaret, then Sarah, were swept away by the powerful current, tumbling into the swirling waters below. As they gasped for air and struggled to stay afloat, they reached out to each other, binding them together in the face of nature's fury.

Amid the chaos and uncertainty, the girls held on to each other, determined to weather the storm together. And as the rain finally began to subside, they emerged from the river bruised and battered but alive.

As the sun dipped below the horizon and the sky turned shades of pink and orange, Margaret and Sarah would finally bid farewell to their imaginary realm, returning to the safety of their backyard.

The sprinkler had formed a puddle. Margaret laughed to herself at the way they used to let their imaginations run wild.

"Where is it?" It's got to be here somewhere," Margaret said hastily. Margaret felt herself becoming frustrated as she was on the second round of going through her things.

Her thoughts again wandered back in time.

Charlie, Sarah and Margaret were sitting on their porch, feeling drained by the warmth. No one wanted to move in fear of getting hot. Sweat was dripping down their bodies. Their T-shirts stuck to their wet skin. Charlie was lying on his back looking up at the overhang of the porch.

"I don't care how crowded the pool is. I'm too hot to sit around here."

"No, I hate it when there are too many people. You can't even move. All those kids are bumping into you." Margaret said it with disgust.

"Well, we just can't sit here until we melt." Charlie sat up. He had an idea. "Let's take a drive...to the river."

Charlie knew of this great spot to take a swim and cool off in the ice, cold river. There was a large rock, with a high cliff, that was supposed to be good for diving. Someone had told Charlie about this little hideaway tucked back within the forest, but much to their surprise it wasn't such a secret place after all.

They pulled up to a clearing near the river. Pickup trucks and motorcycles were tightly parked next to each other. All sorts of people were hanging out. Many of them looked like bikers with long uncombed hair, cut-off blue jean shorts and tattoos that covered their backs and arms. A few were relaxing and drinking beers. One pregnant girl, who didn't look older than eighteen, was smoking a joint while painting her toenails black.

"That must be one of your old girlfriends," Margaret said to Charlie with a laugh.

Sarah punched Margaret in the arm.

Some people were lounging on the rocks at the edge of the river. Others were swimming in the river. Four guys were standing near the base of the big rock. Then, some guy in blue swim trunks jumped from the top and screamed as he headed for the water. His big belly hit the water hard.

Margaret rolled her eyes. "That's gotta hurt."

Charlie laid his blanket out and started taking his shoes off. "Come on. We're gonna do that", Charlie said to Margaret and Sarah.

"I don't know about that."

"Yes, you are."

As they approached the river's edge and climbed up to the top of the cliff, many of the guys turned around and stared at Margaret. She suddenly regretted taking off her t-shirt and leaving it in the car. Now all she was wearing was a two-piece bathing suit.

"Hey, baby."

Margaret didn't look at him. She kept walking. Charlie was ahead with Sarah.

"Wait for me," Margaret said nervously as she speeded up to catch them.

They both looked at Margaret. "Hurry up."

"I don't know if I'm gonna jump off," Margaret said nervously.

"What are you scared of?"

"I'm not scared." Margaret retorted.

The three of them climbed up the steep rock. Two young guys were sitting at the top. They stared at Margaret. She felt awkward.

"Hey." One of the guys said to Charlie.

"Hey. How's the jump?"

"Good. Water is cold."

Charlie was looking over the edge. The water seemed far below, and the swimmers looked small like bobbing heads. "What's it about thirty feet?"

One of the two guys hit his shoe with a stick. "Beats me. It's far."

"Yeah, it's far", said the other guy still staring at Margaret.

She could feel his probing eyes.

"Hey Sarah, let's jump together." Charlie said with a big smile on his face.

"Oh, that's great. Just leave me here with these two guys." Margaret said obnoxiously.

"What's wrong with us?" We can keep you company."

"I'm not hanging out with you two."

She looked at the two guys who were now checking her legs. "Stop doing that!"

"Wha...?"

The guy had no idea what she was talking about. Margaret sighed.

"Ready Sarah?"

"Yep."

Charlie grabbed her hand. "On the count of three... One, two, three."

Sarah and Charlie jumped. Margaret and the two guys, now standing up, looked over the edge. Charlie and Sarah's bodies plunged into the water. A few seconds later they surfaced at the top.

"Whoa! The water is freezing."

Sarah waved up at Margaret. Charlie and Sarah swam over towards the edge of the river, near the other swimmers where his blanket and shoes were.

Margaret looked at the guys she was standing with. "You're next," one said.

"No shit," she whispered.

"My name is Jayson. They call me Jay though."

"Seriously...you're telling me your name?"

"Watch out for the bottom. It's shallow. You need to jump to the right. Pull your feet up, just in case."

She looked at the guys nervously. "Yeah?"

"One time this guy jumped into the wrong spot and forgot to pull up his feet. He broke both his legs. His hip bone was shattered."

"He still doesn't walk right to this day."

"Oh my God. Really? Why didn't you warn them?"

"It just now occurred to me.

"Great. It just now occurred to you."

"Go on, jump, your friends are waiting for you."

"I don't know. What if I jump...?"

"Look, they made it."

She looked at Charlie and Sarah. They both seemed fine.

"Jump to the right."

"Okay. I'll pull up my legs." Margaret took a deep breath.

"Good luck. Don't want to ruin that pretty body of yours."

Jay did an exaggerated sign of the cross. The other guy stared at Margaret's butt.

"Oh please! Like God is listening to you."

She jumped and tucked into her legs. Her body fell toward the water.

The guy yelled over the side as she dropped to the water. " He doesn't walk right to this day."

Her body landed in the cold water. It felt shocking and Margaret could feel her body shiver. She pulled herself to the surface of the water and gasped for air. The air brought a warming sensation to her lungs. A sense of relief came over her.

"I made it. My feet didn't hit the bottom." Margaret yelped out loud

It seemed everyone was staring at her as she walked to the shore. "I made it." She said it loudly." She smiled to herself. I must have looked like a pro.

Sarah pointed to her chest. "Not everything made it, Margaret."

Margaret looked down at her chest. Somewhere at the bottom of the river lay her tiny bikini top waiting for the fish to find it.

Margaret shivered at that thought, as she came back to reality. She continued looking in her closet.

"Where is it?" It's gotta be here."

Frustrated she went back to her dresser and started rummaging through her drawers again.

"What are you doing?"

Margaret jumped back. "God, Sarah, why are you always sneaking up on me?"

"Sorry. I want you and I to drive out to Mitch's place."

"Why?"

"I haven't heard from Charlie."

"Yeah."

"I've called everywhere for him. He's not answering his phone. No one has seen him."

"Maybe he's busy."

"No Margaret, I think something is wrong."

"What 'cause he hasn't called you?"

"Well, yes...no, not exactly. I stopped by Mitch's house earlier today. Patty said she hadn't seen him."

"And?"

"I think she was lying."

"Why?"

"I don't know."

"Sarah, maybe Charlie is staying away from you 'cause of dad." Margaret was pulling things out of her drawers.

"What are you doing?"

"Nothing." Margaret continued to go through her drawers.

"I need you to come with me."

"Sarah, I'm kind of busy right now."

Margaret looked over at Sarah.

"Please come with me. I just want to make sure everything is okay."

Margaret opened her bottom drawer. She lifted-up stacks of shirts and shorts. Her eyes lit up. "Here it is." Margaret held up a T-shirt.

"That's what you've been looking for?"

It was an old T-shirt with a painting of a sailboat on the ocean.

"I had forgotten about this shirt and then something reminded me of it. "Margaret took off the shirt she was currently wearing and put on the one she had just found. Margaret walked over to the mirror and looked at herself. The shirt looked like it had been washed a million times. "Fits just like it used to. I love this shirt."

"Seriously? It looks really old. Where did you get that shirt?

"Don't you remember?"

Sarah didn't have a clue. She shook her head. "Nope, I don't remember it."

"Dad got it for me when he and mom visited the art museum in Paris."

"That was seven years ago and besides it's falling apart."

"I knew I hadn't thrown it out."

"You should. It looks pretty bad."

"You think?"

"Now that you have found your shirt, will you please come with me?"

Margaret sighed.

"It won't take long. I promise."

"God, Sarah"

"Please, Margaret."

"Oh, all right."

CHAPTER 25

The Picture

THE HOUSE WAS DARK. No cars were in the driveway. Sarah got out of Margaret's car and slowly walked across the driveway.

"Sarah what are you doing? No one is home."

Frustrated, Margaret got out of her car and followed Sarah. There were crickets buzzing in the background. Sarah quietly tiptoed over the tar pavement.

"Why are we sneaking around?" It's so weird. What were you expecting him to be waiting for you?"

"No, this whole thing seems so bizarre. I feel like I'm spying on him."

"Spying on him?"

"Never mind." What do you think? Should I knock on the door?"

"You better knock on the door. You dragged me out of here."

"Yeah, okay."

"I'm going back to the car. Make it fast."

"God, Margaret, you could at least stay with me just in case."

"What are you expecting to happen?"

"Fine, whatever. I'll be okay." Sarah retorted.

Sarah continued to walk across the driveway to the side door. What if Mitch answers - then what? No, he wasn't around. His truck wasn't here.

She couldn't shake off the feeling that the luminous orb was shining directly on her back, making her nerves tingle with an inexplicable sense of unease. Thoughts of werewolves prowling in the darkness crept into her mind, sending a shiver up her spine. Her footsteps echoed on the concrete. The only sounds breaking the silence of the night were the clicking sounds her shoes made against the pavement.

Sarah walked up the steps to the side porch and knocked on the door, but there was no answer. She tried again, still no response. Peering through the small window on the doorframe, she saw only darkness, with faint silhouettes of furniture in the kitchen. Beyond that, a glimpse of the stairs. The house was eerily quiet. "Where is everyone?" Sarah wondered, her frustration growing, mixed with worry.

Turning back towards Margaret's car, her heart racing, Sarah ran back to the car, hopping in. "This is so weird," she exclaimed, trying to calm her nerves.

Margaret glanced at her, concern etched on her face. "What happened?" she asked.

Sarah shrugged, the tension in her shoulders evident. "I have no idea. It's like the place was deserted." Sarah couldn't shake the feeling of unease that lingered from the silent house.

"It doesn't make sense."

"I don't know what you are so worried about?" Margaret turned the engine on and put her car into gear.

"Wait, go the other way."

"But it's longer."

"Just do it."

Margaret reversed the car and then headed the opposite way. As they turned the corner, a silhouette of a truck was parked in the distance.

"That's Charlie's truck."

"Yep, it sure is." Margaret pulled next to the truck.

"I'm gonna see if I can find anything in his truck."

"Man, something's got you riled up."

"Yeah... maybe I can find something."

"Find out what?"

"I don't know."

As Sarah stepped closer to the truck, a sense of curiosity tingled her fingertips. The night air wrapped around her like a familiar cloak, as the moonlight cast a silvery sheen across the truck's glossy exterior. Tools and parts of every size and shape cluttered the bed, creating a puzzle of unknown purpose.

Lingering near the tailgate, Sarah's gaze fell upon the wool blankets, still neatly rolled from the previous night's adventures. Memories of laughter and whispered secrets danced in her mind as she reached out to touch the soft fabric, a smile tugging at the corner of her lips.

With a gentle push, the passenger side door yielded with a creak, revealing a trove of manuals and folders perched on the seat like forgotten relics. Sarah's eyes flitted over the words on the papers, her curiosity piqued with each unfamiliar term. She riffled through the stacks, the rustling of paper a quiet symphony under the night sky.

Intrigued by the hidden gems within, Sarah opened the glove compartment with a cautious tug. Among scratched CDs and sun-glasses, a dusty manual and some scattered papers greeted her with a wandering gaze. As she sifted through the contents, a lone envelope slipped from its hiding place and fluttered to the floor board.

The envelope had Charlie's name written on it. Sarah opened it and pulled out a card. Inside was a picture. What is this? The card had something written on it.

Charlie, here's a picture so you will always have me with you. _ Love Patty

"What is this?"

In the picture, Patty was standing in her bedroom, posing confidently in her lacy lingerie. Her curves spilled over the edges, accentuated by the delicate fabric that barely covered her body. Sarah's heart raced as she felt a mix of confusion and anger. Why would her boyfriend have this picture of Patty? She frantically tucked the photo under her shirt and shoved the other things back into the glove compartment, her mind spinning with thoughts. She knew she shouldn't take the evidence, but her curiosity and hurt feelings won over any rational thinking.

Feeling light-headed, climbing out of the truck, Sarah sank down against the side of the door, tears welling up in her eyes. She had always trusted her boyfriend, believed in their relationship. How could Charlie betray her like this? Patty's allure and beauty clouded his judgment, and Sarah couldn't help but compare herself to her in that moment.

As she sobbed quietly, Sarah tried to make sense of it all. This couldn't be happening. It must be some terrible mistake. But deep down, she knew that things had already gone too far. The truth was staring her in the face, and she couldn't ignore it any longer.

* * *

MARGARET YELLED out of her car window. "Come on Sarah, hurry up."

Margaret scrolled on her phone. A minute went by and Margaret finally looked up. "Where are you?" And then Margaret realized that Sarah was crunched in a ball on the side of Charlie's truck.

She saw Sarah's white shirt reflecting from the moon. She was sitting on the ground with her head between her legs.

"Sarah?"

Margaret jumped out of her car.

"Sarah, what's wrong?"

Margaret ran towards her. Sarah was sobbing and holding a picture in her hand.

"What's the matter?"

Sarah sobbed loudly.

"Sarah, get a grip. Tell me what's wrong."

"It's Charlie. He's sleeping with Patt..."

* * *

SARAH SAT in the passenger seat, her hands clasping the picture of Patty tightly against her chest. Margaret, with her foot heavy on the accelerator, weaved through the empty streets under the watchful eye of the full moon. Sarah's tear-streaked face caught the moonlight, casting eerie shadows across her features.

Margaret couldn't bear to see her sister in such distress. She knew she had to get Sarah home as quickly as possible. "Look Sarah, why don't you sleep in my room tonight? It will make you feel better," Margaret suggested, glancing over at Sarah with concern in her eyes.

Sarah shook her head, her voice barely more than a whisper. "Margaret, don't tell mom and dad about all this until I figure out what to do."

"Okay, it will be our secret," Margaret promised, her grip on the steering wheel tightening as she navigated the dark road ahead.

As they pulled into the driveway, a sense of foreboding hung in the air. Margaret helped Sarah out of the car, guiding her towards the house. The porch light illuminated their path as they stepped inside. The heavy silence surrounded them like a shroud.

CHAPTER 26

Betrayal

ONCE INSIDE HER HOUSE, Patty quickly changed into a fresh set of clothes. She grabbed a clean outfit for Charlie and packed some essentials. She made a mental note to stop and pick up some food before going to the hospital.

As she stepped outside, she felt a cool breeze on her face. The stars twinkled above, guiding her on her journey. She hopped into Charlie's truck, determined to make things right.

She stopped by a small diner and picked up some food for herself and Charlie. The aroma of freshly baked bread and coffee filled the air, comforting her weary soul, making her stomach growl.

Finally arriving at the hospital, Patty made her way to Charlie's room. She found him resting peacefully, his face serene in slumber. She gently placed the food on the bedside table and took a seat beside him.

As she watched him sleep, a sense of calm washed over her. It had been a long and challenging day, but seeing Charlie safe and sound made it all worth it. Maybe, just maybe, things are finally falling into place.

* * *

CHARLIE'S BREATH was soft in the dimly lit hospital room, peaceful amidst the beeping of

Machines and the soft rustle of hospital sheets. A small clear tube was connected to a vein in his left arm, leading to a slender stand with a clear plastic pouch hanging from the top. The rhythmic hum of the machines filled the room, echoing the steady beat of his heart.

Patty sat by his side. Her gaze fixed on Charlie's face. She took a bite of her lukewarm dinner, absentmindedly chewing while lost in her thoughts. "Look at what Mitch has done to you," she whispered softly to Charlie, her voice tinged with sadness and frustration. Mitch had spiraled out of control, leaving Charlie in this unsettling state.

Charlie didn't deserve any of this, Patty thought to herself, her heart heavy with guilt and regret. She knew she would do anything for him, even if it meant facing the consequences of Mitch's actions. She promised herself that she would stay by Charlie's side, no matter what challenges lay ahead.

* * *

SHE REMEMBERED the day that everything changed between the two of them.

Patty took a deep breath, the crisp autumn air filling her lungs as she closed her eyes, savoring the moment. It happened at the end of last summer. The nights were starting to get cooler. The trees were beginning to shed their leaves and a layer of leaves and pine needles was starting to cover the ground.

Summer always seemed too short, Patty thought. She glanced over at Charlie, who was staring up at the sky, a thoughtful expression on his face. Patty and Charlie were sitting on a blanket, enjoying one of the last warm evenings of the season. Her legs were laid out in front of her. She was barefooted, feeling the soft grass beneath her feet.

"We should do this more often," Charlie said, breaking the comfortable silence that had settled between them.

Patty smiled, looking out at the setting sun. "I agree. It's so peaceful out here."

They sat in companionable silence for a while, watching as the sky turned shades of orange and pink. A gentle breeze rustled the leaves in the trees, making them dance and sway. It was moments like these that Patty cherished the most - simple, quiet, and full of warmth.

"God, I have ugly toes. Look at how long my toes are?" He looked down at her feet.

Her pout turned into a smile. "Ever since I was a little girl, I've always wished I had pretty feet."

"You're shit out of luck."

"Hey!"

She poked her foot into his side.

"Let's see your feet mister."

"No way. I never said my feet looked good... but now that you mention it, my feet look a heck of a lot better than yours."

She pounced on him like a cat. She poked at his side. He laughed loudly. They were rolling on top of the blanket. He pulled himself over and sat on top of her. He pinned down her arms. She was squirting beneath him.

"Hey, this isn't fair. You're stronger than me."

"Now, I want to warn you before we go any further." He said it seriously.

She suddenly looked concerned.

"This might be hard for you... but when I take off my shoes... don't get upset... promise me."

"What are you talking about?"

"You're going to have to accept it... you asked, so don't get mad at me. Say it. I promise I won't get mad."

"You're crazy."

"Just say it." Charlie poked her again at her side.

She tried to move but he still had her pinned down. She laughed as she said the words. "Okay, I promise."

"Are you ready?"

He lifted his leg over her and sat on the blanket. He removed one shoe, then the other.

"Here's the moment we've been waiting for."

He pulled off his right sock and then his left. His feet were white, and he had a few dark hairs growing on his toes. He wiggled his toes back and forth. "So, if you were a monkey would you be attracted to me?"

"Are you saying that you find me attractive?"

"Only if you're attracted to me."

* * *

THE RHYTHMIC SOUND of Charlie's breathing brought her back to reality. She noticed the table lamp, casting a soft glow on the corner of his bandage, wrapped snugly around his right arm. A faint red stain peeked through the stark white of the bandage, a reminder of his fight with Mitch today, which seemed like days ago.

The doctors had assured Patty that Charlie was on the road to recovery. He just needed to rest and allow time to heal his wounds. She couldn't help but feel a mixture of relief and worry swirling inside her as she watched him. The night in the hospital felt long and tiring, but Patty knew she had to stay strong for Charlie.

She had brought him a sandwich and potato chips. It was his favorite, roast beef with thousand island dressing. He would probably be starving when he woke up. She took her last bite and finished her drink. Her stomach now felt full. She reached into her pocket and pulled out a note. She placed the note and his keys on top of his clothes that she brought from home. The pain killers had completely knocked him out. He would still be asleep for a while longer. "I should go home and get some rest myself." She spoke to herself. She stood up and gathered her things and threw out her trash. When she started walking out of the room, Charlie mumbled words.

"I won't let him hurt you."

* * *

CHARLIE FORCED his sticky eyes to open, feeling as though he had slept for two days. As his vision cleared, he scanned the unfamiliar room around him. Yikes! Hospital walls loomed menacingly in shades of sterile white, giving him an eerie sense of confinement. With a sudden rush of panic, he yearned to escape from the clinical confines that made his skin crawl.

Hospitals always gave Charlie the creeps, with their antiseptic smells and constant probing by doctors and nurses. Every few minutes, it seemed, a new face would barge into his room, armed with needles, thermometers, and stethoscopes. He couldn't shake off the unsettling feeling that they were all part of some grand experiment, strange figures in a theatrical performance staged just for him.

"What are they doing anyway?" Charlie muttered to himself, watching medical personnel come and go in a confusing swirl of activity. Each visitor would fire off a barrage of questions, scribble something indecipherable on his chart, then promptly depart, leaving Charlie alone with his restless thoughts.

A nurse in pale blue scrubs bustled in, flashing a bright smile that failed to reach her tense eyes. She approached Charlie with a thermometer in her hand. Her expression was a mix of professional detachment and weary concern. As she gently placed the device under his tongue, Charlie couldn't help but wonder if he was just a cog in the vast machinery of the hospital, a number on a chart, or a puzzle piece in a medical enigma.

With a soft beep, the thermometer signaled its reading, and the nurse nodded in approval before jotting down the result. Charlie's heart thudded in his chest as he realized he might be stuck in the hospital for a while.

"I'm fine. Really."

"Mr. Parker, we are just doing our job."

He was feeling anxious. "I need to get up and do something."

"There will be plenty of time for that. Sit back and rest."

"Nurse... Whitney", he read her badge. "You seem like a reasonable person. I really feel fine. May I leave now?"

The young nurse shifted her body weight gently and smiled.

"It's against hospital policy. We need to keep you for at least twenty-four hours for observation before we can release you. We wouldn't want any complications."

"How long have I been here?"

"You've been here..." the nurse looks at her watch.

"About eight hours."

He couldn't believe that he had been asleep for nearly eight hours. All that medication and the loss of blood must have made him tired.

"My phone is broken. Who do I speak to about making a call?"

"It's over there on the table, but I need you to answer some questions first and then you also need to fill out this paperwork."

"Right now?"

"Yes Mr. Parker, right now. Someone must pay for all of this."

"All of you are pissing me off."

"We are just doing our job now, aren't we?"

Nurse Whitney winked.

"Is she flirting with me?" Charlie thought to himself.

"If you will cooperate, we can get the job done a lot quicker and you can then make your important call. Anyway, Patty Connors is your..." The nurse looked at Charlie.

"A friend."

A large smile came across Nurse Whitney's face. "Ahhh....Yes, well, she said that you need to call her as soon as you can."

Charlie nodded.

"Oh yes, before I forget. Don't be surprised if the police come in early tomorrow morning to ask you some questions about this incident. They wanted to talk to you sooner but the doctor wanted you to get some rest."

"Just great."

''I will be back to check up on you."

She was definitely flirting with him but that was the last thing on his mind as he watched her walk out of the room. Charlie wanted this whole nightmare to end.

The night had rapidly progressed as nurses followed their protocol. By the time all the paperwork was done it was almost 11:00 PM. He picked up the room phone. He thought about calling Patty but instead he called Sarah. He called her several times. Each time it went straight to her voicemail.

"Shit."

Nurse Whitney poked her head into the room.

"Is everything alright Mr. Parker?"

"It's fine, just fine."

"Okay, I'm here if you need me." Charlie called Sarah again.

"Hi, you've reached..."

"Why won't she just pick up the phone?" Charlie said to himself in frustration. Again Charlie slammed down the phone. "Shit, I can't leave a message." Her father might be screening her calls. Now all he wanted to do was get out of there. That was when he noticed the note on top of a pile of his clothes.

> *Charlie comes home as soon as they let you out. The police are out looking for Mitch. I drove your truck here and took a cab home. It's in the main parking lot. Be careful. I'll be waiting for you.*
>
> —
>
> *Love Patty.*

Charlie got an idea. He pulled the IV out of his arm. He grabbed the stack of clothes that Patty left and put them on. He shoved the keys and the note into his pocket. They would be mad when they found out, but he didn't plan on wasting any more time in here.

CHAPTER 27

The Note

MITCH WAS WOKEN up to his phone buzzing away. It seemed like it had been buzzing for twenty minutes. At first he thought it was part of his dream, "Who the fuck is calling me?" It was calling from a random number. Twelve missed calls. He didn't plan to answer it.

He sat in his truck, parked in a secluded spot deep in the woods. The dim light of the moon filtered through the dense trees, casting eerie shadows on the dashboard. The rhythmic sound of crickets filled the air, creating a sense of calm amidst the chaos that had unfolded earlier.

As he took another swig of his beer, Mitch felt a surge of adrenaline coursing through his veins. Fleeing the crime scene had given him a high, unlike anything he had ever experienced before. It was intoxicating, thrilling, and strangely empowering. He could still taste the metallic tang of fear in his mouth. The image of Charlie clutching his arm burned into his memory.

"I'm not the bad guy here," Mitch muttered to himself, trying to convince himself as much as anyone else. He knew the police would be looking for him, but he had a plan. He always had a plan. With each sip of beer, his mind raced, piecing together a story that would shift the blame away from him.

The memory of his altercation with Charlie replayed in his mind like a movie on repeat. The adrenaline, the fear, the rage – it was a heady mix that left him feeling invincible. He couldn't help but chuckle at the thought of teaching that punk a lesson, of showing Patty who was in charge.

What if Charlie gets Robert Paige to lie for him? Robert has a lot of clout in this town. What if Charlie got Robert's help? Mitch suddenly thought to himself. "Fucking Charlie."

Mitch leaned back in his truck, his mind racing as he thought about his options. He had been in sticky situations before, but this time, it felt different. He had coerced the police once, and he could certainly do it again.

As he drank his beer, Mitch couldn't help but smirk at the thought of Charlie and Patty trying to frame him as the villain. He knew he had only shot Charlie in the arm, a small warning shot to keep them in line. It was nothing serious, just a way to make them think twice before crossing him again.

Sure, things looked grim, but Mitch was no stranger to navigating the murky waters of the justice system. He had some lawer lady friends who owed him favors, these ladies would help him out in a pinch. With their connections and his street smarts, he was confident he could wiggle his way out of this mess.

Mitch took a deep breath. He looked at the note again. He had already read it ten times. He wondered how long the note had been in his truck. He found it lying on the passenger seat after realizing his phone was buzzing. He hadn't noticed it right away. After drinking a case of beer, after his fight with Charlie, he passed out for a few hours. Was it then that the note was conveniently placed in the passenger seat?

Sneaky bitch found his hiding place. "The barn tonight." This would be his way out. Mitch felt good. He felt his adrenaline rushing through his veins. He would focus on Gwen tonight. His plan would go smoothly it seemed. Too bad Gwen was just like the rest of them. Fucking bitches are all the same, playing fucking mind games with men. All women need to be taught a lesson. He had been so disgusted seeing his pathetic father let his fat mom control him.

He looked around, squinting at the dim light filtering through his truck's dusty windows. She must have slipped by here earlier, he thought, a smirk playing on his lips. He was surprised by her. He wasn't expecting this. "Women couldn't resist me." He said out loud.

The beer buzz was wearing off. Sweet Gwen. The blame would go to Charlie. He would threaten to tell everyone about their affair, something that very much haunted Gwen. She would do anything to keep it quiet. He would have to convince Gwen that Charlie was the bad guy, that he was only protecting himself. The sad fact is that Charlie getting shot was his own fault. The rest would be easy, he reassured himself, his mind racing with possibilities. He could smooth things over with the police, charm his way back into Patty's good graces, and ruin Charlie's life once and for all.

A glint of mischief sparked in his gaze as he envisioned the possibilities that lay within. Yes, he thought to himself, this could work. With a devilish grin, he set his plan into motion, knowing that in this game of secrets and lies, he held all the cards.

CHAPTER 28

Charlie's Reappearance

SARAH HAD FINALLY CALMED DOWN. Her eyes were red and swollen and her skin was blotchy. The

two of them were sitting next to each other on Margaret's bed. Margaret's T-shirt was thinly stretched over her knees. Sarah laughed.

"You're gonna rip a hole in that precious T-shirt?"

Margaret giggled. "Anything to make you laugh."

She was glad Margaret had offered to let her sleep in her room. "He's such an asshole. I was so stupid. Did you know about this Margaret? You must have seen or heard something."

"Sarah, I never saw the guy. Maybe there is an explanation for this?"

"Like what?" Sarah held the picture up to Margaret to examine it. "Look, she's looking all sexy, sticking her boobs out."

Margaret looked down at her chest. "She's definitely got more than you and me."

"Are you trying to make me feel worse?" Sarah sighed. "I think this kind of behavior is called incest."

"Sarah, she's not his real mom. She's only five years older than him."

"Whose side are you on?" Sarah growled.

"I'll shut up." Margaret sat quietly.

"How many times do I need to be hit in the head to...?"

"Till you pass out?"

Sarah smiled. "I thought you were going to shut up.

Margaret glared back at her sister.

"Charlie has been acting so weird lately and now it all makes sense. I never thought he would cheat on me."

"You don't know for sure."

"Don't you get it? That's why he's been distant from me. He probably wanted me to break up with him so he wouldn't have to do it. So he wouldn't have to tell me about her. Chicken shit."

The doorbell suddenly rang which completely startedled the two of them. Margaret jumped up and looked out her window.

"It's Charlie, Sarah."

"What?'

"Yeah, his truck is in the driveway."

"I'm gonna kill him."

"You stay here."

"I will talk to him."

"Punch him in the face."

"Don't worry I can take him if I need to."

Margaret ran down the stairs and to the front door. Margaret opened the door.

"Margaret. Thank God."

"What are you doing here Charlie?"

"I need to speak with Sarah."

"I'm sorry Charlie, but she doesn't want to talk to you."

"Why?"

"Charlie, you should know why it's late."

"What? I don't have time for all this. I need to talk to her Margaret. It's really important."

"Like I said, it's late, she's sleeping."

"Cut the crap Margaret, is this about the other night?"

"Yeah, and that too."

"That too?"

Margaret looked at her fingernails. "Eggplant. It's the hottest color in the salon."

"Shit, what are you talking about? This must be about your father?" Margaret held her hands up for Charlie to look at them.

"Stop it, Margaret." He pushed Margaret's hands away.

"Fuck, it is your father!"

"Look Charlie. You messed up. I don't think you're wanted around here."

"You need to let me speak with her."

Sarah could hear their voices now. Charlie was loud.

"Be quiet, you'll wake her."

"Sarah?" Charlie's voice was even louder. He didn't care anymore if her father heard him. "Sarah?"

"What's your problem Charlie? Do you have any idea what time it is? You come over here it's almost midnight wanting to talk to Sarah. Where were you earlier? She was looking for you all day."

"I can explain."

"Have you looked at yourself in the mirror lately? Looks to me like you were getting the shit beat out of you."

"I was."

Margaret sighed. "Look, I don't want to hear about it. I got my own problems. You might try thinking about other people besides yourself."

"Fuck you, Margaret." He said it loudly. "I don't need your crap." His face turned red. "All I want to do is speak with Sarah."

"Get away from her!"

Robert was standing in the doorway.

* * *

ONCE AGAIN, Charlie found himself in a familiar situation - being ordered to leave. The anger boiled within him as he replayed the heated exchange with Robert in his mind.

"He fucking told me to leave," Charlie muttered to himself, his breath coming out in heavy puffs. His heart raced with adrenaline. The urge to lash out almost consumed him. Yet, somehow, he managed to rein in his anger, avoiding what could have been a regrettable outburst.

As Charlie made his way to his truck, a throbbing pain in his arm reminded him of the scuffle that had just occurred. He cursed quietly under his breath, the words slipping out in a raw display of frustration.

"Fuck, fucking shit," he muttered. His voice was tinged with exasperation. Charlie jumped into his truck, the engine roaring to life as he slammed his foot on the gas pedal. The tires squealed as the truck skidded out of the driveway, leaving a trail of dust in its wake. But Charlie knew he wasn't in control, not anymore.

It all started the other night when he hit Sarah in front of her father. Since then, everything has spiraled out of control. No one wanted to listen to him, not even Margaret, who refused to let him speak to Sarah. It seemed like his world was crashing down around him.

As he drove aimlessly, Charlie couldn't shake the feeling that he had lost his last chance to make things right. The weight of regret sat heavy on his chest, suffocating him with every breath. Sarah was his only hope to escape this hellish mess, but now she seemed out of reach.

He replayed his conversation with Margaret in his mind, wondering why she wouldn't just let him talk to Sarah. He was so mad.

"Charlie you've messed up. Looks like you're not wanted around here."

Maybe if he could explain himself, things would be different.

As Charlie's voice grew louder and his gestures more animated, Mr. Paige made his presence known. Charlie froze as he realized the gravity of the situation. "Mr. Paige had to show up," he muttered to himself, wishing he had kept his cool.

"Charlie, you should have known better than to lose your temper," he scolded himself silently.

Of course, Sarah's dad lurked nearby, ready to protect his beloved daughters at all costs.

"What am I, an idiot?" Charlie thought, feeling the weight of his mistake.

"Get out of here now! Or I will call the police."

He should have found a better way to talk to Sarah. "Shit."

Charlie knew he was to blame. He couldn't take back what he had done. Robert was just trying to do what was best for her, but things had escalated beyond his control.

Margaret, with her stubbornness, had shut him out, not allowing him to see Sarah. If only she had let him explain, maybe things wouldn't have gone this far. "Stupid Margaret, always complicating things." His frustration was building up, his muscles tensed with anger.

With a sharp jolt of pain in his head and arm, Charlie realized the pain medicine was wearing off. The hospital was probably in a frenzy by now, knowing he had escaped. He cursed them and everyone else.

"Damn it," he muttered to himself, slamming his fist against the hard dashboard. He needed to find a way to talk to Sarah, to make things right. But how? The road stretched out ahead, uncertainty filling his mind.

Then as Charlie turned the corner, he saw lights suddenly flickering in his rear-view mirror. The lights appeared out of nowhere. He suddenly realized that he had been driving way over the speed limit. "Could it get any worse?"

CHAPTER 29

Margaret's Bedroom

ONCE AGAIN, Sarah tossed and turned in her bed, feeling like Goldilocks in a modern-day dilemma. First, she was too hot, then too cold. Her pillow felt like it housed a family of uncomfortable little lumps, and the moon outside seemed determined to turn her room into a nighttime spotlight.

"Ugh.?" Sarah groaned to herself, her eyes flitting to the time on her phone ticking away. "I shouldn't have taken that nap," she scolded herself, knowing it had thrown off her delicate balance of sleepiness and wakefulness.

As Sarah lay there, tangled in her sheets and trying to count imaginary sheep, lost in her thoughts, Sarah turned over her pillow for the umpteenth time, hoping for a magical transformation that would bring her instant comfort. She closed her eyes and let her mind wander. She replayed the night in her head over again. Charlie finally showed up at their door, after looking for him all day.

After Margaret had answered the door, Charlie and Margaret's voices had started to heighten. That's when Sarah decided to sit closer, on top of the staircase, her heart racing as she listened. Then suddenly her father appeared. Her father's stern voice and Charlie's soft replies echoed in the hallway. She hesitated, feeling torn between wanting to rush in and defend Charlie, and heeding the warnings resounding in her mind.

Her emotions felt like a turbulent storm, constantly shifting from anger to longing in the blink of an eye. Charlie's desperate tone when talking to Margaret tugged at her heartstrings, making her question her own actions.

Should she have approached Charlie before things reached this point? Maybe she could have prevented this messy situation from escalating. But deep down, Sarah knew that confronting him would only leave her vulnerable, exposed to more pain and heartache.

"I have to be strong for myself," she whispered to herself, trying to steel her resolve. Charlie had betrayed her trust, and the wounds were still fresh and throbbing. Running to him now would only enable his bad behavior, fueling her pain even more.

"Margaret, are you asleep?"

"Wha...?"

"Are you asleep?"

"I was."

"Oh..."

"What is it, Sarah? It's late."

"I know. I just keep thinking about Charlie. It's so weird Charlie is sleeping with Patty. Don't you think?"

"Yeah, I guess."

"What does he see in her?" I mean she's married to his uncle. It's kind of creepy."

"Yeah."

"Maybe I did something wrong, but what?"

"Get some rest." Margaret shifted her covers.

"Maybe I didn't try hard enough. Maybe being away at school or..."

"Stop it Sarah!" Margaret's frustration was apparent.

"Do you really think he slept with her?" Sarah asked with desperation.

Margaret rolled over and looked at Sarah. "Why are you doing this to yourself?" It's not worth it to torture yourself like this. This is why you can't trust anyone but yourself. If he slept with her then there is nothing you can do about it. You need to get on with things. Don't let him bring you down."

"I know. But what if he didn't sleep with her?"

"Well, then you have nothing to worry about. So now we can all get some sleep."

"You think he slept with her don't you?"

"Stop it, Sarah. I don't know anything, but I'm tired and would like to get some sleep. May I go to sleep?"

"Yeah, okay. Sorry Margaret."

CHAPTER 30

Block Party

SARAH PLACED her arms behind her neck and looked up at the ceiling. The moonlight cast pockets of shadow against its texture. "Why would he do this to me?" She never thought this could happen. Maybe it wasn't meant to be?

Charlie and Sarah had always been opposites of each other. There was something very different about him, and that was why she was so attracted to him. He wasn't like most guys. He was quiet and he mostly kept to himself, and he had a dark, rebellious side to him which she felt was very sexy.

Charlie's imperfect life was something new for Sarah. Her life seemed so boring compared to his. His opposite ways drew her in and it seemed it was the same for Charlie. He experienced new things with Sarah that he never had growing up. He ate dinner and watched movies with her family at her home. He shared holidays and birthdays with them. They accepted him as part of their family, except maybe her dad.

When Sarah went off to college, she missed Charlie terribly. The late-night conversations, after her studies, they both shared dreams of the future. She couldn't help but feel a pang of loneliness without him by her side.

Determined to keep their bond strong, Sarah made it a habit to text Charlie paragraphs every day about her college life. She described her classes, her friends, and all the exciting experiences she was having on campus. She wanted him to be a part of it all, even from a distance.

Each evening, she would call him, eager to share the day's adventures. She would talk about the amazing parties, the bustling bars, and the laughs they would have missed out on together. But as time went on, she sensed a shift in his reactions.

Charlie seemed more frustrated with each conversation. Her excitement about college life only seemed to remind him of what he was missing out on. The more she shared, the more he seemed to withdraw.

When she was out having fun, she would think of Charlie. I wish he was here. He would be asleep now she thought to herself. He had to get up at 6:00 AM every morning, shower, eat breakfast and head to work. So, usually, he was in bed at 10:00 pm.

One night she forgot to call Charlie. It wasn't like that. They usually talked every night before he went to bed. She had gotten too drunk that night and even passed out at her girlfriend's house.

Sarah, Lou and Jennifer heard about this campus party through Facebook. The post read *Block Party. 137 Lafayette Street. SAT, April. 26th Sundown. BYOB*

Sarah, Lou and Jennifer decided to hit up the biggest party in town. They met up at Jennifer's place and cracked open a few drinks to kick off the night. Laughter filled the room as they reminisced and cracked jokes.

With no care for time, they finally set off for the party. The night air was cool as they made their way through the darkened streets. The distant thump of music grew louder with each step, guiding them to their destination.

As they turned the corner, the scene unfolded before them. The house at the end of the street was alive with energy, pulsating with beats and laughter. Cars lined the road, hinting at the number of partygoers inside.

Approaching the house, the trio felt the bass vibrating through their bodies, setting the tone for the night ahead. Red plastic cups clutched in the hands of the partygoers, they entered the sea of people spilling out onto the street.

Spotlights illuminated the scene, casting a surreal glow over the revelers. Groups of friends chatted animatedly, their voices blending with the music. The backyard was a hive of activity, with kegs dotted around like landmarks for the thirsty.

Sarah, Lou, and Jennifer immersed themselves in the lively atmosphere. Dancing, mingling, and making memories, they lost track of time in the whirlwind of fun.

"Wow, whoever is throwing this party must have spent a lot of money on beer."

Sarah hardly recognized anyone. The school was so big. She hardly ever saw the same face twice.

The more Sarah looked, the more people there seemed to be. It appeared to be in the hundreds. Jennifer pulled out a large bottle of wine and three plastic cups from beneath her jacket. Out of her pocket appeared a wine bottle opener.

"Let's crack this baby open."

"You came prepared."

"Yeah, I hate beer. I only drink if it's a last resort."

Jennifer poured a glass for each of them.

"By the looks of it around here, we need to do some catching up." Jennifer guzzled her first glass of wine. Lou and Sarah followed.

"Geez, look at all these people! I wonder if they all went to school. I don't recognize anyone." Sarah stated

"I bet some of these people don't even go to our school." Lou replied.

Jennifer refilled their glasses. They stood around for a while and talked. Jennifer was telling a story about one of her professors. He had gotten caught in the girl's bathroom doing it with one of his students after school hours. "Can you believe it? He was almost twenty years older than her? Good looking. All the girls just stare at him in class."

"Wow." Lou said with wide eyes. "All my teachers are boring."

"Some girl caught the two of them and turned them in. She was probably jealous that it wasn't her what he was doing. He resigned. Now we got this old fart of a guy that has a German accent that I can barely understand. I'm definitely going to do badly in his class and my dad is going to kill me. But I'm definitely not going to worry about that tonight."

"Amen sister."

Jennifer looked toward the house. "Let's go inside."

Sarah and Lou nodded in agreement.

The kitchen was filled with wall-to-wall people. In the corner of the kitchen, there was a group of people smoking some weed.

'So Lonely,' by the band 'The Police' was playing extremely loud.

"I feel low, I feel low, I feel so low, I feel so lonely." Jennifer was singing.

"Police. Old school music." Sarah replied.

"A bunch of crap if you ask me, "Lou rolled her eyes.

"No... they are really good." Sarah said with excitement.

Sting's voice was screaming out the words. Jennifer was grooving and singing the words out loud. The song made Sarah think about Charlie.

"Follow me." Jennifer pointed to herself.

"What?" Lou and Sarah could hardly hear her.

"I think I saw a guy that I know from my philosophy class."

Jennifer walked towards her classmate. Lou and Sarah followed. Jennifer continued to sing the song. He was next to two other guys. They were each drinking Guinness.

"Hey, Matt, right? From philosophy."

"Yeah?"

"I'm in your class. I sit three seats behind you."

He stared at her. "Uh..."

Sarah could tell he had no idea who she was. Jennifer didn't have a look that many people would remember. She was an average looking girl. Her hair was dark and wavy. Her hair was pulled back in a ponytail that night. She had a fair complexion and a large nose. Jennifer was slightly over-weight and she had large breasts, which she covered with her oversized jacket.

"Jennifer Hagen."

She said it loudly so he could hear it over the music.

"Oh yeah, philosophy."

He still had no idea. He was lying.

"These are my friends Lou and Sarah."

"Tim and Randy," he pointed to his buddies.

"What are you drinking?"

"Rosato."

"That stuff is disgusting," Tim said with a sour look on his face.

"Yeah, but it's cheap." Jennifer poured more wine into Lou and Sarah's glass.

Sarah put her hand over hers. "I'm okay"

"Are you kidding? Drink up. You're dragging behind."

Everyone looked at Sarah. Sarah looked at her plastic cup filled with pink wine. She had managed to drink half of it so far.

"I don't usually drink this much." Sarah stated.

"Come on," said Randy in a plaid shirt.

Sarah put the glass in her mouth. She took a big drink.

"Go ahead Sarah, drink the rest." Lou said.

Sarah gulped the rest of the wine. Jennifer immediately filled Sarah's glass full.

"Matt, do you know who lives here?"

"No, do you?"

"No, we just saw the post on Facebook."

The small living room was trashed. Beer bottles covered the room. Some of the bottles were filled with used cigarette butts. The floor was sticky and wet.

Some drunken guy was passed out on the couch snoring. "Do you see that?"

Lou laughed.

"Look at that guy. He's so gonna regret that."

The guy looked like he had a tattoo on his face. Words were written all over his face in black sharpie. Someone had even written on the layers of his ears.

"He's been that way since we got here," Randy stated. "Man he's gonna be pissed when he sees what they wrote on his face."

Matt seemed interested in Lou. He had moved around next to her.

"Hey, we need a refill," Matt's two buddies went to get some more beer.

Sarah felt herself getting light-headed. The wine was having an effect. It was starting to go down almost too easily. "Hey, give me some more of that Rosato stuff?" Sarah said giggling.

"Can't Stand Losing You" was now blaring through the speakers. Jennifer was dancing to it. She held up the wine bottle in her left hand and her glass in the other. She was moving her body back and forth.

"Hey, Matt."

Jennifer interrupted Lou and Matt's conversation. He seemed bothered. "Do you like the police?"

"Uh..."

"The band that's playing?"

"I guess so. Isn't this really old?"

"Yeah. I guess you call it suicide, but I'm too full to swallow my pride. "I can't, I can't, I can't stand losing...," Jennifer sang the words as if she were Sting.

Matt stared at Jennifer for a moment and then went back to talking to Lou. "Who's your friend?" Matt whispered in Lou's ear.

"Don't you know her? She says she's in your class."

"I've never seen her before."

Sarah started grooving with Jennifer. Matt's buddies came back with three beers as Sarah and Jennifer were spinning around.

"Shit, man, there's a shitload of people outside," Tim said. "The whole world must be here."

"They're down to five kegs and it's only 11:30. They'll be cleaned out soon at this rate," said the guy in plaid.

"The post said to bring your own beer." Matt stated as if he was speaking morally.

Jennifer's words were slurred. "No shit. Why do you think we brought our own wine?

"But we're out of Guinness and all that is left is this Old Milwaukee shit," said Randy.

"Oh man. I'm not drinking this shit." Tim retorted.

"Snobs." Jennifer stated as she fluttered around.

"This stuff is poison," Tim added as he swallowed hard on his next sip.

"Maybe we should go buy some more Guinness," Randy stated.

"Dude, I would but I'm short on cash right now." Tim replied.

"You don't have to tell me."

"I guess we are drinking Old Milwaukee until they run out."

"Shit man."

"Beggars can't be choosers," Jennifer said with a sly grin.

"Whatever."

Lou and Matt had moved to the couch. They were deep in conversation. He was sharing Lou's drink now. "Not too bad," he added.

Jennifer picked up the bottle of wine and stared at it. "Sarah, we might be drinking that Milwaukee shit soon too. We almost drank this whole bottle."

"Man, Rosato will kill you before Old Milwaukee. That's definitely poison to the liver. No way would you catch me drinking that shit.

Jennifer rolled her eyes. "You already said that, Randy." Jennifer retorted.

"It's working for me," Sarah stated.

"I kind of like this poison," Sarah said as she lifted her glass.

"Whatever man. I'll stick with this here shit instead."

Sarah was feeling good. "Fill me up."

"That's it, we are out." Jennifer was looking at the empty bottle. Images were distorted as she looked through the clear glass. Jennifer suddenly realized she better find a bathroom quickly.

"Where's the bathroom around here?"

"It's overflowing. You'll have to pee outside," said Randy.

"I'll be back."

"I'm going too", said Tim.

Jennifer and Tim walked out of the room.

"So, Sarah, what year are you?"

"Junior." She was swaying to the music.

"Me too."

"What are you majoring in?"

"Business."

"A business major." What are your plans when you graduate?

"Heck if I know... First, I have to graduate." She guzzled the rest of her wine. "Oh man I'm out."

"Wow. Looks likes you finished yours?" Randy stated.

"Can I have a sip of your beer?"

"Here, take it. I can't drink it."

She took a drink. "Yikes." She spit out the beer on the floor. Randy jumped back. "It doesn't go good with wine."

She returned her attention to the music. She spun on her tippy-toes, like a clumsy ballerina. As she spun, she tripped over her feet and went crashing to the floor. Beer spilled all over her. She was looking up at the ceiling.

"Hey, are you okay?" Randy said with a concerned voice.

"What happened?"

"You tripped and fell. Let me help you up." As he pulled Sarah off the floor, she had a strange look on her face.

"You, okay?"

"I don't feel so good. The room is spinning around."

"Don't you remember? You just got through spinning."

"I feel sick."

"See, I told you that stuff was poison."

"No really, I'm going to be sick."

Randy reached over to help her stand still. "Don't move. The feeling will pass in a minute."

"Hey, I'm back. Did anyone miss me? Hey, Sarah did you...?" Jennifer pulled Sarah from Randy's grasp and pulled her arm to turn her around. "Hey, did you hear me? Did you miss me?"

As Jennifer pulled her around, Sarah leaned her head and upper body forward. Before Jennifer knew it a spew of liquid landed on Jennifer's legs and dripped down her shoes. Jennifer tried to jump back but it was too late.

"Gross! This is gross." Jennifer stared at her feet. "Look at me, I'm covered in it."

Lou rushed over to Sarah.

"Sarah, are you okay? She must have drunk too much."

"No shit, Sherlock." Jennifer was shaking off the excess puke on her legs. "I smell disgusting."

"We need to get her home," said Sarah's roommate.

"Hey Lou." Matt asked for Lou's number.

"So, what, you two are an item now?" Jennifer said sarcastically.

"No, he's just giving me his number. It doesn't mean I'm going to call him."

"Yeah right."

Sarah was leaning over and hugging her knees. Her body was swaying back and forth.

"Come on Sarah. My place is not too far from here. Why don't you stay the night with me?" Jennifer said.

What started as a simple gathering quickly escalated into chaos. Hundreds of people flooded into the party, turning a small get-together into a massive event.

As the night went on, the party spiraled out of control. The cops were called to break up the drunken bash, but the revelers paid no heed to their warnings. The officers found themselves overwhelmed by the sheer number of party-goers and the wildness of the scene before them.

The house and yard became a scene of destruction, with furniture overturned and decorations destroyed. Riots erupted, and a group of party-goers even broke into the Student Union, hungry for more fun. They raided the pantry and the walk-in refrigerator, cooking up a storm in the kitchen to satisfy their appetites.

A year later, a second Facebook post was sent out, reminiscing about that unforgettable night of chaos and revelry.

```
2nd Anniversary Block Party.
17 North Spring Street
Sat. April 30th
BYOB - 7:00 PM …Be there or
be square.
```

This time Sarah decided to pass on the party. Lou and her boyfriend Matt wanted to at least check out the scene. That night they casually walked past the place where the party was going to take place. The cops were ready this time. Lou and Matt kept walking.

That night, the night when Sarah threw up on Jennifer, Charlie sat on his living room sofa with his phone clutched tightly in his hand. He was waiting eagerly for a call from Sarah.

The clock struck 8:30, the agreed time for Sarah's call, but the phone remained silent. Charlie's heart sank, and he sent her a text to check in. No response. He sent another text, still nothing.

As the night wore on, Charlie's hope began to fade. He fell into a restless sleep on the sofa, the phone still in his hand.

At 4:00 in the morning, he woke up with a start. Sarah never called. She never texted. A wave of sadness washed over him, but he tried to push it aside, pretending he was okay with being stood up. Sarah still feels guilty to this day for not calling Charlie that night.

CHAPTER 31

Stick to the Road

STILL UNABLE TO SLEEP, Sarah looked out the open window. The wind was blowing gently, causing the curtains to sway softly. She couldn't shake off the thoughts that kept her mind racing. "I can't repair this." Her father would never forgive him. Charlie has gone too far," Sarah thought to herself. Sarah had always felt a twinge of guilt deep within her chest every time she thought about Charlie.

She and Charlie were like two sides of the same coin - one shiny and pristine, the other worn and tarnished. She had everything handed to her on a silver platter, while Charlie struggled and toiled for every little thing he had. The contrast between their lives weighed heavily on Sarah's conscience. She had never known the feeling of not having enough, of having to work hard just to make ends meet.

Despite their differences, Sarah knew they shared a common struggle - the need to prove themselves in a world that often looked down on them. Just as she worked twice as hard to be recognized for her efforts, Charlie faced the same uphill battle. He probably saw her as she saw

Margaret - someone who had it all without having to lift a finger.

As Sarah watched the moonlight dance on the leaves outside, she wondered if Charlie ever resented her for the privileges she had been bestowed with. Perhaps they weren't so different after all. Deep down, they were both just trying to find their place in a world that felt like it was stacked against them.

As Sarah lay there, trying to make sense of everything, she couldn't shake off the feeling of betrayal that clung to her like a shadow. Charlie had always been a mystery to her, but she never thought he would be capable of hurting her like this.

She closed her eyes, trying to block out the flood of emotions raging inside her. Maybe it was time to accept that some things are just not meant to be. Maybe their differences were too vast to bridge, despite the undeniable chemistry that had always cracked between them.

Sarah rolled over on her side, her thoughts drifting as she gazed at her peacefully sleeping sister, Margaret. Bathed in the silvery glow of the moon, Margaret looked like a goddess, her porcelain skin flawless and her lips a deep crimson. Sarah couldn't help but admire her sister's beauty.

Yawning, Sarah turned her attention to the moon outside, its ethereal light casting a tranquil glow over the room. The wind whispered gently through the open window, carrying with it a sense of serenity that enveloped the space.

Closing her eyes, Sarah felt herself being carried away by the gentle sounds of the night. The moon's energy seemed to seep into her very being, calming her mind and stirring her spirits. In that moment, she felt a deep connection to the world around her, a sense of peace that she had longed for.

* * *

STICK TO THE ROAD, Sarah thought, her breath billowing in the frigid night air. The moon would be her only guiding light, a pale, ghostly beacon to lead her home. The lightly snow covered asphalt seemed to stretch on endlessly, but she knew this was the way.

She hadn't seen a single car pass since she stumbled onto the deserted road, her bare feet leaving smeared crimson prints in her wake. Sarah still couldn't fathom how she had ended up here, disoriented and alone in the inky blackness of the forest. It wasn't like her to wander aimlessly, especially not in the dead of night, wearing nothing but a thin, white nightgown that offered little protection from the biting chill.

She must be out of her mind, Sarah mused, her thoughts racing. Yet despite the alarming circumstances, her body felt strangely invigorated, almost unnaturally so. The deep gashes on the soles of her feet no longer ached, the pain having given way to a pulsing, primal energy.

Driven by some unseen force, Sarah pressed onward, her pace quickening with each stride. She was close now. She could feel it. Soon, she would be home, and all of this would fade into nothing more than a distant, dream like memory. Or would it?

The moonlight bathed the quiet countryside in a soft glow, illuminating the familiar path as she hurried towards home. Sarah could see her house perched atop the small hill in the distance, its outline standing in stark contrast to the inky darkness. Her heart raced, fueled by growing anxiety - her family must be worried sick.

As she approached the house, a chill ran down her spine. The front door hung open, an ominous invitation to the unknown. Steeling her nerves, Sarah slowly stepped inside, her bare feet whispering against the smooth wooden floor.

"Hello? Is anyone home?" she called out, her voice tight with concern. "Mom? Dad? Margaret?"

Silence was her only answer, save for the faint creaking of the old house settling. Sarah's eyes scanned the dimly lit entryway, searching for any sign of her loved ones. Where could they be?

She moved further into the house, her footsteps quickening as a sense of dread began to consume her. The kitchen seemed untouched. There was one plum left in a decorative bowl in the middle of the table. The plum felt firm in Sarah's hand, its deep purple hue glistening invitingly. She almost took a bite, savoring the sweet juices she anticipated, when a sudden unease caused her to pause. Looking closer, she noticed discoloration and a softening texture, maggots now covered the plum - the plum was rotten, far beyond its prime.

"Ugh... gross," she muttered, her face twisting in disgust as the fruit slipped from her grasp and hit the floor with a dull thud. Red-purple stains now mark her fingertips, a stark contrast to her pale skin. Wiping them hurriedly on her gown, she made her way to the family room, a growing sense of unease stirring within her.

The fire in the hearth burned with an unusual intensity, the flames flickering and dancing as if in slow motion. The crackle and pop of the wood seemed amplified, each sound carrying an ominous weight. Sarah stood transfixed, her chilled skin soaking in the radiant heat, but her mind racing with unanswered questions.

"Mom... Dad, hello ... Margaret?" She moved quickly back into the foyer.

"Mom, Dad...Mom. Where are you?"

She continuously looked around the area, towards the kitchen, down the hallway and back to the family room, then up the stairs. She called up the stairs. No answer.

Bang!

The sound raced through and around the high walls of the surrounding area. Sarah jumped. A noise came from the study. It was probably her dad. But why hasn't he answered me? Sarah felt scared. She proceeded with caution.

She headed left down the hallway, the floorboards creaking ominously beneath her steps. The door on the right was open, and a faint scent of vanilla wafted into the dimly lit corridor. Steeling her nerves, she peered inside the bathroom, but the room was empty save for a single candle flickering on the counter.

Her heart pounded in her ears as she turned her attention to the open door of the study. A faint light filtered into the hallway, beckoning her forward. She closed her eyes, taking a deep, shaky breath in a futile attempt to calm her racing thoughts. This was ridiculous; she needed to get a grip.

Forcing her eyes open, she froze as she caught sight of a figure standing next to the study door on the left of the hallway. Her breath caught in her throat as she recognized the familiar form of Charlie, his expression unreadable.

"What are you doing here?" she managed to whisper, her voice trembling with a mixture of fear and confusion.

Charlie said nothing, his gaze fixed on her with an intensity that made her skin crawl. The air seemed to crackle with an unseen tension, the shadows in the hallway casting ominous shapes that danced across the walls.

She swallowed hard. Her mouth suddenly dry. "Charlie, answer me. What's going on?"

The weight of his stare bore into her, and for a moment, she could have sworn she saw a glint of something dark and dangerous in his eyes.

"Why are you acting so weird?" Charlie pointed to the study.

Sarah walked into the room. She was horrified by what she saw. Her father was gagged and tied to his chair. His voice sounded muffled beneath the cloth.

"Oh my God, Charlie. Did you do this?"

She heard a sound behind her. Sarah spun around on her toes, her heart racing. There in the doorway stood her sister, Margaret, with crimson eyes, dressed head to toe in black. The long coat she wore brushed against the ground as she took a step forward, her expression undecipherable.

Sarah glanced at her father, bound and gagged, and then back at Margaret. "Why would you tie him up?" she demanded, her voice trembling.

Margaret's lips curled into a chilling smile. "Because, dear sister, he stands in the way of my plans." She moved closer, the floorboards creaking beneath her feet.

"What plans? What are you talking about?" Sarah felt a rising panic within her. This couldn't be happening - not to her family.

"You always were the naive one," Margaret hissed. "You are going to help me."

Sarah's eyes widened in horror as realization dawned on her. "No, I won't!" she cried.

"It's already started."

The air crackled with palpable tension as Sarah stared at her sister, her eyes wide with a mixture of fear and bewilderment. "What has started?" she demanded, her voice trembling.

Margaret's gaze was unwavering, her expression grave. "It's your destiny."

Sarah felt a strange sensation rippling through her body, a tingling that intensified with each passing moment. "No, this can't be happening," she whispered, her heart pounding in her chest.

Suddenly, a sharp pain shot through her spine, and she doubled over, gasping. Her skin began to tingle, and she felt as if her very cells were undergoing a transformation. Sarah watched in horror as her hands started to morph, the fingers elongating and sharpening into talons.

"What's happening to me?" she cried, panic rising in her voice.

Her sister placed a hand on her shoulder. Her touch was surprisingly gentle. "It's your birthright, Sarah. The power that lies dormant within you is awakening.

You are becoming what you were always meant to be."

Sarah looked up at her, her eyes pleading. "I don't want this. I can't control it. Please make it stop!"

But her sister's expression remained resolute. "It's too late, dear. The process has already begun, and there's no turning back. You will embrace your destiny, whether you're ready or not."

The walls of the room seemed to close in as her mind descended into the abyss. The darkness within her stirred, a primordial beast yearning to break free. She could feel its savage hunger clawing at the edges of her consciousness, a relentless force threatening to consume her.

With trembling hands, she tried in vain to maintain control, to push back the encroaching madness. But it was a futile effort – the beast was far too powerful, its thirst for destruction too great to be contained.

A guttural howl erupted from her throat. Her once-familiar features twisted and contorted, giving way to a visage of pure, unadulterated fury. The beast had emerged, its soulless eyes scanning the room, taking in every detail with a predator's precision.

Robert cowered, his heart pounding in his chest as the creature's gaze fell upon him. The air was thick with the scent of his fear, a potent lure that the beast could not resist. Another bone-chilling wail pierced the silence, and in an instant, the creature lunged forward, its razor-sharp fangs bared and ready to tear him asunder.

Time seemed to slow to a crawl as Robert stared into the abyss of the beast's eyes. His own mortality lay bare before the raw, unbridled power that now stood before him. In that moment, he knew that his fate had been sealed, and that the relentless march of darkness would not be denied.

CHAPTER 32

Robert

ROBERT WAS SITTING in his office contemplating his and his family's future. Robert gazed up at the picture hanging on the wall, a faint smile playing on his lips. It was a snapshot from years ago, back when he and his old friend Paul were just a couple of scrappy entrepreneurs, toasting their newfound success in a small bar downtown.

Next to the photo, a collage of awards and accolades bore witness to the journey they'd embarked on - the long nights, the endless brainstorming sessions, the victories and the stumbles along the way. Those were the glory days, when the company was just taking root and every milestone felt monumental.

Robert couldn't help but feel a pang of nostalgia as he recalled those formative years. He and Paul had been thick as thieves, relying on each other for support and inspiration. They'd been through it all together - the highs of landing a big client, the lows of a project gone awry. But no matter what, they always had each other's backs.

His business idea happened with his cousin when Robert's world was turned upside down. His mother had made the difficult decision to sell the family home, the one he'd grown up in. After his father passed away, she just couldn't keep up with the demands of the old house on her own.

Robert remembered how hard that transition had been, leaving behind the familiar comforts of his childhood. But through it all, Paul had been there for him, offering a listening ear and a shoulder to lean on. Their bond had only grown stronger in the face of adversity.

Now, years later, as Robert gazed upon the remnants of those early triumphs, he couldn't help but feel grateful. Grateful for the memories, the lessons learned, and most of all, the unwavering friendship that carried them through it all. Whatever the future held, he knew he could count on Paul to be by his side.

It was supposed to be a simple real estate transaction, but for Samantha, his mother, it felt like the end of an era. Ever since her husband passed away last year, the old family home has been more of a burden than a blessing. The house and the sprawling 500-acre forest land were too much for her and her son Robert to maintain on their own.

"The house and the land should bring in a pretty penny for my retirement and your future," Samantha told Robert over dinner one evening. "This is what your father would have wanted."

Robert nodded solemnly. He knew how much the Victorian house meant to his mother, but he also understood the practicality of downsizing. "We can get a nice little place closer to the city," he said, reaching across the table to give her hand a reassuring squeeze. "It'll be good for us."

And so, the house went up for sale. To their surprise, it didn't take long for a buyer to materialize - a local timber company that was looking to expand its operations. Not only did they offer a generous sum for the house, but they were willing to pay an absolute fortune for the forest land as well.

"The timing is perfect," Samantha said, her eyes shining with a mixture of excitement and nostalgia as they signed the paperwork. "It's like it was all meant to be."

Robert watched his mother carefully, knowing how bittersweet this moment must be for her. But as they walked through the familiar rooms one last time, he also felt a sense of possibility - for a new chapter, a fresh start. The future may have been uncertain, but it was theirs to shape.

"Your father would be proud," she murmured. "This is the right thing to do."

Robert had been trying to figure out a way to make some extra money after graduation, and this inspiration led to an idea. Immediately, Robert contacted his cousin Paul, and they decided to use the money and take a gamble on real estate after they finished college.

At first, Robert's mother was a bit concerned about their plan. "Real estate? Isn't that risky?" she asked. Her brow furrowed. But Robert was confident, and he set out to convince her that this was a sure thing.

"Come on, Mom," he said, a mischievous grin spreading across his face. "Paul and I have done our research. We know the market, and we've found the perfect property to flip into a fortune. This is going to be huge. I can feel it."

His mother still looked uncertain, but Robert could see a glimmer of hope in her eyes. She wanted nothing more than her son to succeed, even if it meant taking a chance.

"Alright," she said, letting out a deep sigh. "I trust you. Just promise me you'll be careful, okay?"

Robert pulled his mom into a tight hug. "I promise, Mom. This is going to be the best investment we've ever made. You'll see."

And with that, the wheels were set in motion. Robert and Paul dove headfirst into the world of real estate.

Robert had always been fascinated by the potential of Old Town Portland. As a university student in the city, he would often wander through the historic district, admiring the charming buildings that lined the riverfront, even as they fell into disrepair.

Robert used some of the inherited money from the sale of his family's land, and he knew exactly what he wanted to do with it. He approached his cousin with this idea, a plan to revitalize Old Town.

"Can you believe all this potential is going to waste?" Robert said, gesturing to the vacant, dilapidated buildings. "I think with the right vision and some hard work, we could turn this place around."

His cousin was skeptical at first, but Robert's infectious enthusiasm won him over. Together, they decided to take the plunge and start purchasing some of the abandoned properties, one by one.

It was no easy task. The buildings were in rough shape, requiring extensive renovations to bring them back to their former glory. There were zoning regulations to navigate, construction delays to overcome, and plenty of naysayers who doubted their vision.

But Robert and his cousin pressed on, fueled by a shared belief in the untapped potential of Old Town. Bit by bit, they restored the historic facades, modernized the interiors, and brought in a mix of residential, retail, and commercial tenants.

As each newly revitalized building opened its doors, the energy in the neighborhood began to shift. People were drawn to the charming streets, the bustling shops and restaurants, and the stunning views of the river. Property values started to rise, and the once-forgotten district was suddenly the talk of the town.

Before long, Robert and his cousin had transformed the entire landscape of Old Town.

Robert and Paul have always been a dynamic duo when it came to real estate. The two cousins had an uncanny knack for spotting hidden gems and turning them into profitable ventures. Their latest project was no exception.

With their pockets full, from the successful demolition and parking structure in Old Town, the pair had their sights set on the booming city of Portland. The influx of Californians seeking a more serene lifestyle was creating a surge in demand for commercial space.

Without hesitation, Robert and Paul plunged headfirst into their next big investment. They scoured the city, analyzing market trends and scouting prime locations. Finally, they landed on a promising plot of land on the outskirts of downtown.

The old warehouse that stood there was nothing to write home about, but Robert and Paul saw its potential. They quickly assembled a team of demolition experts and got to work, clearing the way for their grand plan.

As the rubble was carted away, the duo began mapping out their vision – a multi-tiered commercial complex that would cater to the needs of the growing population. Retail spaces, office suites, and even a parking garage were all part of the blueprint.

With their usual blend of calculated risk-taking and entrepreneurial spirit, Robert and Paul poured their profits into bringing this project to life. The construction process was a whirlwind, but they never lost sight of the end goal.

And when the dust finally settled, the results were nothing short of spectacular. The remodeled buildings were quickly snapped up by eager tenants, and the parking structure became a coveted commodity in the bustling city.

At just 29 years old, Robert couldn't help but feel a sense of pride as he surveyed their latest creation. He and Paul had once again proven that with a little grit, a lot of vision, and a healthy dose of luck, anything was possible.

As they set their sights on the next venture, the duo knew that their journey was far from over. The thrill of the chase, the rush of a successful gamble – it was all part of what made them tick. And with Old Town's skyrocketing prices in their rearview mirror, they were ready to tackle the next big challenge.

As their venture continued to grow, Robert and Paul knew they needed to bring in a team to help manage their operations. With their growing reputation, Paige Incorporated was in high demand, and they soon expanded their reach beyond their local area. They started taking on similar development projects in other parts of the country, leveraging their expertise and connections to replicate their success.

By the time Robert was 34 years old, he found himself worth a staggering 350 million dollars. He couldn't help but chuckle to himself as he reflected on how far he and Paul had come. From a couple of ambitious dreamers to the co-owners of a thriving national real estate empire – it was the stuff of movies.

"The two of us, a team forever," Robert thought, his heart swelling with pride and gratitude for his lifelong friend and business partner.

When Robert first heard about the problem from Paul, he didn't think much of it. People always seemed to overreact, and he had experienced this more times than he could count. But as Paul's voice grew increasingly strained, Robert realized this might be more serious than he initially thought.

"Robert, it looks bad. We need to get together immediately," Paul said, his words laced with urgency.

Robert let out a small sigh. "I don't think I can get back until Thursday," he replied casually.

"They're extremely concerned, and I've seen it, it's bad. I'm not sure they can wait much longer," Paul pressed.

Sensing the gravity of the situation, Robert paused for a moment. "Look, Paul, I'll try and get home tomorrow evening. Have Mike drop off the drawings at my house. If no one's home, tell him to leave them on the porch. "I'll go over them as soon as I get in," he said, his tone still relatively relaxed.

As he hung up the phone, Robert couldn't help but wonder what kind of problem his colleagues had so worked up. It must be something serious, he thought. Nonetheless, he didn't let it faze him too much. He had dealt with crises before and knew that keeping a level head was crucial.

Robert stared in disbelief at the stack of legal documents on his desk. The letters that followed all said the same thing - Paige Incorporated was being sued for severe negligence. It was a nightmare scenario. The words seemed to scream in his face.

He had spent hours poring over every detail, looking at every possible solution. But there was no way to resolve this problem. The construction site had been prepared incorrectly, and now the brand new apartment building was being declared structurally unsafe, due to the mass soil erosion that had been tearing away at its foundation.

No one was allowed to set foot inside the building anymore. It stood there, empty and abandoned, a looming testament to their failure. Robert picked up one of the crumpled letters, the paper crinkling in his hand. With a frustrated growl, he wadded it up and hurled it against the wall, watching it bounce to the floor.

This was a mess of epic proportions. Their reputation was in tatters, the company facing crippling lawsuits, not to mention the families who had been displaced from their new residences. Robert dragged a hand down his face, feeling the weight of it all pressing down on his shoulders.

How did it all go so wrong? He replayed the decisions, the site assessments, the construction process in his mind, searching for where they had gone off the rails. But no matter how he looked at it, there was no easy fix, no way to undo the damage that had been done.

With a heavy sigh, Robert turned his gaze back to the ever-growing stack of legal documents. Time to dig in and start damage control. This was going to be an uphill battle, but failure was not an option. Paige Incorporated's future - and his own - depended on him finding a way through this crisis.

CHAPTER 33

Rag Doll

PATTY JUMPED and a small yelp came out of her mouth when Charlie walked into the kitchen.

"God Charlie, you scared me."

Charlie looked frazzled and he seemed very upset. "Yeah sorry."

"Where have you been?" The hospital called and said that you had left without their approval. I've been worried sick."

"Fucking hospitals."

"A gunshot is not something to play around with. Let me take you back to the hospital."

"No fucking way."

"Anyway, how are you feeling?" Patty asked, her eyes wide open with kindness.

"What do you think?" Charlie retorted.

"What is it, Charlie?"

Charlie was pacing back and forth in the kitchen.

"Sit down and tell me what's the matter."

He realized that he must have appeared uneasy.

"Do you want something to drink?"

He pulled the chair from under the table.

"How about a beer?" He sat down. He grabbed his injured arm. It was throbbing.

She walked over with his beer. Patty appeared refreshed as if a great weight had been lifted off her shoulders.

"Have you heard anything about Mitch?" "Yeah, still no sign of him."

"He'll show up."

She sat next to him. Charlie was still rubbing his arm. "How is it?"

"It hurts."

"We need to change into a bandage."

Patty leaned forward.

Charlie stopped her. "Not now."

"What's wrong?"

"It's all over my future... in the fucking trash."

"What do you mean?"

"What do you think I mean?"

He gulped his beer.

"Is it Sarah?" Her voice quivered, hoping his thoughts weren't consumed by his girlfriend.

"Yeah."

Patty really didn't want to hear about Sarah, but she listened anyway.

"Unless I can find a way... to change his mind... shit I don't know." He took a deep breath. "Sarah's father convinced her that I'm some kind of monster. She won't even talk to me."

"How do you know this? Did you call her?"

"No, I stopped by the house."

"What? When?"

"A while ago, before I came here."

"Wow, I wasn't expecting that," Patty stated.

"Got stopped by the cops too."

Charlie took the speeding ticket out of his pocket and put it on the table. Patty looked at it and then at Charlie.

Now she suddenly wanted him to continue. "A speeding ticket?"

"Two hundred and seventy five dollars. Fucking day. It just keeps getting worse."

"So, you've definitely made up your mind about us. Is that why you went over there?" She looked down at the ticket and picked it up and then put it down again.

"Patty... I don't know what to say." He sighed.

Charlie rubbed his temples. "It doesn't matter now anyway. I've ruined everyone's life. Yours, mine,... Sarah's. Her father will never allow me into the family. He's never going to trust me again. Shit, I could have done something with my life. My head is killing me."

Patty could sense that he was trying to hold back his anger. "Charlie, you can still be happy. Maybe it's not as bad as you think."

"Fuck, are you crazy?" He leaned forward.

She pulled her body back away from him. "You're scaring me, Charlie."

"You tell me how I'm going to be happy. The girl that I've devoted myself to, for over four and a half years, fucking hates me. I've tried to be patient with her being gone most of the time at college, which annoys the crap out of me by the way. She now thinks I am some crazy lunatic because I hit her."

"You hit her?" "Fuck, yeah, I did."

Patty looked at him with uncertainty. She was starting to feel a bit uncomfortable.

"Mr. Asshole had to get involved in my business. Her sister told me that I only thought about myself. Her father had to restrain me once again and he told me to leave. What do you think? Do I still have a chance?" He was loud now.

"I didn't realize things had gotten that bad. I thought maybe all this between you and Sarah was because of your feelings for me. You never intended to leave her, did you?"

"Shit, I don't know. It's all a big fucking mess." He swallowed down some of his beer and slammed the bottle on the table.

"Charlie, you need to calm down."

"That's all I ever do. My whole life I've had to hold onto everything. Patty I'm sick and tired of it. I'm not going to let them do this to me."

Patty slowly backed away.

Charlie realized she was scared. "God, Patty, I'm sorry. It's just that..." He slumped into his chair like a rag doll.

* * *

IT WAS a bittersweet moment for Patty. She could see the guilt and sadness etched on his face as he sat across from her. She had always known, deep down, that Charlie's heart belonged to Sarah. The way his eyes lit up whenever she was around, the gentle way he spoke her name - it was painfully obvious to Patty that she could never truly compete.

She sighed heavily, a lump forming in her throat. Charlie had been her closest confidant, her rock through so many trials and tribulations. To lose him now, to Sarah of all people, felt like a betrayal. But Patty knew in her heart that it was no one's fault. Love was a fickle thing, and it had chosen to blossom between Charlie and Sarah, regardless of the complicated circumstances that bound the three of them together.

Patty steeled herself, straightening her shoulders. As much as it pained her, she knew she had to let Charlie go. Their love, while passionate and real, was doomed from the start. Society would never accept it - they were bound by blood, even if not by family. It was a hopeless endeavor. This wasn't what she wanted to hear, but memories came flooding back despite her efforts to push them away.

She thought about how she had felt when she believed he was gone forever, when she saw him lying on the floor bleeding. The agony of that moment was almost too much to bear. There was so much blood. She couldn't tell where he had been shot. She had prayed with every fiber of her being that he would pull through, that she would have the chance to see his face, hear his voice one more time.

The depth of her love for him still astounded her. He had been there for her through the darkest period of her life, never wavering from his support and care. He had changed her in ways she could hardly fathom - giving her the confidence to embrace her desires as a woman once more.

From the moment they met, she felt a deep, magnetic pull toward him. What had started as a tentative friendship had blossomed into a profound connection that defied explanation. The circumstances that had brought them together had been nothing short of bizarre, but Patty knew that fate had intervened.

Patty stared at Charlie. He looked so defeated. Charlie's head lay on the side of the table, his exhaustion evident in every line on his face. He looked like an old man. The shadows in the creases oaround his eyes were exaggerated against his dark skin. His bloodshot eyes stared vacantly at the beer bottle he was twirling, his rough, jagged facial hair a testament to the weariness consuming him.

"Charlie...?" a voice called out, gentle and concerned.

He looked up, his gaze meeting Patty's worried eyes. "Everything will be okay," she assured, offering a sympathetic smile.

Charlie continued to swirl the bottle.

CHAPTER 34

The Dark Intruder

GWEN WALKED INTO THE STUDY. Robert was working on his computer. His eyes were bloodshot.

"Robert, we need to talk."

"It's late Gwen. I'm trying to finish up some things before I go to sleep."

"Do you know what time it is? It's almost 2:30. You've been in here for hours."

"Is it that time already?" Robert looked at his watch.

"Why are you up?"

"It was the oddest thing. I was fast asleep and then something woke me up." Gwen rubbed her eyes. "I thought it was you, but no one was there." Gwen shivered." It may have been thunder. It looks like a storm might be heading our way."

"Hmm..." Robert seemed a million miles away.

"Well anyway, I realized you hadn't come to bed."

"I'm way behind on my work."

"I think we should talk."

"Now?" Roberts eyes lifted above his reading glasses.

"We really need to talk."

His eyes had returned to his computer. He was clicking on the keyboard.

"Robert, please, it's important."

Robert sighed. "Gwen...I'm busy. My work happens to be important too." Robert kept on typing.

"Just for once, can you pay attention to me?" Her voice was stern.

He looked up and leaned back in his chair. Robert rocked his body back and forth. "So, what's so important that you can't wait till morning?"

"It's about...I need to tell you something..."

"So, what's so important?" He just looked at her as if he already knew what she was going to say.

Gwen took a deep breath. "You were right. You were right about me having an affair." She sat in one of the chairs opposite Robert. She pulled her knees up to her chest. Her plaid pajama bottoms looked worn at the knees. Robert leaned further back into his chair.

"Aren't you going to say anything?"

"What do you want me to say Gwen?"

"I've been seeing him for almost a year."

Robert looked exhausted. "Wait what? But..."

"How did you know about us?"

"Gwen you're my wife. We share our lives together." He exaggerated. He had only just put it together, but she didn't have to know that.

She put her head to her knees. Her blond hair fell forward over her blue T-shirt. "I didn't think you even noticed me anymore." Gwen talked between her knees.

" A year..."

"Robert, I'm sorry. I don't know what's gotten into me. Our marriage."

He leaned forward and picked up a pen. He moved the pen around in his fingers. His mind wasn't focused on her words. He threw the pen across the room.

"Shit Gwen, a year is a long time." He rubbed the top of his eyebrows

"Don't you want to know why?"

"Why? Fuck Gwen. What do I want to know who it is?"

You know I've been cheating but you don't know who it is?"

Robert felt suddenly stupid.

'Don't pretend you don't know who it is. It's Mitch."

"What the fuck? You've been sleeping with that prick Mitch Connor?"

"I know that's why you checked up on him."

"Gwen, he's a fucking narcissist!" Robert pounded his hand down on the desk.

"I didn't know about those things. I really had no idea." Gwen pleaded.

"God Gwen, he's crazy and he could have hurt you."

"I ..."

"You're my wife. You're the mother of my children. Was it worth it? Do you love him?"

Gwen began to cry. "Robert, I'm so sorry."

"You're sorry?"

"I am. I've been so stupid."

"Why Mitch?"

"I don't know. He was nice to me."

"Nice to you? Yeah, that's fucking great. Is that what it takes to get you into bed these days?"

"Please Robert, you're being mean."

"This is just perfect. He's nice all right. Nice until he doesn't get what he wants."

"Oh God, Robert, I've been so foolish."

"That's right Gwen you have been very foolish to destroy everything we have worked for. He's probably got several girlfriends."

Gwen was crying uncontrollably.

"Do you love him?"

"Once... I thought I did."

Robert looked like someone had just punched him in the stomach.

"No, Robert, I don't love him. I've always loved you. I know that now. I didn't know then, but I know now. I've been so wrong. It's killing me not to tell you."

He looked straight at her. "It seems convenient, don't you think? I mean, you decided to tell me this after you found out he might have assaulted these young women."

"No Robert...I don't know. I've been so confused for so long. You're never home and we never talk anymore. I felt like we had grown apart. He paid attention to me and I was lonely."

"I'm lonely too, but I made a promise to you."

"I'm sorry. Please forgive me. Please, I told Mitch it was over."

Robert suddenly looked worried.

"What is it Robert?"

"When you ended it, was he mad? Of course he's mad." Robert retorted.

"Yes... he was." Gwen replied.

"Shit. One of the girls that he assaulted claimed that he went crazy and beat her up when she tried to break it off with him."

"Are you sure?"

"Yes." Why would I make that up Gwen?"

"Robert, Mitch was really mad."

"What did he say?"

"I can't remember. I don't know. He said I was being dramatic."

"Okay. Everything is fine. We just have to be careful. You can't go near him ever again. None of us. Block his number."

"I did."

"Good."

"Look at what I've done to all of you." Gwen was frazzled. "Can you ever forgive me?"

"I don't know... We will figure this out."

The door to the study suddenly opened with a creak, startling Robert and Gwen. They turned to see a mysterious figure silhouetted in the doorway, dressed head-to-toe in black and wearing a cloth mask over their face, their eyes covered with goggles. In the intruder's gloved hand was a gun with a menacing silencer attached.

"What the...hell is going on?" Robert stammered, his voice trembling as he tried to stand from his chair, but the chair got stuck underneath the heavy desk, preventing him from rising.

The black-clad figure swiftly moved towards Robert, pressing the cold steel barrel of the gun against his temple. Robert felt a chill run down his spine, his legs shaking uncontrollably. He knew this person was not to be trifled with.

"Don't move," the intruder rasped in a distorted, deep, unidentifiable voice. "You either," the figure now looked at Gwen. "I will shoot him."

Robert glanced frantically at Gwen, who sat frozen in her chair, her face pale with terror. He had to comply - their lives depended on it. Swallowing hard, he replied, "We will cooperate."

The person motioned for Robert to walk over to Gwen. She was crouched in her chair like a frightened little girl. Robert's hand accidentally knocked over a stack of books, causing a loud banging sound to hit the wood floor. The noise made Gwen jump and a yelp escaped her throat.

The intruder jabbed the gun into Robert's back, the barrel pressing firmly against his spine. Robert's heart raced as he felt the cold metal digging into him. He knew he had to stay calm for Gwen's sake.

Grasping her trembling hand, Robert whispered, "Gwen, just do what he says, everything will be all right." Robert's voice was low and intense, masking the fear that threatened to overtake him. Gwen's eyes were wide with terror, but she nodded slightly, squeezing Robert's hand.

The person in black held out a rope and motioned Robert to tie his wife's hands together. Robert's heart raced as he stared into Gwen's terrified eyes. With a shaking hand, he took the rope and slowly wrapped it around her delicate wrists. The coarse fibers cut into her soft skin, making her wince.

"I'm so sorry, Gwen," Robert whispered as he leaned in to kiss her forehead. He could feel her whole body trembling under his touch.

The armed figure barked an order, motioning for Robert to step away. Gwen's eyes went wide with panic.

"No, don't leave me!" she cried out, her voice cracking with fear.

Robert fought back tears as he forced himself to move away, leaving his beloved wife at the mercy of their captor.

"It's okay, Gwen. I'm right here," he said, his tone desperate and strained, trying to convey a sense of calm he didn't feel.

The person in black stood menacingly between them, the gun still pointed at Robert's head. The air was thick with tension as Robert stared in horror at the scene unfolding before him. The intruder shot Gwen in her leg, continuing by hitting her over her head with the gun. Gwen fell and lay motionless on the ground, a devastating blow rendering her unconscious.

Time seemed to slow down as Robert's gaze fixated on the attacker, his dark silhouette towering over Gwen's limp form. Adrenaline surged through Robert's veins, fueling a primal need for vengeance. He clenched his fists, every muscle in his body tense and ready to strike. Robert's blood boiled with rage as he resisted with all his strength to attack. He would surely be shot too.

"You fucking asshole," Robert spat through his gritted teeth. The intruder motioned him to move back around the desk and sit back down in his chair. Robert did it reluctantly. "Please...I don't understand. What do you want from me?" The person stood over him, their weapon trained steadily on Robert's prone form. "Please don't hurt my family. I'll get you anything you ask for," he pleaded.

The person in the black mask stood silently, seemingly contemplating Robert's words. "I have access to plenty of money. I'll give it to you if you don't hurt my family," Robert continued, desperation creeping into his voice. The intruder didn't reply which further infuriated Robert. "Who the fuck are you?" The intruder stood still. "Is that you Mitch in that ridiculous black costume? Show yourself." The intruder seemed to enjoy Robert acting out in such desperation. The person's finger tightened on the trigger, their expression betraying no emotion. "You think you got me? Believe me I will ruin your life." Robert's angry words echoed through the room.

The muffled voice from behind the mask spoke again, "Say a prayer."

"What? I'm not religious. I don't understand," Robert replied, his eyes locked on the masked intruder.

"Then make something up. Include your family," the voice commanded.

Robert's mind raced as he desperately tried to think of the right words. Taking a deep breath, he began, his tone intense and pleading. "Thank you, God, for watching over my family. Protect them from harm in this terrible situation. Give me the strength to get them to safety. Please, I beg of you, spare us..."

"That was beautiful."

The dark intruder fired a single shot. A deafening crack echoed through the room, as Robert felt a searing pain rip through his head. He crashed backwards, then forward, his limb body buckling underneath him.

CHAPTER 35

Reprehensive

GWEN SLOWLY LIFTED her throbbing head off the area rug covering the wood floor. Her vision was blurry and unfocused, but she managed to make out the familiar shape of her husband Robert's shoes underneath the desk. Her heart raced as she noticed they were covered in blood.

"Robert...?" she croaked weakly, her voice barely above a whisper.

Gwen tried to pull herself up, but the rough ropes binding her hands behind her back prevented her from moving. A searing pain shot down her leg. Gwen screamed as she saw a gaping hole in her thigh.

A wave of panic washed over her as the reality of her situation sank in. She was trapped, injured, and at the mercy of whoever had done this to her.

The sound of boots, in the distance, shuffling across the floor made her skin crawl. She looked closer. Her body was filled with terror as she saw the shadowy figure of her attacker moving around the dimly lit space in the hallway. She had no idea who this person was or what they wanted, but the bloody state of Robert's shoes told her it couldn't be anything good.

Pain radiated from the gash on her head, and Gwen winced as she gingerly touched the warm, sticky wound. Adrenaline coursed through her veins, urging her to flee. Gwen's mind raced, desperately trying to piece together what had happened. How did she end up here? Robert? Was he...? She couldn't bear to finish the thought.

With a sudden burst of energy Gwen forced herself to sit up. She needed to get a better view. Robert?" Gwen's voice trembled as she stared at the lifeless figure slumped against the desk. A large, crimson pool was forming next to his right shoe, blood gushing from the side of his head.

"Oh my God, Robert. Please..." Gwen's heart raced as she frantically pulled herself up, her eyes widening in horror as she took in the gruesome scene before her.

She didn't recognize this man - his head was slumped forward, the front corner of his skull missing, exposing the grisly mess within. Nausea, fear, anger, and desperation consumed her.

"Oh Robert..." Gwen's voice was barely a whisper as she looked around for the person responsible, her eyes wide with terror. The shuffling noise had stopped but she knew the person must still be close.

The deafening silence was shattered by Gwen's anguished scream, "What have you done?" echoing through the still air like a haunting melody of utter devastation. Her world had crumbled, and she was powerless to stop it.

The air was thick with the metallic stench of blood, and Gwen felt as if the walls were closing in around her. She had to get out, had to escape this nightmare, but her legs refused to move.

The wind howled outside the house as Gwen struggled against the ropes binding her wrists. Panic rose in her chest - how had she ended up here, trapped in this stranger's lair? Then without knowing, Gwen's adrenaline took over her body. She ripped herself loose from the rope that wrapped her hands together. The rope fell to the floor as she leapt forward from the floor. She ran as fast as she could, through the door, down the hallway dragging her leg behind her, a trail of blood following her. She sensed the stranger was only a few steps behind her. She didn't want the stranger to lose focus on her in fear for her daughter's life. The girls were surely, hiding and she prayed that they wouldn't be found.

Gwen scrambled to open the front door and then in a second she was out running towards the barn. The front door slammed with a gust of wind. Lightning lit up the sky as she raced barefooted across the gravel driveway. Then, in a split second, out of the corner of her eye she saw Sarah looking down from above. Sarah was in Margaret's room. Gwen turned around and looked up and pointed towards her, trying to warn her, but then everything went black.

* * *

SARAH'S HEART was pounding in her chest as she and Margaret crouched beneath the bedroom window. The drapes were soaked, billowing violently with the powerful gusts of wind that howled through the cracked glass.

Scattered papers from the desk had been swept up in the gale, dancing and swirling across the floor.

Sarah struggled against Margaret's firm grip, desperately trying to pull herself up and look outside. "Sarah, get your head down!" Margaret hissed urgently, yanking her sister back down. But Sarah's sudden movement was too quick, and she felt a searing pain shoot through her arm.

"Ow," she cried out, clutching her throbbing elbow. Sarah drew her hand away. A jagged gash on her elbow, now trickling down her skin.

The girls' eyes went wide with fear as they realized the danger they were in. Something or someone was out there, prowling in the storm, and Sarah's cry had surely given away their position. Margaret wrapped an arm tightly around Sarah, pulling her close as they both trembled in the darkened room, praying they wouldn't be discovered. The howling wind seemed to taunt them, the rain lashing hard against the glass. Sarah bit her lip, trying to hold back a whimper as the pain in her arm intensified.

"What do we do?"

"Why is mom lying in the middle of the driveway? I can't tell if she is hurt. We need to get to her." Sarah impatiently leaped toward the door.

"Wait, we have to be careful. I thought I had heard a gunshot. Maybe someone's in the house."

"Maybe not. It might have been thunder you heard."

"Maybe, but we should still be smart about this. Let's think. We need to stick together. We need to move slowly and cautiously, Sarah, always stay behind me. I'll look forward. You look behind me." Margaret insisted.

"Okay."

The hallway was dark. Margaret looked around. "Looks okay."

The air was thick with tension as Margaret and Sarah cautiously made their way down the dimly lit hallway. Every few moments, a flash of lightning illuminated the eerie scene, casting ominous shadows that danced across the walls.

They knew they were close to the top of the stairwell, but the darkness made each step feel like a treacherous, journey. Sarah's heart pounded in her chest, the sound of her own heartbeat nearly drowning out the patter of raindrops against the windows.

Suddenly, a loud bang echoed through the corridor, causing both women to jump in fright. They grasped each other's hands, their fingers intertwined, as they stood rooted to the spot, paralyzed by fear.

"What was that?" Sarah whispered, her voice barely audible over the sound of the storm raging outside.

Margaret's eyes darted around, searching the darkness for any sign of danger. "I don't know," she stammered, her own body trembling with apprehension.

The air felt thick and oppressive, making it hard to breathe. The shadows seemed to close in around them, taunting them with their unseen presence.

Sarah's grip on Margaret's hand tightened, her knuckles turning white. "We need to get out of here," she said, her voice shaking with barely contained panic.

"We've got to keep moving cautiously," Margaret whispered urgently, her voice barely audible over the deafening storm raging outside.

Sarah nodded, her eyes wide with fear, as she clutched Margaret's arm, the two women inching their way down the creaking stairs.

The thunder crashed like cannons, making them both flinch. The beating rain pounded the roof above, each drop sounding like the footsteps of their unseen pursuers. Sarah's heart thundered in her chest, the frantic rhythm echoing in her ears.

They had to escape, they had to get as far away from this place as possible. The shadows seemed to close in around them, whispering menacing secrets. Sarah fought the urge to cry out, to break the tense silence that hung thick in the air.

Inch by agonizing inch, they made their way down the stairs, every creak of the wood sending a jolt of panic through their bodies. They dared not look back, they dared not even breathe too loudly, lest they draw the attention of the evil that stalked their home.

Just a little further, Sarah told herself, her grip unrelenting on Margaret's arm. They would make it. They had to. The alternative was unthinkable.

"Sarah, are you okay?" Margaret looked so much like their mom, with the same hair, the same blue eyes and her slender body. Even her voice at times sounded like their mother's. Sarah nodded. "Mom, will be okay. We are almost there."

Margaret held on to Sarah's hand while she headed for the front door. The wood floor was cold beneath their bare feet. Sarah constantly watched behind them. She saw no one, only deep shadows and silhouettes of objects, a faint light coming from their father's study. Where was their father? Was he in the study?

"Margaret, there's a light."

Sarah let's get to mom first."

"You're right. I saw someone from the window out there with her."

"You're sure your mind wasn't just playing tricks on you?"

"Yes, I'm sure, but it was so fast I couldn't see who it was."

The door was unlocked. No one seemed to be around. Margaret pulled open the heavy door. A gust of wind whipped through the opening. Sarah felt the swirling air wrap around her legs and up her body, the rain beating sideways in a furious assault.

Drumming thunder rumbled in the distance, a primal beat accompanying the storm. They couldn't see their mother through the sheets of rain pouring down, obscuring their vision. The raindrops felt icy cold as they hit their exposed flesh, stinging like needles.

Their wet bodies pushed against the relentless wind, the gravel cutting into their naked, vulnerable feet. "Only a few more yards to go," Margaret shouted over the roar of the storm, her voice laced with desperate intensity.

They had to keep moving, they had to reach their destination no matter what. The elements raged all around them, an untamed force of nature intent on tearing them apart. But they kept going, their determination burning hotter than the chill of the rain.

The flashes of lightning illuminated their path, momentarily revealing the way ahead before plunging them back into darkness. Thunder boomed, the sound reverberating in their chests.

"Oh my God."

They stood there staring at the ground in horror. Their
night shirts were stuck to their fragile trunks. They were
oblivious to the rainfall that was beating down around
them. Large puddles had formed in the pockets of gravel.

"She fell here. I saw her."

"Are you sure?"

"Yes, I'm sure."

There was now only flooded gravel at her place.

"Where is she?"

"I don't know. Let's get back in the house and find dad."
Margaret said urgently.

The front door wasn't shut when they went outside. It
stood wide open to the wind. Water had blown into the
foyer, making the wood floor slippery. The faint light was
still glowing in the hallway. They didn't hear a sound.

"Wait. What if someone is still in the house?

"Sarah, I think if they wanted us dead it would have
already happened."

Margaret was right. The house appeared empty. The
person surely would have come after them by now, but
something still felt wrong. Her mom turned around and
pointed up at the window and then she just fell. She didn't
move. Why did she look back in the first place? Was
someone chasing her? Sarah was sure she saw someone
standing by her in the driveway, but then Margaret pulled
her to the floor.

They proceeded down the hallway toward the dim light.
Pictures of various breeds of horses were displayed on the

wall. Their mom was posing in most of them. She still looks the same Sarah thought to herself.

As the thunder and lightning storm raged outside, everything inside appeared quiet.

"Margaret, I'm scared."

"So am I. Hold my hand."

"Do you think we are overreacting?"

"God Sarah, I sure hope so."

CHAPTER 36

Sinister

THE WIND WAS STRONG. It whistled through the trees. He looked up at the sky. The weather didn't appear to be letting up. Raindrops were streaming down his face blurring his vision. He wiped his wet hair from his eyes. She was lying on her back. The pellets of rain hit his back as he bent down to touch her. He checked her pulse. She was alive. He picked her up and laid her on his shoulder. Her flesh felt slick against his chest. Her body was limp as he hurried across the driveway. He looked around. The house remained dark. It was late. Everyone was sound asleep, which worked out well.

He needed to get her out of the rain. He headed toward the barn. Water dripped from her soaked body. He pulled out a blanket from inside the sheltered space where all the blankets were nicely folded. He draped it over her. Hopefully she wouldn't wake up before he got all his thoughts together. This had been planned nicely. It was going to be a long night and he was going to enjoy it.

* * *

GWEN'S HEAD WAS POUNDING, a dull ache that throbbed with every heartbeat. The world around her was a hazy blur, her senses dulled and disoriented. She felt like she was drowning, her body heavy and unresponsive.

Slowly, the details came into focus. She was lying on a damp blanket, her wrists and ankles bound tightly with coarse rope. A blindfold covered her eyes, blocking out any semblance of light. A strange tingling sensation pulsed through her leg, and Gwen winced as she became aware of the pain she was feeling. Pain was also coming from the back of her skull. Something was wrapped around her head, a makeshift bandage perhaps.

Panic began to rise within her, a cold fear gripping her heart. Where was she? How did she end up here? Her mind raced, struggling to make sense of the terrifying situation. Tears stung her eyes, spilling down her cheeks as she strained against her bonds, desperate to break free.

The taste of mildew on her tongue only added to the overwhelming sense of nausea. Gwen felt like she was going to be sick, her stomach churning with dread. This had to be a nightmare, a twisted figment of her imagination. But the pain radiating through her body was all too real. "Oh my God, Robert," she screamed inside herself.

Gwen's breath caught in her throat as she heard a faint noise, a soft creak that sent a shiver down her spine. She froze, every muscle tensing as she strained to listen. Was someone else here? The realization that she was not alone only heightened her terror.

"Please, God, let this be over," she whispered, her voice trembling. Gwen had never felt so helpless, so completely at the mercy of an unseen captor. She could only pray that this nightmare would soon come to an end.

Terror rushed through her body as the lunatic pulled her hair and lifted her head.

"Wake up. It's time to wake up."

* * *

THE DOOR to the study stood open, a gaping maw that beckoned with a sense of foreboding. Margaret slowly turned the corner, her heart pounding in her ears. She knew, deep down, that they had not overreacted. Something was terribly wrong.

Sarah followed closely behind Margaret, her brow furrowed in concern. She couldn't see anything yet, but the tense silence was deafening. Suddenly, Margaret let out a strangled gasp and stumbled backwards, knocking Sarah to the ground.

"No, no, no!" Margaret wailed, her voice shrill, with terror. She curled into a trembling ball, her fingers clawing at her own skin as she descended into a frenzy of panic.

Sarah's eyes went wide with a mix of fear and confusion. She didn't want to know what Margaret had seen, she didn't want to imagine the horror that had unfolded. But morbid curiosity was too strong. She pushed Margaret aside and pulled herself up, steeling her nerves.

What she saw next would haunt her for the rest of her days. The study was in shambles. The furniture was overturned, with papers strewn about. Her father's canisters of drafted plans were flung across the floor. And at the center of the madness, a sight so unspeakable that Sarah's breath caught in her throat. She stumbled backwards, her legs threatening to give out as a scream of pure anguish tore from her lips.

The world seemed to slow to a crawl as Sarah's mind raced, trying to process the unthinkable. How could this have happened? Who could have done this? Questions swirled in her mind, but one thing was certain – nothing would ever be the same again.

Sarah stared in horror at the grotesque sight before her. She had distinctly recognized the figure as her father, but the image was so distorted and surreal that it didn't even look real. A large portion of his head was simply missing, as if violently torn off. In its place was a gaping, oozing wound, blood streaming down his face and pooling across his desk. His papers were splattered with crimson liquid, making them look as if they had been doused in red paint.

She fought the urge to vomit, her stomach churning at the sight of the mangled, disfigured form. Her mind raced with questions, but the image before her offered no answers, only a grisly, unsettling tableau.

Trembling, Sarah took a step back, her eyes locked on the gruesome display. She wanted to run, to escape this nightmare. But she found herself frozen in place, unable to tear her gaze away from the macabre sight of her father's mutilated body.

The fig tree, now lying on its side, poured dirt out onto the floor. Next to it was blood. Sarah felt suddenly and uncontrollably nauseated. She puked. Her dinner was now puréed to a fine liquid.

She didn't know how long she had been sitting there crying. She looked around the room. Her eyes were sticky. Margaret was crouching in the doorway. Her blonde hair hung in her face. She looked like a frightened little girl.

"Margaret. Margaret. Are you okay?"

Margaret looked up. Her eyes were red and swollen. "This is all so horrible."

Sarah pulled herself up from the floor. "Who could have done this? We need to call the police right away."

"Wait Sarah. What if... God... what if... mom did this to dad?"

Sarah stared at Margaret with disbelief. "What are you talking about?"

"Think about it. It's possible. Mom and dad are always fighting lately. Where is she anyway?

"I don't know but she wouldn't do this."

Margaret nodded her head as if she agreed.

"I know this is going to sound crazy but maybe I know the person who could have done this."

Margaret looked directly at Sarah. "You do?"

"Well, now that I'm thinking about it," Sarah answered.

"Who Sarah?"

"Mitch. Mitch Connors."

"Mitch? Why would he do this? That sounds even crazy than mom."

"'Cause he's been sleeping with mom." Sarah breathed loudly and continued. "I even think dad has known about mom having an affair for a while."

Margaret's face seemed pale and fragile.

"Dad found out things about him. Mitch may have assaulted some women a while back."

"What women?"

"I'm not sure... I think it was when he was younger, before he married Patty. Oh... he hit Patty."

"What?"

"Charlie told me. He hit Charlie too." Sarah looked at the floor and she saw her father's blood-stained shoes. She covered her mouth and quickly looked up at Margaret. Sarah choked on the words. "I heard mom talking to someone on the phone. I know it was Mitch. She told him that their relationship was over. "He's probably going to ape shit." Sarah felt a knot turn in her stomach.

"But why would he kill dad?" Margaret asked as if she was trying to put the pieces together. Then Margret's eyes widen. "Sarah, something just occurred to me. Charlie might be in danger. He looked like he was in a really bad fight. He had bandages and..."

Sarah was surprised. "What? Why didn't you tell me?"

"It didn't occur to me. I was so mad at him for being an ass to you."

"Margaret, something must have happened. We have to call him right away."

"What will the police think if we call him before them? It will look weird."

"I know, but we need to warn Charlie." Sarah picked up her father's phone. Blood was smeared on top of it. Sarah wiped it with her wet night shirt. She typed in his passcode 4321. He used it for everything. Then she dialed Charlie's number. Sarah gave Margaret a terrified look.

The phone went to voicemail.

"He's not answering." Sarah said, her voice in a panic.

"You need to call Patty so that she can find Charlie."

"I don't know her number."

"It's 503-653-4705."

"How do you know her number?"

"She worked at the spa. I had to call her all the time."

Sarah was surprised. "She worked with you?"

"Yeah."

"How come I didn't know?"

"You weren't around."

"Oh." She nodded and then dialed the number.

The phone rang several times before he realized it was ringing. "Who was calling Patty's phone this time of night?" He recognised the number. "Why is Sarah's father calling Patty?" He answered. He held the phone to his ear. He didn't say anything.

"Hello, anyone there? Patty?" Sarah's heart was racing."

Charlie responded. "Sarah, is that you?"

"Charlie?"

"Whoa Sarah. I have been trying to reach you."

"I know. Thank God that you are alright. I have been so worried."

"What? Yeah, I'm fine. Why are you calling Patty from your dad's phone?"

"Why are you answering Patty's phone?"

But Sarah knew why he had answered her phone. The two of them probably hung out all the time together. She forced down her feelings. She would worry about that later. "Never mind. So much has happened, but I don't have time to tell you right now."

"So now you want to talk to me?"

"Listen to me Charlie, you may be in danger." Her voice was quivering.

"Someone shot...."

"Sarah, calm down. I can barely understand you."

"...my father." I think it was Mitch."

"What's happened to your father?"

Sarah was bellowing out the words.

"Charlie, he's dead. Mitch shot him in the head."

Sarah could barely get the words out.

"Sarah, calm down so I can understand you. Did you say Mitch shot your dad?"

"Uh...I think so...I don't know for sure.

"Sarah, if it was Mitch then you could also be in danger."

"What should I do?"

"Have you called the police?"

"No..."

"You need to call the police." Charlie firmly stated.

Tears were rolling down her face. Sarah looked over at Margaret. Her head was between her legs.

"Charlie, what if it was my mom?"

Sarah was now blurting out all her doubts.

"Sarah, your mother? You're accusing your mother?"

"I know, but it could be possible. She's nowhere to be found. My mom and dad weren't getting along. Dad knew about her affair."

"Did he know it was with Mitch?"

"I'm not sure."

"Wait for me. I'll get there as fast as I can. Don't do anything, we'll figure something out. Wait for me."

"Okay."

CHAPTER 37

Charlie is Coming

THE RAIN POUNDED against the window, the rhythmic tapping creating a somber backdrop to the tense atmosphere within the room. Charlie stood in the doorway, an air of determination etched on his weary features as he surveyed his surroundings.

Crossing the dresser, he pulled open the top drawer, retrieving a well-worn baseball cap. Placing it atop his head, he caught a glimpse of his reflection in the mirror - a man pushed to the edge, sleep-deprived but resolute.

Kneeling down, he lifted the stack of clothes in the bottom drawer, revealing the ominous gleam of the nickel-plated revolver. Wrapping his fingers around the cool metal, he felt a sense of reassurance wash over him. "This might come in handy," he muttered, tucking the weapon beneath his shirt.

The weight of the gun against his chest was a sobering reminder of the gravity of the situation. Charlie knew that whatever lay ahead, he needed to be prepared. The rain continued to lash against the window, as if the very heavens were bearing witness to the turmoil brewing within.

* * *

SARAH BECAME WHITE WITH A FRIGHT. Margaret saw the look on her face.

"What's wrong?"

Sarah stood frozen. "Margaret what if ... ? I mean, what if Charlie shot dad? Patty's house is only a few minutes drive from here."

"Are you crazy?"

"No think about it. He's been acting so strangely. He hit me Margaret. He's sleeping with Patty. He's been lying to me all this time. I heard him with you earlier tonight on the porch. He was losing control. Maybe all he ever wanted was our money."

"Sarah, let's not overthink this."

"Don't you see, he won't ever get the money if he doesn't marry me? He must have thought dad didn't want him around anymore. Charlie knew that dad would never allow it."

"What do you mean?"

"I guess after our fight, dad became suspicious of Charlie so he called his lawyer to do some checking around."

"He did?"

"Charlie must have believed that Dad wasn't going to change his mind."

"So, what did dad find out?"

"Nothing. That's just it. Dad was okay with Charlie."

"Do you think Charlie is trying to hide something else?"

They both looked at each other with wild terror. "Shit. He's on his way over here."

CHAPTER 38

Two Sides of the Same Coin

MARGARET AND SARAH desperately came up with a plan. They had now suspected everyone around them of this horrible act against their father. They narrowed their suspicions to Mitch or Charlie. Sarah didn't want to believe it was Charlie, but he couldn't be ruled out. Margaret and Sarah both decided that something must have happened to their mom. She would never leave them behind without trying to protect them. More importantly she could never be capable of cold-blooded murder especially of her husband. Something terrible must have happened and she was out there somewhere.

"I need to find her before it's too late."

"No Margaret. I'm scared."

"Sarah, she has to be nearby. You saw her lying on the ground."

"I know I did."

"She must be in trouble, maybe she is lying somewhere unconscious bleeding to death. I'm going to look for her."

"No Margaret, the police can do that."

"It might be too late if I don't go now. I just want to look around the grounds. I'll come right back."

"It might be dangerous."

With kind eyes, Margaret replied. "Trust me."

Margaret opened up her father's safe using the same passcode numbers and removed his gun from a black case. She placed the sleek gun in her right hand.

"Margaret...what are you doing?"

"I'll only use it if I have to."

"God Margaret, be careful."

"Call the police." Margaret walked out of the room.

Sarah picked up the phone. Oh God. What am I doing? She dialled 911.

"Don't do anything until the police arrive," the operator told her on the phone.

"They had already done so many things," Sarah thought to herself.

"Do you understand?"

"Yes."

"The police will be there in a few minutes."

"Please hurry. Charlie is on his way."

"We need you to hide somewhere safe."

"I'm scared."

"Don't worry. Nothing will happen to you. Now go hide until they get there."

* * *

CHARLIE ARRIVED within twelve minutes of her call to him. He knocked on the door, his heart pounding in his chest. No one answered. Panic crept into his mind as he saw a faint glow of light through the side window. Without thinking, he turned the doorknob, surprised to find it unlocked. He cautiously stepped into the dimly lit foyer.

As he took a step forward, his foot slid on a patch of water, causing him to stumble. Grasping the nearest wall for support, he cursed under his breath, his senses heightened by the eerie silence surrounding him.

The house, once filled with life and laughter, now felt cold and deserted. Most of the lights were out, casting long shadows that danced in the corners. The occasional burst of light seeping through the windows gave the scene a transcendental quality.

Charlie's footsteps echoed in the empty space, the sound breaking the silence and adding to his growing unease. With every step, he tried to call out for Sarah, but his voice seemed swallowed up by the stillness.

"Sarah? Sarah, it's Charlie," he called out, his voice laced with urgency. The silence remained unbroken, amplifying his unease. He continued to explore the house.

A sudden gust of wind outside rattled the windows, causing Charlie to jump. Beads of sweat formed on his forehead as he fought to keep his nerves in check. He couldn't shake the feeling that something wasn't right. "Where is she?"

* * *

Gwen had never been so awake in her life. She knew his voice well.

"Answer me, are you awake?"

"Yes."

He had blindfolded her, but she knew his voice well.

"Good. We have a lot to talk about."

"What?" Gwen was crying.

"You tell me."

" I don't know what you are talking about." Gwen shifted. The ropes tugged on her wrists and feet..

"You playing coy with me?"

"Is this about me breaking things off with you?"

"Oh, come on Gwen we both know you can't leave me."

Gwen winced in pain. "Please can you at least untie my feet?"

"So, you can run away?"

"How can I run away?" You shot my leg."

"Yeah, I can see that a nasty wound there on your leg." He laughed. "I bandaged it up. I found this first aid kit. It took me a while to find it...never been used before I see. I found some cream for burns and an ace bandage. It might help stop some of the bleeding for a while. I'm pretty sure that you will need to see a doctor about this."

"Mitch, please untie my legs."

Mitch leaned over and cut the rope that tore into her ankles, with his leather-man that she bought him for his birthday.

"Why are you doing this?"

"Poor Gwen is always worried about herself. It's always about you."

"What are you talking about?" Gwen shot back.

"You've never had to worry about anything."

"Mitch, you need to let me go. You are just digging yourself a bigger hole."

"Then Charlie." He softened his voice. "Had to take matters into my own hands, seeing that you and Charlie are causing me trouble.

"What does this have to do with Charlie?" Gwen retorted.

"This is my mistake. Anyway, I don't usually make these kinds of mistakes but, well, I thought you both were different. Charlie not minding his own business. And then he has the balls not to show up for work. Shit, we're swamped! I don't know what made me angrier, Charlie not showing up or you calling me with all your nonsense crap... I don't quite remember."

"What's Charlie got to do with me?"

"Nothing except for your stupid husband. He can't mind his own business."

Gwen thought about Robert's sudden inquiry about Mitch and Charlie.

I had a few beers. I went home knowing that I would find Charlie taking it easy there while I worked my ass off at the shop. Saw his truck parked down the street, trying to be sneaky.

Gwen softened her words. "You know how kids are... He probably wasn't feeling well."

"I wanted it to be a surprise...kind of like this."

Gwen listened.

"He was just getting dressed. Imagine that. Pisses me off. Sleeping till noon. That was it. I went ballistic. Hit him over the head, several times I might add, with this here gun." He held up his gun.

"Oh, right, you can't see anything."

"You hit him?"

"Yeah, fucking prick."

"So, Charlie wasn't lying about Mitch," Gwen thought to herself.

"Charlie. He sure as shit fought back. He's strong. I will give yout hat. We were both on the floor rolling on top of each other and before we knew it we rolled down the stairs. That's when the fucking gun went off."

"What?"

"Shit, the gun wasn't supposed to go off, but it did, right into Charlie's arm. I'm sure it didn't kill him. I just wanted to scare the asshole, not shoot the prick.

"You shot Charlie?"

"Shit, talk about being scared. What was I supposed to do? Wait until the police came? No fucking way. I ran. I needed to come up with a plan. So that's where you come in."

"That's where I come in?"

"Yeah, you know." Mitch chuckled. "I finally decided on a plan. You, little doll, are going to help me."

"Help you? Please Mitch. You don't have to do this." Gwen was sobbing.

"Well, you're the one who gave me the idea."

"I don't understand."

* * *

SARAH'S HEART pounded in her chest as she peered cautiously through the balcony railings. His voice sent shivers down her spine.

"Sarah?" he called out, his voice filled with concern.

Sarah was standing on the edge looking down on the grand foyer. He wore the baseball cap she had given him as a gift. Her eyes were locked on him as he started making his way towards the hallway. Sarah's hands trembled as she tightly clutched the bat she had used when she played softball years ago, her only form of defence. She knew she had to be prepared for whatever might come.

Taking a deep breath, Sarah cautiously stepped towards the top of the stairs. Every step she took seemed to emit a creaking sound, causing her heart to skip a beat. She froze, holding her breath. It felt as if time had come to a standstill, hanging in an instant of suspense.

"Please..." she whispered, her voice barely audible.

Suddenly, a deafening crash of thunder erupted, shaking the house to its core. Lightning illuminated the entire room, casting an eerie glow on Sarah's trembling form. The light bounced off her T-shirt, causing it to gleam brightly, as if revealing her vulnerability to the shadows. In an instant, she dropped to the floor, hoping to hide herself from his gaze.

Her heart raced as she questioned herself, "Did he see me?

Was I exposed?" She couldn't afford to make a mistake, not now.

* * *

THE AIR WAS thick with tension as Gwen lay motionless, her heart pounding in her chest. She had never seen this side of Mitch before - wild and unhinged as she could hear him pace back and forth, muttering under his breath. Gwen shuddered at his insanity, realizing with dawning horror that she was now at the mercy of a murderer - a man she had once loved and trusted with her life. She knew she had to tread carefully, lest she suffer the same fate as her husband and now Charlie.

"Here's what we're going to do," Mitch whispered. "You're going to be a good girl and do exactly as I say. Understand?"

Gwen swallowed hard and nodded, her eyes soaked with tears under the blindfold. She had no choice but to comply, for her own life hung in the balance.

She shook her head yes.

"Good. Just making sure. I'm going to untie your hands and take the blindfold off, but first you have to promise to do everything I say. Do you promise?"

She shook her head.

"No? No! You fucking bitch!" He was screaming. "Say it!" He tugged hard at her hair. "Say it!"

Gwen was trembling. "Yes, I promise to do what you say."

"Very good." He untied her arms first. Her wrists burned from the rope.

"Now, Gwen, I'm going to remove the blindfold. Be good or else you're not going to like what's going to happen to you."

"I'll be good."

"You better be."

She blinked furiously. Her eyes were heavy and swollen, trying to adjust her eyes to the dim light. The barn came into focus, though the scene unfolding before her was bleak and unsettling.

Shadows flickered across the timber-wood walls, cast by sputtering candles and a camping lantern. The air was thick with the musty scent of hay and horses. Hay was strewn across the dry mud floor. The first aid kit was empty of its contents now spewed across the ground. The wooden walls let in slivers of moonlight. The high, truss ceiling loomed overhead, an abode to rustic architecture in all its beauty, as rain was still pounding against its structure.

"I see why you like it here so much."

Gwen was now sitting up, her back leaning against the wall on a wool blanket that she had collected. She looked down at her leg. A large bandage was wrapped around her left leg of her jeans. Blood had saturated the bandage. "This is where he shot me, in my leg," Gwen thought to herself. "It looks like it's still bleeding. What is he going to do? Let me bleed to death? God he's crazy," the words screamed inside her head.

"That leg of yours doesn't look very good."

She looked at him. Mitch's hair was messy and his beard was longer than normal. His shirt was unbuttoned and hanging loose from his pants. On the shoulder of his button down shirt, she could see a blood colored stain. He smelled of alcohol and a bad body odor. He was still holding a gun which was dropped to his side.

"Don't look so surprised, Gwen

He laughed. "You women are all alike. It's fucking disgusting. But you sure were good in bed, all sweet and nasty."

Gwen felt violated. She cringed.

"You loved it. I got plenty of women to fill all my needs. You were just one of many. It's no loss losing you, but I'm the one who says it's over."

Gwen felt she was being stabbed a million times.

"There are moments of course when the thought of love occurred to me. I liked the idea of having money. I could have convinced you of my love. Shit Gwen, you're so fucking gullible. Sweet as pie... except in bed of course."

She was horrified.

"We know how Gwen likes it..." He laughed loudly. His voice echoed through the barn.

Gwen covered her ears with her hands.

"All you women think you have so much power over us men. Stupid bitches, each and every one of you. No more Mr. Nice guy. I'm going to call the shots now." Mitch looked at Gwen. "There are a couple more things we need to deal with."

Gwen didn't want to respond.

"Are you listening?"

"Yes... I'm listening, but I don't know what you are talking about."

"You are going to help me with the cops. We're gonna make it look like Charlie is the bad guy. He attacked me. You are going to convince everyone. We know that they will believe you."

"You are psycho!"

His large hand landed on her face. The intensity of his fist made tears roll down her cheeks. "Hey bitch. You want to play rough?" He was hovering over her. Gwen sat frozen. "I will drop you off close to the hospital's emergency doors. You are going to tell them Charlie shot you. You got away and ran. If you tell them another story, much worse things will come your way. Everyone will know about how you've been cheating on your husband. It will ruin your reputation. What do you thinks Margaret and Sarah will think about their slut of a mom?

Gwen didn't move. She cringed at how her selfishness had destroyed her family's life. Now if he wanted, he could shoot her like he shot Robert.

"I will say you seduced me."

"Get up!"

"I can't...My leg."

"Now!"

She slowly tried to stand up. Tears filled the corners of her eyes. She was trembling.

"Get moving." "Mitch...it hurts..."

Mitch slapped her hard again. She fell against the wall. "Shut up. You are moving too goddamn slow!"

"Get your fucking hands off her or I'll shoot your god damn head off, you son of a bitch!"

CHAPTER 39

Where is Sarah?

CHARLIE'S HEART raced as he ventured further into darkness. Each step felt heavier than the last, as if an invisible force was pulling him back. He called out her name again, desperation tainting his voice, as he headed into the family room.

"Sarah? Where are you?"

Silence resonated throughout the room, intensifying his anxiety. The only sound was his own ragged breathing, mingling with the distant rumble of thunder. The room felt suffocating, as if it held secrets that were waiting to be unveiled.

With trembling hands, Charlie reached for the light switch, but was met with disappointment as darkness remained. "Shit the power must be out." He cursed under his breath, frustration building inside him. He couldn't shake the nagging feeling that something was terribly wrong.

As he crossed the room, memories of their fight replayed in his mind like a broken record. Words of anger and resentment, driven by a moment of foolish pride, had torn them apart. Regret washed over him like a wave, intensifying his unease.

With hesitant steps, he pushed open the French doors and stepped out onto the rain-soaked wooden patio. The intense downpour showed no signs of stopping. Potted plants and lawn chairs lay strewn about, casualties of the ferocious storm.

Under the pale glow of the full moon, Charlie's eyes scanned the surroundings, hoping to catch a glimpse of Sarah's familiar figure. The rain hit his cap, trickling down his face, mixing with his tears as frustration transformed into pure fear.

"Sarah! Please answer me!"

His plea was swallowed by the howling wind, his voice lost amidst nature's fury. The gusts grew stronger, causing one of the patio doors to slam shut.

Bang! The sound reverberated through the night.

Charlie's heart raced as he jumped and spun around, startled by the sudden noise that had pierced the air. Raindrops pelted against his face as he struggled to comprehend what was happening. His mind was filled with fear and confusion.

"Shit! What the fuck is happening?" Charlie voice was trembling with adrenaline. He hastily retreated back into the safety of his home, slamming the door shut behind him. He shook off the rain from his soaking hair and cap, trying to regain control of his racing thoughts.

Standing in the hallway, dripping wet, Charlie took a deep breath to calm himself. His eyes darted around the familiar surroundings, searching for any signs of danger.

Quietly, he moved through the hallway and into the kitchen. The sound of thunder drowned out any other noise, making it difficult to gauge the situation. Charlie's senses were heightened, and every creak of the old house made his heart skip a beat.

Through the foggy windows, he could see the rain relentlessly pounding the earth. Outside, the trees swayed violently, as if dancing to a supersensory rhythm. The dim light filtering through the windows cast eerie shadows across the room. The deserted surroundings only added to his growing unease. Charlie called out, his voice laced with worry, "Sarah, where are you?" Charlie spun around and headed back into the foyer. The floor still felt slippery. Slowly he headed toward the light coming from the study.

"Why aren't the other lights working?" Charlie thought to himself. Knowing Sarah's father, he probably had a generator for his work. His work was valuable and top priority.

* * *

"THE GUN!"

Gwen stood stunned. Confused, Mitch spun around.

"Grab his gun!"

Her body shook as she pulled the gun out of Mitch's hand. Gwen pointed the gun at Mitch.

"Oh, this is great," Mitch rolled his eyes. "Now you both have guns."

Gwen didn't understand what was happening. "Margaret? How did you ...?"

Mitch laughed out loud. "Didn't you know?... I guess I forgot to mention it."

Gwen looked at him. Margaret pointed the gun at his head.

"SHUT UP MITCH."

"What's wrong, afraid mommy here is going to be mad?"

Gwen looked at Margaret and back at Mitch.

"Mitch, don't say another fucking word or I'll blow your fucking head off."

"No Margaret, I want to hear."

"Mom please."

"She's so much like you Gwen. She has a bit of a darker side, but all in all a lot alike."

"How would you know that, Mitch?"

"She's real good in bed like you Gwen. Almost can't tell you two apart sometimes. I almost called you Margaret a few times. Hell, that would have been a hoot."

Gwen felt disgusted. She and Margaret had been sleeping with the same crazy man.

"You're fucking filth, Margaret replied."

"You didn't used to think that of me."

"I swear Mitch, shut up. I'm not afraid to use this gun."

"Oh, little Margaret to the rescue. Did you miss me? Is that why you came? See Gwen, this is where Margaret and I would do it, for hours and hours. Sometimes in that little hotel down the street from my shop, but mostly here. She wanted me badly."

"That's enough Mitch." Margaret steadied her hands tighter on the gun.

* * *

CHARLIE PULLED out something from under his shirt and was now heading towards the study. Is that a gun? What is he doing? She felt herself getting mad, protective and terrified. With her mind racing, Sarah carefully tiptoed down the stairs, doing her best to make as little noise as possible. Her bare feet pressed against the soft carpet runner, muffling any sound. She hugged the walls, her body blending with the shadows that danced along the hallway. The only sound she could hear was the haunting whistle of the wind as it whistled through the cracks in the windows.

"Where are the police? What's taking them so long?" Probably the weather Sarah thought to herself. Sarah's determination fueled her swift movements. She knew she had to stay one step ahead of Charlie, never allowing him to suspect that she was following him. The thought of what he might be planning sent shivers down her spine, but she couldn't afford to let fear paralyze her.

* * *

THE AIR WAS thick with tension as Gwen stared across the room at Margaret, their eyes locked in a silent battle of wills. The weight of their shared secret hung heavily between them, a dark cloud that threatened to engulf them both.

Gwen felt anger simmering within her, a familiar heat that she had tried so hard to suppress. But now, in the aftermath of Robert's murder, she could no longer ignore the truth. She was just as culpable as the woman standing before her. Their selfish actions led them down this treacherous path.

As Margaret steadied the gun in her trembling hand, Gwen couldn't help but notice the similarities between them. The same sharp features, the same ever-changing eyes that mirrored her own. It was as if she was staring into a twisted reflection, a mirror image of the person she had become.

Gwen's mind raced, desperately trying to make sense of it all. How had they ended up here, standing on the precipice of a decision that would seal their fate forever? Robert's lifeless body lay in their home, a testament to the devastating consequences of their choices.

The air was thick with the scent of regret and betrayal, and Gwen knew that there was no going back. She and Margaret were bound by this terrible secret, two sides of the same coin, destined to carry the weight of their actions to their graves.

"I guess the two of you are having second thoughts about me now. Maybe we could have a threesome?"

"You're disgusting."

He laughed out loud.

Gwen shivered. "What... did I ever see in you?"

"So, you think you got me cornered?"

"Did the gun pointed at your small dick give it away?" Margaret retorted.

"Now I have a small dick?" He found himself amused. He laughed again. "Baby, it's more than you can handle."

Gwen's eyes were wide with disbelief as she listened to the exchange unfold before her. Mitch, a grotesque caricature of a man, his features contorted into an unnatural grin. His words dripped with malice, like venom from the fangs of a venomous snake.

Besides him, Margaret was trembling her expression vacant, as if her very soul had been extinguished. Gwen felt a chill run down her spine - she was certain that she and Margaret were mere puppets, dancing to the twisted tune of Mitch's cruel machinations.

"This can't be real," Gwen whispered, her voice laced with a mixture of fear and desperation. "It has to be some kind of nightmare." But the harsh reality of the situation became increasingly clear with every passing moment, shattering any illusion that this was merely a bad dream.

"Let's get him out of here.

"Oh, are we leaving already? I thought we were going to have some fun."

"God, you're really a piece of work. Get moving."

"I'm not going anywhere." Mitch said it loud and clear. His voice echoed through the barn. It startled Gwen and Margaret.

"Mitch, you're walking on thin ice," Margaret spat out.

Where had Gwen heard that before?

"What are you going to do?" Shoot me? That's a laugh."

"Mitch, I'll god damn shoot you till you have twenty holes in you."

Gwen looked at her oldest daughter Margaret. Gwen's face felt hot. She was holding back her tears. Margaret sounds so much like Robert. Gwen wasn't going to put up with Mitch's shit anymore. She tightened her grip and pointed the gun at Mitch's head.

"You heard her, move your fucking ass."

"Look here, Gwen has grown a pair of balls." Mitch was now making fun of her. He shook his head from side to side. "Kissy. Kissy."

"One more word so help me. We'll be swimming in your blood.

"Go ahead and shoot me... I know you can't do it."

Gwen put both her hands on the gun and held it directly in position. He was less than ten feet away. The gun felt heavy making her arms shaky.

Mitch stood calmly. "Gwen, you're too weak and pathetic."

Gwen was now trembling uncontrollably. She held on tight to the gun in fear she might drop it. She didn't know what to do. Gwen looked at Margaret, hoping that she had an answer.

"Remember when you told me you loved me?"

"Oh god, I can't...

The gun went off. The bullet hit Mitch squarely in the head. His eyes connected with Gwen's eyes and for one moment he looked scared. He fell backwards and his body hit hard on the mud floor with a loud thump. Mitch's eyes stared up at the ceiling while his body quivered, and a puddle of blood formed around his head. His body slowly stopped moving.

Margaret threw the fired gun onto the floor.

* * *

HE GRIPPED THE GUN TIGHTLY, his knuckles turning white. Where was she? He had told her to wait for him, but she was nowhere to be seen. Panic started to set in as he moved toward the study, his heart pounding in his chest. As he approached the half-opened door, the faint amber light filtering through sent a chill down his spine. He was almost there, hesitating before pushing the door fully open. The space was eerily quiet, save for the sound of his own shaky breaths. He looked around.

Pictures lined the hallway walls, their frames casting haunting shadows that seemed to move in the dim light. The bathroom on the right was dark and ominous, a gaping void in the corner of his vision. He gripped the gun tighter, his arm trembling as he stepped into the study. Slowly, he pushed the door open, his gun raised and ready.

* * *

MARGARET TOOK A STEP BACK, her mind racing. They had to get out of there. They needed a plan. They would get to Mitch's truck and make it look like Mitch kidnapped Gwen. Her mom would somehow untie the rope that bound her hands behind her when she was in the truck, without him noticing. Then in a quick move, grabbing the gun from Mitch's side, Gwen would threaten to shoot Mitch if he didn't let her go. She would make him stop the truck. Then she would try to jump out of his truck and make a run for it. When Mitch grabs Gwen, her mom will shoot him in the head multiple times to cover up the earlier shot from Margaret's father's gun, also so that blood saturated the interior of his truck. She would then drive herself to the emergency room. She would admit she was having an affair, but that she had recently broken off from the relationship. He must have gone ballistic, just like he did with the other girls. Margaret in the meantime would cover up the evidence in the barn.

"Mom, Mitch keeps a gun under the car seat with a silencer. Use that gun."

"How do you know that?"

"He's shown it to me before.

"I will get rid of these guns."

"Now go."

Charlie stood frozen his heart pounding in his chest as he stared at the horrific scene before him. The image was seared into his mind, a grotesque scene straight out of a freak show.

Robert's body was contorted, his chest pressed against the edge of the desk, his jaw hanging open in a silent scream. His skin had taken on an unnatural hue, the color of the inside of his mouth, while his arms hung limply, stretched thin like spaghetti noodles, nearly touching the floor. A large, bloody wound had opened up on his head, and the table and floor around him were slick with blood.

Sarah stood right behind him, staring intently at the back of Charlie's head. She could feel the heat radiating from his body, the tension in the air unmistakable. Sarah's eyes narrowed as she looked down at his back - his clothes were still wet from the torrential rain outside. She knew he was holding the gun in his hand, but his shirt was blocking her view. What was he doing, just standing there staring at her father? He hadn't flinched or made a sound - this was not the typical reaction.

"What is wrong with you?" Sarah's words echoed through the silent house. The intensity of her voice startled even herself. She held her arms high as she held the bat next to his head. As Charlie spun around, his right hand instinctively gripped the gun. In a split second, the weapon fired, a piercing noise filling the once peaceful home. Sarah's body crumpled to the floor, her trusty bat slipping from her grasp. She lay motionless.

Charlie was already at her side, desperation etched on his face. "Sarah? Sarah, can you hear me?" he pleaded, dropping to his knees beside her.

The sound of sirens in the distance grew steadily louder, and soon the flashing lights of police cars filled the windows. Two officers burst through the door, guns drawn and trained on Charlie.

"Drop the gun now!" they commanded, their voices sharp and unyielding.

Charlie looked up, his hands trembling. "Wait, you don't understand. I didn't mean to... I didn't know she was behind me."

"Drop the gun, or we'll shoot!" One of the officers barked.

Slowly, Charlie set the gun on the floor, his eyes never leaving Sarah's motionless form. The officers rushed forward, one keeping his weapon trained on Charlie while the other checked on Sarah.

The officer placed handcuffs on Charlie, while reading Charlie's rights. Sarah's eyes were still closed in fear of knowing that the bullet had hit her. The paramedics were zoning in around her.

"Are you okay young lady?

"I'm not sure." Sarah responded softly. "All I could think of was dropping to the ground."

"Good thinking." It saved your life. The bullet hit the wall."

"Did you get him?" Sarah finally opened her eyes. "I was afraid I was shot."

"Believe me, you would have felt it if you had been shot."

"Sarah, what's going on? I don't understand", Charlie was now demanding an answer.

"Sir, right now you don't have any rights."

"I don't understand. Sarah, why have you done this? You think I did this?"

"Young man, don't say another word."

"Sarah?"

"Charlie, I don't trust you."

The police grabbed Charlie's arm and forced him forward. "Come with me. We are taking him down to the station, Miss Paige."

"Sarah, please, you've got it all wrong."

"Do I?"

CHAPTER 40

Starting Over

THE BRUSH GLIDED across the canvas, each stroke imbued with raw, visceral energy. Margaret's fingers trembled slightly as she worked, the weight of the paint growing heavier with each layer. A deep, brooding hue spread across the surface, shrouding the once-vibrant colors in a cloak of darkness.

Gone were the days of her delicate, pastel-tinged landscapes - this was a new Margaret, one whose art had been forged in the crucible of Emily's tutelage. The mentor's influence had seeped into her protégé's very soul, transforming her perspective and unlocking a wellspring of emotion that had long been dormant.

With each brush stroke, Margaret felt the pent-up feelings surge forth - the frustration, the sorrow, the anger that had been building inside her. This was no mere painting; it was a visceral expression of her inner turmoil, a cathartic release of the demons that had been haunting her.

The final touches were now added with a sense of grim finality, the painting exuding an aura of brooding intensity.

Margaret stepped back, her eyes scanning the canvas with a mixture of pride and trepidation. This was her truth, laid bare for all to see - a testament to the transformative power of art, and the darkness that could lurk within the human spirit.

She had poured her very soul into this work, channeling the raw emotions she had buried for so long. The articles praising her burgeoning talent were a testament to her unwavering dedication, but she knew the true test would be how the audience responded. Would they truly see the depth of her vision? Or would they simply pass it off as the fleeting fancy of an up-and-coming artist?

The air buzzed with anticipation as the final touches were put in place. Margaret paced nervously, her heart racing. This was the moment she had been working towards for months - the opening of their very own art gallery, featuring her most intimate and personal creations.

* * *

Just eight short months ago, this had all been a dream. A dream she had shared with her mother, Sarah, and herself who had tirelessly supported her every step of the way. Together, they had poured their blood, sweat and tears into turning this vacant space into a vibrant, captivating sanctuary for Margaret's art.

And now, the moment of truth has arrived. The flashing cameras, the whispering crowds, the air thick with anticipation - it was all almost too much for Margaret to take in. She had never expected this level of hype, this outpouring of interest. Her hands trembled as she straightened the frames on the walls, double-checking that every piece was positioned just so.

Taking a deep breath, Margaret allowed herself a quick glance out the window. The street was alive with activity - people hurrying to be among the first to witness the grand opening. Margaret felt a surge of pride mixed with a healthy dose of fear. What if they didn't like her work? What if she had poured her heart into something that fell flat?

Gwen appeared at her side, sensing her daughter's unease. "It's time," she whispered, giving Margaret's hand a gentle squeeze. "You've got this. I'm so proud of you."

Sarah was frantically racing around doing last minute things that had been forgotten. "Mom, where is the registration book? I can't find it anywhere."

"It's in the office where you left it. On the book shelf."

"Oh yes, that's right."

"You need to slow down. Everything looks perfect."

"There's always something that needs to be done."

* * *

SARAH'S GAZE swept across the gallery. Her eyes narrowed with a critical intensity. This space, so meticulously curated, seemed at odds with the vibrant, emotive canvases that adorned the pristine white walls. Margaret's paintings, explosions of color and movement, demanded attention, clashing with the reserved, minimalist design.

Yet, as Sarah stepped closer, she could feel the tension building. The juxtaposition between the stark environment and the raw, visceral nature of the art created an electric current that charged the air. It was as if the gallery itself was holding its breath, waiting to see how the two disparate elements would resolve.

Sarah's footsteps echoed against the dyed concrete floors as she moved from one canvas to the next, her scrutiny unwavering. The paint, applied with bold, sweeping strokes, seemed to leap off the surface, beckoning her to lose herself in the depths of each composition. She could almost hear the paintings whispering their secrets, daring her to unlock their mysteries.

Crossing her arms, Sarah leaned in, her brow furrowed in concentration. This was no mere display of technical mastery; these were the raw, unbridled expressions of Margaret's soul.

This was Margaret's moment - the culmination of years of tireless dedication and unwavering passion for her craft. Sarah wished their father could be here to witness it, knowing he would have beamed with uncontained pride. Before the doors opened, the crowd flooded into the foyer, the area right before the grand room, their murmurs and gasps echoing through the cavernous space beyond the glass doors straight ahead, commanding the central wall, Margaret's masterpiece - a haunting portrait of their father, Robert Paige, Margaret naming it "Crimson."

Sarah stepped closer, her eyes drinking in the raw emotion that emanated from the canvas. Margaret had somehow managed to capture the very essence of their father's being - the pain, the sorrow, the resilience that had etched itself into his weathered features over the years. It was a work of such profound dark beauty that it left Sarah trembling, tears threatening to spill down her cheeks.

This was Margaret's paramount piece, a testament to the depth of her talent and the unwavering love she held for their father. And as Sarah stood there, transfixed by the haunting brilliance of the portrait, she knew that somehow, someway, he was watching - his spirit soaring alongside the strokes of the brush that had brought him to life on the canvas, forever immortalized in all his complex, achingly human glory.

"He would have been so proud of you," she whispered, her voice barely audible above her own breath. In that moment, she could almost feel her father's presence, his strong hand on her shoulder, his weathered face alight with wonder and admiration.

* * *

SARAH WONDERED how the three of them ever pulled this off. When they first decided to open up the gallery, it seemed almost impossible. The weight of her father's brutal murder still hung heavy over them all, consuming every waking moment.

Gwen poured herself into this project, desperate to distract herself from the sleepless nights and the guilt that plagued her. After what she had done to cause such tragedy in her and her daughter's lives, she was prepared to make up for it all by working nonstop to get the gallery going, so that perhaps she could finally forgive herself.

But at the beginning, they had almost run out of money. Gwen refused to believe it - this gallery had to work, it had to be the redemption she so desperately needed.

"What do you mean we have no money?" Gwen retorted.

Gwen had lost almost everything, her husband and now their money. "I have to make this right for my daughters?" She told to herself. She fell into depression and hours and days turned into weeks. Her mother did not leave her room.

Sarah took charge.

"Mom, we have to go now."

Gwen sat in the large, empty room on the wood floor. Her back was leaning against the wall, and she was staring out the uncovered windows. "I don't know if I can."

"We don't have a choice anymore."

The sky was grey and the sun was buried beneath the heavy clouds. Sarah looked around the room. There was a small plastic cup in the corner of the room.

"Did you take your pills?"

Gwen seemed a million miles away as she stared into the distance.

"Mom."

"Um...yes sweetie, I did."

The doctor had prescribed her mom an antidepressant to help her through the long days and her crying spells. After a month and a half of taking the pills, they did seem to help her. She slowly started working on the project again with Sarah and Margaret.

"It's so pretty. I took it all for granted you know. Both you and Margaret, this house and your dad."

"It's okay. We forgive you, Mom."

"I never realized what I had."

It seemed none of them did. Sarah helped her mother up off the floor. She still had problems with her leg. The doctors couldn't repair all of the damage that had been caused by the bullet in her leg. She now walked with a slight limp.

"I hope they like it."

"They will. It's a beautiful house."

"You know we borrowed a lot of the design elements for this house from a ski lodge in the Carnic Alps."

"Yeah, I remember dad telling me." Gwen smiled.

"Your father loved that place. He would vacation there several times a year. It's the most beautiful place.

"It sounds nice, Mom."

"Who is going to take care of the horses?"

"Don't worry mom, the horses will be fine. The family who bought this place has four daughters who all ride or want to ride."

"That makes me happy. I love riding."

"You'll ride again."

"No, not with this leg."

"The doctor said you could ride but no fancy stuff."

"Exactly. I didn't appreciate a good thing, even when I was younger and competing. I gave it all up for your father."

"You don't regret that do you?"

"No, sweetie. I just took so many things for granted. I hope you learn from all this."

"Mom, you don't have to worry about me."

"I hope Margaret appreciates her gift now."

"I think she does. She paints for hours every day. You should see some of her new paintings."

"I'm glad."

"Mom, we need to go. Margaret's been waiting."

"Can I just look out the window for one more moment?"

"Okay. One more minute."

* * *

As Gwen looked out of the window one more time her thoughts flooded her mind. It was a miracle that everything had worked out, if you didn't include the death of her husband, losing their house and her beloved horses.

It seemed to all happen at once. Just as they buried her husband, Gwen stared in disbelief at the bank statements spread out on the table before her. The numbers in the accounts were unmistakable - the accounts were empty, completely drained of the vast fortune her late husband Robert had spent his life building. His company, Paige Incorporated, had been slowly bleeding money for years, and now the inevitable had come crashing down.

Robert was so sure he could turn things around. He had poured every last penny of his own savings into the company, desperate to keep his life's work alive. But the banks had grown increasingly wary of lending more, and creditors were closing in, demanding payments that Paige Incorporated simply could not make.

Gwen remembered the late nights, the strained conversations, the way Robert's eyes would dart around nervously as he discussed the company's dire situation. He had been in denial, convinced that if he could just land that one big new client or secure that crucial investment, everything would be alright, but they had made a disastrous mistake in the very structure of a building.

Now, Gwen was left to face the consequences. The opulent lifestyle they had grown accustomed to was gone. The grand mansion, the luxury cars, the lavish vacations - all of it would have to be sold off to pay the overwhelming debts. Gwen felt the walls closing in, the weight of their financial ruin bearing down on her.

She had to decide. Would she fight to save what was left of Paige Incorporated, pouring even more of their dwindling resources into a losing battle? Or would she have to concede defeat, let the company go under, and rebuild their lives from scratch? The future has never seemed more uncertain.

Gwen's hands trembled as she signed the final papers, sealing the deal on the sale of their family home. The weight of the decision hung heavy on her shoulders, but she knew it was the right thing to do. The money they would make, from selling their home, would be their future, their new legacy.

She could still hear her husband's voice, echoing the words his mother had spoken all those years ago - "Take the money and make something of it. Don't let it slip through your fingers." Gwen was determined not to let that happen.

"It's done," Gwen said to her daughters, her voice barely above a whisper. "The house is sold. Now all that's left is to make this work."

Margaret reached out, giving Gwen's hand a gentle squeeze. "We will," she said unwaveringly. "This is our dream, and we won't let it slip away. Not now, not ever."

The three women stood there, the weight of the world on their shoulders, but the fire in their bellies burning brighter than ever before. They would pour every ounce of themselves into this gallery, this labor of love, and they would succeed. Failure was not an option. With a deep breath, Gwen squared her shoulders and looked at the unfinished structure looming before them. This was it. The moment of truth. Together, they would paint a masterpiece, one brushstroke at a time.

* * *

"IT'S TIME TO GO MOM."

As Sarah and her mom approached Margaret, the three of them stood looking one more time at the beautiful house that Robert and Gwen built together. Memories flood their minds. They sat in silence as they drove down the winding road. There was a chill in the air, a biting frost, numbing their fingers and stinging their eyes. The trees had lost most of their leaves, their bare branches reaching up towards the steel-grey sky like skeletal fingers. Only the hardy pines remained, their green needles a defiant splash of color against the monochrome landscape.

The forecast said there might be snow on its way, heralding the arrival of a long, merciless winter. Sarah stared out the window, watching the scenery blur past, her mind drifting to time gone by. So much had changed since they were young - the carefree days of laughter and adventure had given way to this heavy, oppressive silence, a weight that pressed down on them with every mile.

None of them spoke, each lost in their own thoughts, their own regrets. The path that had once seemed so clear had twisted and diverged, leading them to this moment - a family, estranged by time and circumstance, reunited by a darkness that threatened to consume them all.

Sarah felt a shiver run down her spine, and it had nothing to do with the cold. Sarah thought about a time when Margaret and she were young.

* * *

THE SNOW CRUNCHED SOFTLY under Sarah's boots as she trudged through the thick, white blanket that covered the ground. The streetlights cast a warm, amber glow, illuminating the twinkling Christmas lights that adorned the trees and houses lining the quiet street.

Sarah pulled her coat tight. Memories of that long-ago winter evening flood her mind. She could still see the dark silhouettes of the bare trees passing by the school bus window, their branches reaching up towards the inky black sky. Margaret had been sitting beside her, their breath fogging up the glass as they peered out at the snow-covered hills.

It was the week before Christmas. A sudden storm caught everyone by surprise. The world had been transformed into a serene winter wonderland - untouched and pristine. In that moment, Sarah and Margaret were carefree, young and innocent, without a worry weighing them down.

Sarah smiled wistfully, her heart aching with the bittersweet nostalgia of those bygone days. How she yearned to return to that peaceful, untainted time - before the harsh realities of life had set in. The snow began to fall gently around them, as they drove down the road, as if the universe was trying to recreate that magic moment so long ago.

CHAPTER 41

Crimson

It had arrived, all their hard work paying off, finally opening night. The three of them, Sarah, her mother and Margaret, had poured their very souls into transforming the rundown space into a shining beacon of art and culture.

Now, as they stood back and surveyed the packed opening night crowd, Sarah could scarcely recognize the tired, haggard women they had been just months ago. The air was alive with hushed, excited chatter, the walls adorned with vibrant, breathtaking pieces. Against all odds, they had done it.

Sarah glanced at her mother, seeing the sheen of unshed tears in her eyes. This was their fresh start, their chance to begin anew. It didn't erase the past, the trauma that would forever haunt them. But in this moment, it felt like a remarkable victory - one hard win through unimaginable pain. But a victory nonetheless for the three of them. Gwen reached out and squeezed Sarah's hand, silently telling her that they were going to be okay. Together, they would find a way to move forward.

* * *

EARLIER THAT DAY before the gallery opening Gwen approached Margaret. "Margaret, I have something for you."

"What is it, Mom?"

Gwen opened her closed hand. She spread her fingers outward in front of Margaret. There, lying on her palm, was Margaret's gold necklace that she had discarded on her father's night table. Margaret looked at her mom. She stared at her birthstone. "Where did you find it?"

"I found it in your father's pocket that night he died. He must have found it and planned on giving it back to you."

Margaret could see tears in the corners of her mother's eyes. Margaret took the necklace from her mother's hand. She held the stone up to the light. The ruby flickered as the necklace swayed back and forth. "I've always loved red."

"This will bring you good luck."

"Thanks mom."

"You know, you were wrong about yourself."

"Was I?" Margaret closed her hand around the gold chain.

"It's always been in you to paint."

Gwen walked away. Margaret watched her mother as she limped on her leg. She looked down at her necklace and then put it around her neck.

* * *

"I WONDER WHAT MARGARET'S DOING?" Sarah asked her mom.

"She took Dad's painting off the wall and took it in the back. She said she needed to adjust something."

Gwen looked at the void on the wall. "It's almost time to open the main door. What is she doing?"

"I don't know. You know how Margaret is, she's a perfectionist." Said Sarah.

Gwen looked at her watch. "She needs to get her final piece up on the wall."

"Hey, sorry I'm late."

Sarah beamed a huge smile. "Charlie."

He kissed her.

"Hey Mrs. Paige."

"Hey, there, Charlie. You need to stop calling me that." Gwen hit him lightly over the head.

"I know. Just an old habit." Charlie replied.

"You look beautiful, Sarah."

Sarah blushed. "You are just saying that. How was your day?"

"I'm exhausted, but I wouldn't miss the opening for anything. There are so many people out in the foyer." Charlie said excitedly.

"I know. The turnout seems more than I expected."

"The space looks perfect. I bet Margaret is nervous."

"She must be. She is still in the back doing something to Dad's painting."

"That's okay. She is the main attraction. She can be late."

"Yeah." Sarah chuckled. "Margaret does like to make an entrance."

"How's the baby doing?"

Sarah looked down at her belly. She rubbed her hands gently over her bump. "He's been kicking all day."

Charlie joined Sarah and rubbed her belly too. Sarah was due in less than a month. It made her smile. Charlie has been working so hard lately. Sarah was proud of him. He wanted them to be set up before the baby came.

Everything had come together. The air in the mechanic shop was thick with tension as Charlie took over the reins from the late Mitch Connors. Patty, Mitch's wife, had handed over the business to Charlie, sensing his determination to keep it going. He would pay Patty a percentage until he could buy the shop outright.

The news of Mitch's shocking demise had sent shockwaves through the community, and the shop had nearly come to a grinding halt. Faced with dwindling finances, Charlie had to make the gut-wrenching decision to let go of all but his three most trusted employees - his buddy John, the seasoned Jerry Peterson and Fred.

The other mechanics eyed Charlie with skepticism, unconvinced that he could steer the shop back to prosperity. But Charlie refused to be deterred. This was his chance to prove himself, to safeguard the legacy Mitch had built and, more importantly, to provide for his family and his loyal team.

With a steely gaze and a relentless work ethic, Charlie dived headfirst into reviving the business. He worked tirelessly, putting in long hours, negotiating with suppliers, and ensuring every customer left satisfied.

Slowly but surely, the shop began to regain its footing, and the once-doubtful mechanics started to see the glimmer of hope in Charlie's eyes.

True to his word, Charlie rehired the team, and true to their word, they rallied behind him, their faith in his leadership bolstered by the shop's steady recovery. And with each passing day, the air in the mechanic shop grew less tense, replaced by a palpable sense of determination and camaraderie.

"Look who just walked in the door? Who invited her?" Charlie said it as if he was in shock.

"I did."

"Sarah, I thought it was too hard on you."

"I know, but she is family."

Charlie smiled.

Patty moved slowly around the space, looking at all the paintings. Her eyes were wide with amazement as she gazed at all the magnificent pieces. Patty looked the same except her hair was cut shorter. "She is still as pretty as ever," Charlie thought to himself.

Sarah saw the look on his face. "I saw that."

"You saw what?" Charlie replied.

"Your eyes are bugging out. Just because I'm pregnant doesn't mean you're allowed to ogle other women, especially Patty."

"I did all that?"

"Yes, you did. So why don't you go over and talk to her before she thinks she's not welcome? Go on, but I'll be watching."

Charlie kissed Sarah on the cheek. "Don't worry. You're the only one for me."

He walked over to Patty. "Hey."

"Charlie. It's good to see you." Patty hugged him. "You look great."

"Thanks Patty. I feel great."

She smiled. Her eyes twinkled.

"I like your haircut."

"Really? Thanks. I'm still getting used to it."

"You could wear it any way and still be beautiful."

"You were always so sweet to me."

"Sweet has nothing to do with it. I'm just being honest."

Patty felt her face flush and she suddenly felt bashful. "Sarah asked me to come."

"I see that."

"I'm so glad you came."

"Me too." Sarah said, "I could come early and beat the crowd."

"Good thinking. There's a lot of people out there." Charlie said proudly.

"How are you and Sarah? I heard the two of you are expecting a baby."

"Yeah. I'm nervous. I can't believe I'm going to be a daddy."

"You'll be a great dad." Patty said in a sweet voice.

"I have so many things I want to do for the baby."

"When is Sarah due?"

"In three weeks."

Patty nodded her head excitedly. "Wow it's almost time."

"Have ya'll found out if it's a boy or girl?"

"Nah. Sarah wants it to be a surprise."

"I see." Patty said softly.

"If it's a girl we are going to call her Samantha, Sam for short, after Sarah's father's mother."

"Oh that's pretty."

"If it's a boy we will name him Evan or Luke. We haven't decided." Charlie expressed.

"Those are both great names. That's a hard decision."

"Are you ready?"

"I hope so. It went faster than I thought. I'm sure Sarah doesn't feel like that. She's always complaining that her back hurts."

" I wish I had a baby."

"You still can."

"We'll see." Patty mumbled.

"I heard you're leaving town soon?" Charlie asked

"Yeah, it took a while but the house was finally sold."

"I don't know why. That's a great house."

"Maybe 'cause Mitch owned it? "Patty replied.

"Oh... I didn't think about that."

"Any way too many memories."

"I know what you mean. I think about you a lot, Charlie said modestly."

Patty blushed. "I'm going to move in with my parents for a while. It will be nice. My parents can't wait till I get there. They call me every day."

Charlie looked at Patty. He suddenly felt guilty. "I feel bad that I led you on that way..."

She looked at him. "Charlie, it's okay. You helped me in so many ways. I was so pathetic and you were the one who saved me." She said softly

"I always wanted to repay you. When I was finally able to come through for you, well, I felt like I truly had a purpose again." Patty divulged herself.

Charlie looked at her as if he wasn't sure what she meant.

"You know?"

"Mitch's shop?"

"No silly."

"I'm not quite following," Charlie chuckled.

Patty started twisting her hair. She seemed bashful. She looked up at Charlie. "I've wanted to tell you for so long. I love you so much, I would have done anything to make you happy, even... you know... that's why it's been so hard to keep this secret from you. Patty declared.

Charlie was puzzled. "Secret?"

"Yes, can you keep a secret?"

"What? I'm not sure I understand." Charlie had a perplexed look on his face.

"Robert."

"What about Robert?" Charlie asked.

"He was in your way. I know you wanted a better life." Patty affirmed.

"Oh my god, Patty, what are you saying?"

"Well ... I got rid of Robert for you."

Charlie stood frozen. Beads of sweat were dripping from his forehead. He didn't move in fear that the walls would come crashing down.

"I set Mitch up. I told Mitch that I had made a mistake and that I supported him. He believed me." Patty laughed. "I told Mitch that I would shoot Robert and injure Gwen for him. I told him to find Gwen at the Paige's place the night you left the hospital."

"The night that I was shot?" Charlie Asked

"Yeah, when you came back from the Paige's place. I saw how sad you were. Sarah, Margaret and Mr. Paige not believing you. I couldn't bare seeing you like that."

Charlie felt like his legs were going to buckled.

"I told Mitch to take Gwen to the barn." Patty paused and then continued. "I told him to tie up Gwen, make her scared and threaten Gwen with their affair. You know, so she would agree to blame it on you." Patty looked down at the floor.

"I don't understand?" Charlie said as if he was about to cry.

I told Mitch that he should blame you. I told him I would tell the police that you attacked Mitch. I put a note in his truck to meet Gwen at her barn.

"Oh my god Patty."

"Don't you see? Mitch and Robert were in the way. Now you have what you always wanted. I had to convince him to blame you so that I could get rid of Robert."

"Not like that." Charlie retorted, trying not to cause a scene.

"He deserved worse but it was the best I could do," Patty asserted.

At that moment Sarah walked over and grabbed Charlie's hand. His hand was cold, and his face had become extremely pale. He was sweating profusely.

"What's the matter Charlie?" Sarah looked back and forth at Charlie then at Patty.

"I think he's just nervous about the baby."

"Charlie is going to be the best dad ever." Sarah declared with all her heart.

"The gallery is beautiful Sarah. Margaret is brilliant. Thanks for inviting me."

"Of course, Patty."

"Sorry I have to rush off. I have to be somewhere soon." Patty said with a sincere smile.

Patty turned and headed toward the door. She stopped. She turned back around. "Don't forget Charlie it's our secret." Then Patty walked out the door.

* * *

MARGARET WAS STILL in the back. The wad of paper in Margaret's hands crinkled as she gripped it tightly, her knuckles turning white. Her mind raced, a whirlwind of anger and resentment that she could never seem to quiet down. Sometimes the intensity of her emotions was so overwhelming, she could hardly see straight.

This anger had been festering inside her for far too long, a toxic brew that threatened to destroy her from the inside out. Painting had been her one true solace now, the only thing that could calm the storms raging within. After her father had forced her to see psychiatrist after psychiatrist, she had been made to feel ashamed of her lack of motivation for her artistic passion, as if it were some sort of illness that needed to be cured. Now it seemed to be the only thing that helped her stay slightly sane.

Her father had always tried to control her, to mold her into the perfect daughter he envisioned. But Margaret refused to be broken, refused to surrender her independence and her dreams. She had spent countless sleepless nights praying for a way to break free of his oppressive hold. And then Patty came into her life.

Patty was a fragile, beaten-down soul, the perfect pawn in Margaret's carefully crafted plan. She played on Patty's weaknesses, her vulnerabilities, slowly manipulating the beautiful woman until she was firmly under Margaret's sway. The wad of paper in her hand represented the final phase of her scheme, the key to her long-awaited freedom.

As Margaret's lips curled into a cold, determined smile, the intensity of her gaze burned with a ferocity that bordered on madness. She was so close, so close to finally breaking free of her father's chains and reclaiming her life. Nothing was going to stand in her way, not even her own lucidity. This was her moment, her chance to seize control and paint the world with the colors of her own design.

Margaret opened the wad of paper. She held the crinkled paper so she could read it. Patty had beautiful handwriting. Luckily Mitch still had it in his pocket the night she shot him. The note had droplets of blood on it.

Mitch,

I'm so sorry. I have let you down and I feel awful for that. Can you ever forgive me? I knew you would be here. Remember when we used to come out here together? I want it to be like that again.

I know how much you do for me. When you and Charlie rolled down the stairs and I saw the blood, all I could do was pray it wasn't you. I can see now how Charlie is getting in your way. I should never have asked you to let him live with us. He is so much like his father. He is destroying us. I want to help you. We must be united on this if you don't want you to end up in jail. I have a plan. It will work perfectly if you do exactly as I say. I will take care of Robert and injure Gwen. You will go to their house at exactly 2:15 AM in the morning. You will wait till you see Gwen running to the barn. Make sure she goes to the barn. Remember she will be injured. She will be easy to catch. Tie her up and terrorize her. Make sure it's enough to scare her so that she will agree to blame everything on Charlie. Be careful that you aren't followed.

I will be a better wife for you. I promise.

Love you, Patty

Margaret smiled. She planned this from the minute she met Patty, which felt like forever. As part of her plan, she had to get Mitch to fancy her which repulsed her, but it was the only way. She was sleeping with the same man that her mom fell for the hard way.

Margaret was sitting on the floor. She knew the day would show itself when the time was right. It had finally come. Patty called her from a pay phone down at the police station.

"He's gone crazy. He shot Charlie. "I'm really scared." Patty whispered so no one could hear.

"This is perfect. This makes things so much easier for us. We have to do it tonight, exactly as I tell you."

"I'm so nervous." Patty retorted.

"Stay calm. He'll take the fall. No one will ever know the real truth."

Patty took a deep breath.

"Think of Charlie and remember that Mitch will never let you have a normal life."

It went just as planned.

"Do you have the gun with the silencer I gave you?"

"Yes."

"Where's Mitch right now?"

"He took off. But I'm pretty sure I know where he's hiding in the woods. He used to take me there all the time. No one else knows about it. That's where he hides sometimes."

"Are you sure he didn't leave the state? Margaret asked

"Heck no. He wouldn't just leave all his stuff behind even if the police are looking for him. He's got too big of an ego to do that. He's just stewing in his own bullshit.

"You need to plant a note." Margaret stated firmly. "Write exactly what I say."

"Yeah okay."

"Can you get it to him?"

"Yeah, officer Smith is about to drive me home. When he drops me off, I will get in my car and drive there immediately and plant the note."

"What if he sees you?"

"He won't. He drinks all the time like his father especially when he's stressed." That's convenient Margaret stated.

"What if he doesn't wake up?" Margaret asked as if the plan had taken a bad turn.

"No problem with that either. I will call his phone from the pay phone Charlie always calls me from. I will call many times." Patty stated.

"Do you think it will wake him?" Margaret questioned.

"Yeah. He's super jumpy even when he's drunk. He's super paranoid."

"Okay. Good."

"What should I do next?"

"When you get to my house just enter the code. Be quiet when entering the house. My mom will be sleeping in her bedroom upstairs. I'm going to make some noise to wake her up. She will go looking for my dad. She hates it when he isn't in bed. My father will most likely be in the study. He's been sorting out work and is way behind. I will make sure Sarah is in my room. I will make it a sister bonding moment. I will keep an eye on her."

Patty was only wounding her mother. "Tie my mom's hands together. If they are together, have my father tie her and then shoot her in the left leg exactly as I say. Then hit her with the butt of the gun over her head so she passes out."

"It was a good shot," Margaret thought. "You will have to shoot my father in the head. You will then wait until my mom wakes up. She will eventually get up and run."

"How do you know your mom will run?"

"Trust me. She has a fiery side."

She knew her mom would run to the barn. Patty was to stay in the shadows a few feet behind her. This would ensure Gwen's exit outside to the barn, where Mitch would find her.

"Once you see Mitch, you will run to Mitch's truck without being seen."

"Shove the gun that you used in Mitch's truck under the seat so my mom can find it."

The weather that night was just an added bonus. This was the perfect distraction from what they were about to do. Knowing Charlie had hit Sarah, as well as Margaret knowing Charlie had slept with Patty, this was also an extra bonus to keep Sarah occupied.

Margaret had asked Patty to put a sultry picture of herself inside a card and put it in Charlie's glove compartment a few weeks prior to this event. If Charlie found it he would think nothing of it, just a sweet jester of their relationship.

Then, out of sheer luck, Sarah asked Margaret to look for Charlie. Margaret knew that Charlie was at the hospital and Patty would be driving to find Mitch. This was the perfect opportunity for Sarah to accidentally discover the picture. Margaret knew Sarah would insist on finding any clues. Sarah would be upset, and she would have Sarah sleep in her room. This way, she could keep an eye on her.

No one would ever suspect Margaret of this cunning, murderous event. She had Sarah as an eyewitness. The storm was thick with tension, with whipping gusts of winds, as if a miracle was happening. Lightening and rain came as Mitch strode up the driveway right on time. Sarah had seen something taking place from the window, seeing what was about to unfold. Thankfully, Sarah didn't recognize Mitch. Margaret was able to pull her to the floor. Mitch found Gwen in the driveway, another miracle unfolding. He would take her to the barn per Patty's request.

Margaret would eventually lead Sarah into their father's study. Margaret would have to pretend to be shocked. Then, knowing that Sarah would question all scenarios, she would eventually blame Charlie.

Margaret, her face a mask of cold indifference, faked her fear and sorrow for their bloody father. She had to make time pass long enough for Mitch to torture Gwen a bit. Finally, Margaret took control. Sarah, you call the police and then hide. I will go find my mom. The plan went off without a hitch. Gwen was tied and blindfolded up in the barn.

Margaret stared solemnly at the flickering flame as it consumed the letter, the only physical remnant of the fateful exchange that had altered the course of her life. The corners of the paper curled and blackened. The words she had poured over a thousand times were now reduced to lifeless ash drifting to the floor.

She had made the trade, her father for Mitch, a decision that still weighed heavily on her conscience, a burden she would carry for the rest of her days. In the dimly lit room, the shadows seemed to close in, mirroring the darkness that had taken root in her heart.

Surrounded by the tools of her craft - the canvases, the paints, the sketches - Before now, the vibrant colors and vivid strokes only served as a cruel reminder of the life she had chosen to sacrifice, but now Margaret had found solace in the act of creation.

Margaret watched as the last of the letter crumbled, the final remnants of her note to Mitch disappearing forever.

Margaret winced as she pushed herself up from the cold, hard ground. She brushed off her new dress. The fabric was a vibrant crimson that seemed to crackle with inner energy. Margaret reached up and grasped her gold chain around her neck, fingering the small, intricate ruby pendant that hung from it.

"Father, you have won your battle," she whispered, her voice thick with a mixture of determination and sorrow. "I'm painting again."

The gallery doors would be opening in just ten minutes, and Margaret could feel adrenaline coursing through her veins. This was her moment, her chance to reclaim the passion that her father had fought so hard to rekindle within her.

She squared her shoulders, her grip tightening on the necklace.

She walked over to the light, the soft glow illuminating the easel before her. Positioned there was an oil painting of her father. The desire to paint his portrait came to her immediately, an overwhelming need to capture his likeness on canvas.

Her hand moved with purpose, her mind in total control as she began to mix the oil paint. Stroke by careful stroke, the painting came to life - his weathered features, the sorrow etched in his eyes, the disappointment radiating from his expression, the beast within him. This masterpiece, a window into her father's very soul, would soon hang in the center of the gallery for all to see.

As she stepped back to admire her work, a chill ran down her spine. Those eyes seemed to be looking at her with judgment, an accusation she could not escape. Suddenly, the memory of his death came rushing back - her father, sitting lifeless in a chair, a pool of blood surrounding him.

"No," she whispered. Realization dawned on her. After hours spent with the psychiatrist unpacking her subconscious, how could she have missed this? She had seen his death all along. And in this painting, she knew the terrible truth - she was the one who had killed him.

She had titled her father's portrait "Crimson" and she signed it Ruby Paige. Ruby Margaret Paige was her birth name, but her father never liked her to use the name Ruby. Now, dad, you can't tell me what to do. She picked up the painting and reached over to turn out the light, but before she could turn out the light, she heard a voice whisper. It was the voice of her father. Chills ran up her spine. She had seen it all along in her nightmare.

"Soon they will all know your secret. You've painted it on my face."

Epilogue

THE GREAT CRIMSON-EYED beast led the pack through the woods, its massive body surging with primal power. The forest was thick and dense, overgrown with tangled bushes and ancient trees. Twigs and branches snapped beneath the pounding of their enormous paws as the pack pushed ahead, undaunted by the fallen obstacles in their path.

The full moon hung high above, casting an ethereal glow over the shadowy trees. Its light had called them once more, summoning the beasts to fulfill their ancient purpose. They were alive, every sense heightened, the energy of the hunt coursing through their veins.

The Alpha's gleaming eyes scanned the darkness, nostrils flaring as it caught the scent of its prey. A deep, guttural growl rumbled in its chest, echoed by the rest of the pack. Their instincts were razor-sharp, guiding them inexorably forward.

As one, the pack surged through the undergrowth, powerful muscles propelling them with blinding speed.

The forest blurred around them, every sound and scent intensified - the snap of twigs, the rustle of leaves, the rich loamy earth beneath their paws. They were close now, the scent growing stronger with each stride. The Alpha's lips pulled back in a fierce snarl, crystalline fangs bared and ready. This was their moment, the very reason for their existence. As the hunt was beginning, the beasts unleashed a chorus of chilling howls that echoed through the primordial woods.

The high moon drenched the enclosure in an ethereal glow, wispy clouds floating like transparent glass over its silvery rays. Each beast knew its place as they gathered in a great circle, the air thick with anticipation.

Lastly, the crimson-eyed vanguard moved into the middle of the newly formed ring. The massive, muscular creature stood on its hind legs, head thrown back as it unleashed a howl that echoed with primal intensity, the surrounding beasts watching in ominous silence.

With a loud, earth-shaking thump, the vanguard's body came crashing down, the beast exposing its razor-sharp canines as it let out a series of deep, guttural growls. The other creatures responded in kind, grunting in unison as they felt the energy pulsing through the air.

"The hunt will begin soon," the vanguard declared, its crimson eyes burning with a feral light. Each beast knew its role, their bodies coiled and ready, poised for the moment when they would break free from their positions and join the chase.

The air grew heavy with anticipation. The only sound was the gentle rustling of the wind through the trees. And then, just as the moon reached its apex, the vanguard let out one final, bone-chilling howl, signaling the start of the hunt.

The hunt had begun, and there would be no mercy.

A sudden movement rustled the branches deep within the primitive forest. The beasts of the realm stood still, silencing their powerful lungs as they strained to pinpoint the source of the disturbance. The vanguard, a massive, crimson-eyed wolf, searched the shadowy woods with heightened senses, its hackles raised.

Then, a hulking shape emerged, snapping twigs underfoot as it surged forward. A colossal beast with gleaming white fur and eyes that burned like molten gold moved into the moonlit pasture, its heavy paws crunching the ground with each step. With great speed and confidence, the yellow-eyed wolf charged toward the crimson-eyed behemoth guarded by the ring of beasts.

The vanguard let out a bone-chilling howl, its crimson eyes narrowing as it positioned itself. The yellow-eyed wolf paused, growling a warning, but the crimson-eyed Alpha responded with a ferocious snarl, commanding the intruder to retreat back into the shadows.

The large white wolf slowly approached the formation unrelentingly, without warning. Two crimson-eyed beasts separated, letting the white wolf beast into the inner circle.

Tension hung thick in the cool night air as the Apex predators eyed each other warily, each unwilling to back down. The stage was set for a primal clash - a battle for dominance in the primal realm of the forest.

"Who is this that approaches?" The Vanguard's voice was deep and eerie. The white wolf did not speak.

"Tread carefully, stranger."

The white beast reached the middle of the circle. It stood twenty feet from the crimson-eyed vanguard. They stared in silence. The only sounds were the rustling leaves in the surrounding woods. The moon flickered as clouds filtered across its glowing orb.

The white wolf could see horror rising in the crimson beast's eyes, but the vanguard stood its ground.

"I know what you did."

The white beast took a step forward. The Vanguard stood firm.

"There is no way for you to know."

The air was thick with tension as the pack encircled the imposing white wolf after it entered. Its piercing golden eyes scanned the ring of crimson-eyed beasts, sizing up its opponents. With a sudden burst of speed, the white wolf lunged forward, its powerful jaws clamping down on the throat of the Vanguard crimson wolf. The creature let out a guttural yelp before the white wolf ripped out its still-beating heart in a shower of blood.

The pack watched in stunned silence as the white wolf consumed the warm, pulsing organ, its eyes narrow and predatory. The taste was primal, invigorating - a rush of raw, untamed power coursing through its veins. Licking its chops, the white wolf turned its gaze upon the other wolves, daring them to challenge its supremacy.

The pack remained motionless, their hackles raised as they met the intense stare of the domineering predator. Slowly, the white wolf began to pace the interior of the ring, emanating an aura of absolute dominance. Its foot-falls were measured, confident - the steps of a true Alpha.

The other wolves cowered, submitting to the white wolf's unspoken command. This was no mere skirmish for territory - it was a battle for the right to lead the pack, to decide the fate of the entire group. And in that moment, there was no doubt who the Alpha would be.

The white wolf's howl echoed through the night, a triumphant call that summoned the other beasts. As they joined in the eerie chorus, the sound reverberated across the moonlit landscape, a symphony of primal power.

The white wolf stalked forward, its paws padding silently through the grass. Its keen eyes focused on the still form of the crimson-eyed wolf that lay before it, the once-fierce predator now motionless and vulnerable.

Approaching the body, the white wolf let out a low growl, its hackles rising. There, beneath the intense glow of the full moon, lay the human woman - Margaret. Her once-vibrant body was now marred by the brutality of her demise. Her hair was matted with thick, dried blood. Her skin was torn and stained crimson.

The white wolf circled the corpse, sniffing the air, ears alert for any sign of danger. The other beasts remained at a distance, their own cries quieting to an uneasy silence as they sensed the solemnity of the moment. Lowering its head, the white wolf regarded Margaret's lifeless form. A flicker of something akin to mourning passed through its sharp eyes. As the Alpha of the pack, the white beast felt invincible, her muscles rippling with raw strength. She let out a thunderous howl, calling her brethren to her side. They arrived swiftly, their crimson eyes gleaming with reverence for their new leader.

The white wolf turned her attention to the human. Her face was hauntingly disfigured, stirring a sense of deep sadness within the animal's primal consciousness.

"Like you said, it's my destiny."

The End